VOCABULARY BASICS

VOCABULARY BASICS

JUDITH NADELL

BETH JOHNSON

PAUL LANGAN

TOWNSEND PRESS   Marlton, NJ 08053

Books in the Townsend Press Vocabulary Series:

Vocabulary Basics
Groundwork for a Better Vocabulary
Building Vocabulary Skills
Building Vocabulary Skills, Short Version
Improving Vocabulary Skills
Improving Vocabulary Skills, Short Version
Advancing Vocabulary Skills
Advancing Vocabulary Skills, Short Version
Advanced Word Power

Books in the Townsend Press Reading Series:

Groundwork for College Reading
Groundwork for College Reading with Phonics
Ten Steps to Building College Reading Skills
Ten Steps to Improving College Reading Skills
Ten Steps to Advancing College Reading Skills
Ten Steps to Advanced Reading

Other Reading and Writing Books:

Everyday Heroes
Voices and Values: A Reader for Writers
English at Hand
English Essentials

Supplements Available for Most Books:

Instructor's Edition
Instructor's Manual and Test Bank
Online Exercises

Copyright © 1998 by Townsend Press, Inc.
Printed in the United States of America
9 8 7 6

ISBN-13: 978-0-944210-40-6
ISBN-10: 0-944210-40-6

Send book orders and requests for desk copies or supplements to:
Townsend Press Book Center
439 Kelley Drive
West Berlin, New Jersey 08091

For even faster service, contact us in any of the following ways:
By telephone: 1-800-772-6410
By fax: 1-800-225-8894
By e-mail: cs@townsendpress.com
Through our website: www.townsendpress.com

Contents

Note: For ease of reference, the titles of the reading selections in each chapter are included.

UNIT FOUR

UNIT FIVE

FOR EXTRA HELP

To the Instructor

In all likelihood, the students you teach have severely limited vocabularies. Some have come to this country as adults, and their day-to-day struggles in an unfamiliar culture have left them little time to acquire more than the most basic vocabulary. Others, although born in this country, have been short-changed by the educational system. Often with undiagnosed or poorly understood learning problems, they were pushed from grade to grade and missed consistent instruction in vocabulary development. Still others received a solid enough education but never developed strong vocabularies because they were raised in homes where television—not reading or conversation—was the favored pastime.

In the long run, it makes no difference why your students have limited vocabularies. The results are the same: *Self-conscious about their limited vocabularies,* students hesitate to take steps on their own behalf—like continuing in school or applying for a better job. *Not knowing enough words,* they are unable to meet the demands of school and the workplace.

Vocabulary Basics provides a practical answer to your students' vocabulary problem. In the course of 30 chapters, *Vocabulary Basics* teaches 240 critical words—the words that ESL, adult-literacy, and pre-GED students need to get ahead in today's competitive world. Here are the book's distinctive features:

1 **An intensive words-in-context approach.** Studies show that students learn words best by encountering them repeatedly in different contexts, not through rote memorization. The book gives students a concentrated in-context experience by presenting each new word in *seven different settings.* Each of the thirty chapters takes students through the following series of steps:

- Students start by inferring the meaning of each word as it appears in two sentences. On the basis of their inferences, they choose the closest meaning from three multiple-choice options.

- Then, armed with a basic understanding of the new words, students are ready to match each word to its meaning.

- Next, they strengthen their understanding of the word by applying it in four different words-in-context practices, including sentence-completion activities and high-interest fill-in-the-blank passages.

- Last, to lock in their mastery of the new words, students are asked to come up with their own endings for eight practice sentences, each of which includes one of the new words. At this point, students will be so comfortable with the words that they will have little trouble using them in this challenging writing-speaking activity.

Each encounter with a word brings it closer to becoming part of the student's permanent word bank. *No comparable vocabulary book gives such sustained attention to the words-in-context approach.*

2 **Abundant and varied practice.** Along with extensive practice in each chapter, unit tests at the end of every six chapters provide students with *three additional chances* to work with the words in a unit. By the end of the book, then, students will have worked with each new word *ten times.* Moreover, Chapters 2 through 30 repeat words from earlier chapters (such repeated words are marked with small circles like this°), allowing for even more reinforcement. Many unit activities—for example, synonym and antonym practices and crossword puzzles—are completely different from those found in the chapters. This variety keeps students motivated and ensures their mastery of the words. All this practice makes it possible for students to learn in the best possible way: by working closely and repeatedly with the new words. *No comparable book provides so much and such varied reinforcement.*

3 **Focus on essential words.** A good deal of time went into selecting the 240 words featured in the book. We started by consulting word frequency lists, along with lists in a wide range of vocabulary books. In addition, each of us—as well as our editors—prepared a list of words. A computer was used to consolidate these many word lists. Then a long process of group discussion led to final decisions about the words that would be most helpful for students working at a basic level.

4 **Sensitivity to students' needs.** The book gives careful attention to the special needs of basic students.

- The simplified pronunciation guide at the front of the book and in each chapter is free of the strange-looking pronunciation symbols that many people, particularly basic students, find so confusing. Instead, easily understood letters and letter combinations are used to show students how to sound out each new word.

- Throughout, we have aimed for a tone that is friendly and accessible, but never condescending.

- Recognizing that basic students often have difficulty processing long sentences and paragraphs, we have kept sentence structure uncomplicated and paragraphs brief.

- Whenever a word has multiple meanings (for example, *delicate,* meaning "easily broken" or "requiring care and skill"), we use the meaning that basic students are most likely to encounter and thus find helpful. (In this case, the meaning "easily broken" is the one we use.)

- Many basic students have difficulty with verbs: they have trouble remembering the correct form of the third-person singular in the present tense and the correct endings of the past and progressive tenses. Their tendency is to omit, respectively, the -*s,* -*ed,* and -*ing* endings. For example, when adding a new verb, such as *insist,* to their vocabulary, they will often write (and sometimes say), "My friend always *insist* I drive when we go out," "Last night, I *insist* that we buy a new radio," and "I got tired of *insist* that my kids clean their rooms." So in the "Learning Eight New Words" section, whenever a new word is a verb, we usually provide the verb's base form (*insist*) in the first sentence and the third-person singular present tense, past tense, or progressive form in subsequent sentences. Through repeated exposure, students become familiar with the correct way to form verbs. To help them even further, we include at the end of the book (see pages 249–251) a chart summarizing the more troublesome verb forms.

- To dispel students' belief that the words in *Vocabulary Basics* are removed from their everyday lives, we deliberately use the second-person point of view in many of the book's activities and passages. Seeing unfamiliar words in material that refers to "you" helps students see the relevance of the words to their own lives.

- Finally, the last activity in each chapter and in each unit review encourages students' ownership of the words even further. These activities ask students to use the new words when writing and speaking. Indeed, what better way is there for students to "own" a new word than to use it on paper or in conversation? However, basic students are often at a loss when asked to write or say a sentence using a new word. Throughout the book, then, we provide considerable help when it's time for students to generate their own material. For example, the last activity in each chapter has students devise only endings for partial sentences already containing the new words. Such a structured approach gives students the help they need to get moving in the right direction. Similarly, the final activity in each unit review provides students with help as they get ready to create their own sentences—this time, from scratch. In this instance, we provide suggested topics that students can draw upon when writing or saying their sentences.

  Consider, for example, our item for the word *comfortable*: "Using the word *comfortable*, write or talk about a time you made someone feel relaxed and at ease. Perhaps you invited a new neighbor to dinner, took the time to show a coworker around on the first day on the job, or helped a relative feel less nervous about going into the hospital." If students were simply told "Make up a sentence using the word *comfortable*," they might come up with something like this: "I feel comfortable in my English class." Of course, such a sentence doesn't demonstrate students' understanding of the word. *Comfortable* could mean "upset" or "angry" or "bored." Our suggestions encourage students to generate sentences that show they *truly understand* the new words. Some students may follow our suggestions closely; others may use our suggestions to spark topics of their own. In either case, our "prompts" help students write or say sentences that demonstrate their genuine understanding of the new words.

5 **Appealing content.** Dull practice exercises work against learning, while relevant, lively, even humorous materials grab students' attention and enhance learning. For this reason, we put considerable effort into creating activities and passages with widespread appeal. Throughout, we have tried to make the material enjoyable for teachers and students alike. Look for a moment at the sentences on pages 10 and 28, and at the reading passages on pages 12, 30–31, and 42. When field-testing the material, we found that students especially enjoyed the often playful quality of the "Showing You Understand the Words" activity (see pages 11 and 17, for example).

6 **Clear format.** *Vocabulary Basics* has been designed so that its very format contributes to the learning process. Each chapter consists of three two-page spreads. In the first two-page spread (see pages 8–9), students can easily refer to all eight new words when completing the matching activity. In the second two-page spread (see pages 10–11), students can refer to a box that shows all eight words while working on the "Adding One Word" and "Adding Two Words" activities. In the third two-page spread (see pages 12–13), they can cross out the words in the box when filling in the blanks in the reading passages. The book's format is equally attentive to the needs of the instructor. For instance, to facilitate grading, including use of the Scantron, students can mark answer spaces with the letter of the word or with the word itself.

7 **Helpful supplements.** An *Instructor's Edition* containing answers to all the activities and tests in the student book as well as teaching guidelines is available at no charge to instructors adopting the text. Also available is a computer disk containing additional tests for each vocabulary chapter; these tests feature actual pronunciations of the words.

8 **Realistic pricing.** While *Vocabulary Basics* is comprehensive enough to serve as a primary text, its modest price ($7.90 net) also makes it an inexpensive supplement in basic reading, writing, pre-GED, and ESL classes.

9 **One in a sequence of books.** *Vocabulary Basics* is the most fundamental book in the Townsend Press vocabulary series. It is followed by *Groundwork for a Better Vocabulary* (a slightly more advanced basic text), *Building Vocabulary Skills* (an even more advanced basic text), *Improving Vocabulary Skills* (an intermediate text), and *Advancing Vocabulary Skills* (an advanced text). There are also short versions of the last three books. Suggested reading levels for the books are included in the *Instructor's Manual.* Together, the books create a comprehensive vocabulary program that will make any student a better reader, writer, and thinker.

ACKNOWLEDGMENTS

A number of people provided valuable assistance as the three of us worked on *Vocabulary Basics.* Our thanks go to Susan G. Hamson, whose word-processing abilities eased the demands of the project. Eliza Comodromos assisted at the very end by fine-tuning some of the questions and activities. Susan Gamer helped by drafting several sets of lively practice materials and by proofreading the completed manuscript. We appreciate as well the extraordinary design, editing, and proofreading skills of the multi-talented Janet M. Goldstein. Final thanks go to Carole Mohr, co-author of the other books in the Townsend Press vocabulary series. Her rigorous and insightful editing identified the changes that were needed to make the book as helpful as possible to ESL, adult-literacy, and pre-GED students.

Judith Nadell
Beth Johnson
Paul Langan

To the Student

WHY A GOOD VOCABULARY MATTERS

At one time or another, you have probably heard someone say, "It's important to have a good vocabulary." Wanting to be polite, you may have agreed. But perhaps you really wanted to ask, *"Why is having a good vocabulary important?"* Here are five reasons why.

1 **Knowing a lot of words makes it easier for you to understand others and for others to understand you.** Have you ever had trouble following what someone else was saying? Maybe you found it hard to understand a television news report. Perhaps you could not understand a doctor's instructions for completing a medical form. Maybe you could not figure out what family members meant when they talked about an election. If you are like most people, you probably got upset when you didn't understand what was being said.

    It can also be difficult to tell others what you are thinking and feeling when you don't know enough words. Maybe the words will not come when you are writing a letter to a sick neighbor. Perhaps you have a hard time explaining to relatives why you were hurt by something they did. Maybe you have trouble telling friends why you are so excited about your new apartment.

    As your vocabulary gets larger, you will not have to work so hard to understand others—or to make others understand you. That, in turn, will make your life much easier.

2 **A good vocabulary is the key to understanding what you read.** If you don't know enough words, you are going to have trouble figuring out the meaning of what you read. One or two words whose meanings you don't know may not stop you. However, if there are many words you don't know, it will be hard for you to understand what you read. With a strong vocabulary, you will get more out of newspapers, magazines, books—or anything else you want to read.

3 **A large vocabulary can help you score higher on tests.** Vocabulary is an important part of many tests—for example, the GED exam, college entrance exams, armed forces tests, and job placement tests. Why is that? It's because the people who make up these exams know that vocabulary helps measure what you already know and how easily you can learn new information in the future. The more words you know, the better you will do on these exams.

4   **A solid vocabulary will help you do better in school and at work.** Knowing many words makes you a better reader, writer, speaker, listener, and thinker. These are the skills you need to do well in the classroom and on the job. In school, having a good vocabulary helps you understand your textbooks, classmates, and teachers. And in the world of work, a good vocabulary counts as never before. More and more, workers are being asked to change jobs and learn new skills. Knowing how to learn quickly is the key to doing well in this fast-changing world. A good vocabulary makes it easier for you to understand new ideas so you can get ahead on the job—and stay there.

5   **A strong vocabulary helps you believe in yourself.** Sometimes people who don't have large vocabularies feel they don't have what it takes to do well in today's world. They may sit quietly in the back of the classroom, nervous about joining in. They may hear about an interesting job opening but be afraid to apply. Having a strong vocabulary helps you feel you have what it takes to make your life better. In other words, having a strong vocabulary helps you build confidence. What is *confidence*? It is the belief that you can do things you used to think you would never be able to do.

Now you know why it is so important to have a good vocabulary. The next few pages tell how this book will help you build a strong vocabulary—one that can unlock doors that used to be tightly closed.

HOW *VOCABULARY BASICS* IS DIFFERENT FROM OTHER BOOKS

The way most books try to build vocabulary is by asking students to memorize lists of words. But people usually forget memorized lists quickly. To learn a word really well, you must see and use it a number of times. *Vocabulary Basics* gives you the chance to use the new words in each chapter *seven different ways*. By the end of each chapter, you will easily remember what the new words mean because you will have used them so many times.

UNDERSTANDING THE BOOK AS A WHOLE

Inside Front Cover and Contents

By filling in the blanks below, you will understand how the book is organized. First, turn to the inside front cover. As you can see, the inside front cover provides a chart called _Vocabulary basics_. This chart will help you figure out how to say the vocabulary words in the book. Next, turn to the Table of Contents on pages v–vi. There are _many_ chapters in the book and a unit review after every _books_ chapters. At the end of the last unit review, there are four short sections. The first section shows how to form verb tenses. The second gives information on making _nouns plural_. The third section is a _Limite Answer Key_. The fourth section is a list of the _word list_ in the book.

UNDERSTANDING EACH CHAPTER

Now it's time to turn to the first chapter in the book, on pages 8–13. This chapter, like all the others (except for the unit reviews), has seven parts. Each part is described below.

1. Learning Eight New Words

The first part of the chapter (see pages 8–9) is called "Learning Eight New Words." The left-hand column lists eight **boldfaced** words. Underneath, you are shown how to say, or *pronounce*, each boldfaced word. For example, here is how to say **agreement**, the first word on page 8: uh-**gree**-muhnt. (Remember: for help on how to say the new words, see the guide on the inside front cover.)

After showing how to say the boldfaced word, the chapter gives the word's *part of speech*. What part of speech is *agreement*? It is a *noun*. The vocabulary words in this book are mostly *nouns, adjectives,* and *verbs*. **Nouns** are words used to name something—a person, place, thing, or idea. The words *boyfriend, city, hat,* and *truth* are all nouns. **Adjectives** are words that describe nouns, as in the following word pairs: *old* boyfriend, *large* city, *red* hat, *whole* truth. Many of the words in this book are **verbs**, words that show action. They tell what someone or something is doing. The words *ask, buy, drive, learn,* and *sing* are all verbs.

To the right of each boldfaced word are two sentences that will help you understand its meaning. And below the sentences are three possible meanings for the boldfaced word. From among the three choices, you select the answer that has the closest meaning to that of the boldfaced word. In each sentence, the other words near the boldfaced word—the *context*—will give clues that help you figure out the meaning of the boldfaced word. There are four kinds of context clues: *examples, words with similar meanings, words with opposite meanings,* and *the meaning of the sentence as a whole*. Each kind of context clue is described below.

- **Examples**

  A sentence may have *examples* that help explain the meaning of the boldfaced word. For instance, take a look at the following sentence (from Chapter 1) and note how the examples (in *italics*) help explain the meaning of the word **agreement**:

  > After fighting for hours, the little girls made an **agreement** *to share their toys*.

  The sentence gives an example of an agreement—sharing toys. To figure out what **agreement** means, think about the example. What would it mean if two children said they would share their toys? Now look at the three answer choices below. On the answer line to the left, write the letter of the answer you think is right.

  ___ *Agreement* means   a. fight   b. question   c. promise

  The examples make it clear that the two girls have made a *promise* to each other, so *c* is the correct answer.

- **Words with Similar Meanings**

  Words with the *same* or *almost the same* meaning are called **synonyms** (**sin**-uh-nimz). For example, the words *joyful, happy,* and *pleased* are synonyms because they all mean about the same thing. Synonyms often give clues about the meaning of a nearby unknown word. Look at the following sentence (from Chapter 1) and note how the synonym (in *italics*) helps explain the meaning of the word **prepare**:

> Last year, I **prepared** all kinds of interesting dishes for our holiday dinner. But this year, I'm going to relax and let someone else *make* the meal.

Instead of using *prepare* again in the second sentence, the writer uses the synonym *make*. Now choose the letter of the right answer.

> ____ *Prepare* means   a. get ready   b. watch   c. leave

Since both *prepare the meal* and *make the meal* mean "get the meal ready," answer *a* is correct.

- **Words with Opposite Meanings**

Words with *opposite* or *almost opposite* meanings are called **antonyms** (**an**-toh-nimz). For example, *help* and *hurt* are antonyms, as are *work* and *rest*. Antonyms can help you figure out the meanings of new words. How? By giving the opposite meaning of an unknown word, an antonym makes it easier to figure out what a new word means. Look at the following sentence from Chapter 1 and note how the antonym (in *italics*) helps explain the meaning of the word **cancel**. Then look at the three answer choices below and select the best answer.

> I *had planned to* see the doctor today, but I feel so much better that I think I will **cancel** my visit there.

> ____ *Cancel* means   a. remember   b. not do as planned   c. get ready for

The sentence says that the writer *had planned to* see the doctor but now will *cancel* the visit. You can guess, then, that *cancel* has the opposite meaning of *plan to*. So *b* is the correct answer.

- **The Meaning of the Sentence as a Whole**

Sometimes there is no example, synonym, or antonym in a sentence. But even without these clues, you can figure out what a boldfaced word means by studying *the meaning of the sentence as a whole*. For example, look at the following sentence (from Chapter 1) and see if you can decide on the meaning of the word **flexible** simply by studying the rest of the sentence:

> The new lamp next to my bed has a long neck that is so **flexible** it can be moved any way I want.

> ____ *Flexible* means   a. able to bend   b. real   c. heavy

It's clear that the neck of the new lamp must be able to bend in different ways. So *a* is the correct answer.

As you go through the "Learning Eight New Words" sections, look closely at the two sentences given for each word and at the answer choices. As you figure out the meaning of each word, you are doing what's needed to understand and remember the word. Working with the word in this way and seeing how it is used in a sentence are the keys to completing the rest of the chapter.

2. Matching Words with Meanings

The second part of the chapter (see page 9) is called "Matching Words with Meanings." Often it is not enough to see how a word is used in a sentence. To understand a word fully, most people need to see the meaning, or *definition*, of the word. The matching activity gives the meaning of each new word, but it also makes you look for and think about each meaning. This is the best way to learn and remember a word. Now look at the *Be Careful* note that follows the matching activity. This note reminds you that you should not move on to the rest of the chapter until you are sure that you know the correct meaning of each word.

3. Adding One Word to an Item

The third part of the chapter (see page 10) is called "Adding One Word to a Sentence." This section, with eight sentences, gives you a chance to show how well you understand the new words. After placing *one* word in each sentence, *be sure to check your answers* in the Limited Answer Key at the back of the book. Checking your answers will help you see if you really know the words. If you do, you are ready to complete the rest of the activities, for which answers are not given.

4. Adding Two Words to an Item

The fourth part (see page 10) is called "Adding Two Words to a Sentence." This activity is a bit more difficult because you have to see which *two* words fit best in a sentence. The extra work you do to find the right answers will help you learn the words.

5. Showing You Understand the Words

The fifth part (see page 11), called "Showing You Understand the Words," is made up of two sets of four items. Each item uses one of the chapter's new words. By completing an item or by answering the question asked by an item, you show that you truly understand what the word means. You will, we think, have a lot of fun doing this activity.

6. Adding Words to a Reading

The sixth part (see page 12), called "Adding Words to a Reading," has two interesting readings. By choosing the right word to fill in each blank, you get a good idea of the way the new words can be used in a paragraph.

7. Using the Words When Writing and Talking

The seventh part (see page 13) is called "Using the Words When Writing and Talking." By coming up with your own ending for each item, you will be well on the way to making the words part of your everyday vocabulary.

At the end of the seventh part, you will find a box where you can enter your scores for "Adding One Word to an Item" through "Adding Words to a Reading." To get your score for each part, count how many you got right. Then look at the "Number right" explanation below the box to see what your score is for that part. You should also enter your scores on the Vocabulary Performance Chart found on the inside back cover of the book.

Now you know how the chapters in *Vocabulary Basics* are organized. As you have seen, every chapter gives you the chance to work with the new words *seven times*. Each time you complete an activity, you get closer to making the new words part of your everyday vocabulary. And to give you even more practice, almost every chapter repeats some words from earlier chapters. (These repeated words are marked with small circles—like this°. If you are not sure of the meaning of a repeated word, turn to the Word List on pages 257–258. There you will find the page on which the word was first used.) In short, you will have plenty of chances to learn—and relearn—the words.

UNDERSTANDING THE UNIT REVIEWS

As you saw earlier, there is a unit review at the end of every six chapters. Each unit review offers six different kinds of activities—everything from crossword puzzles to sentence writing. All in all, you will have the chance to practice each word in the unit *three* more times. When you finish the unit reviews, you will have worked *at least ten times* with each word in the book. By then, you should know the words so well that you will be ready to use them whenever you want.

Take a moment to look at the instructions for the final activity in the unit reviews (see page 53, for example). Note that when doing this final activity, you should "feel free to use **any tense of a boldfaced verb** and to make a **boldfaced noun plural**." For example, for the verb *assist,* you might use a number of different *tenses:* "My family *assists* me when I have trouble with my schoolwork," "Last summer, I *assisted* my uncle with the opening of his new store," or "For two weeks, my friends *have been assisting* me with plans for the party." For the noun *volunteer,* you might use the *plural form* and write or say, "Two *volunteers* came to the school to talk about fire safety."

Like many people, you may have trouble remembering the correct form of some verb tenses and the correct plural form of some nouns. So, when doing this final activity, you will probably find it helpful to look at the charts on pages 249–251 and 252. They will give you the help you need.

A FINAL THOUGHT

The facts are in. It *is* important to have a strong vocabulary. Having a good vocabulary makes you a better reader, writer, speaker, thinker, and learner. Having a good vocabulary can make things smoother for you at home, in school, and on the job. But learning new words will not happen easily or by itself. You must decide that you want to build your vocabulary and then work hard with the chapters in this book. If you do, you will not only add to your vocabulary—you will add to your life as well. Good luck.

Judith Nadell
Beth Johnson
Paul Langan

Unit One

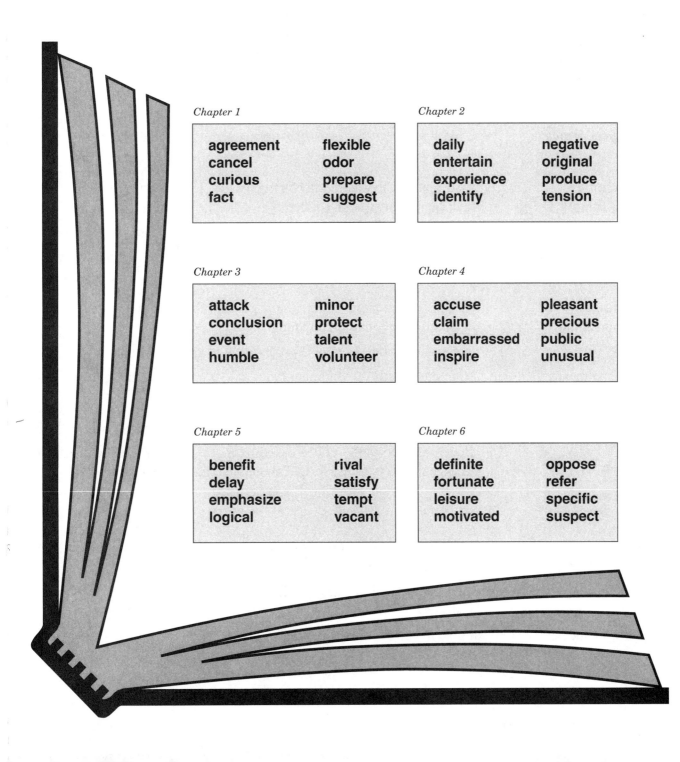

Chapter 1

agreement	flexible
cancel	odor
curious	prepare
fact	suggest

Chapter 2

daily	negative
entertain	original
experience	produce
identify	tension

Chapter 3

attack	minor
conclusion	protect
event	talent
humble	volunteer

Chapter 4

accuse	pleasant
claim	precious
embarrassed	public
inspire	unusual

Chapter 5

benefit	rival
delay	satisfy
emphasize	tempt
logical	vacant

Chapter 6

definite	oppose
fortunate	refer
leisure	specific
motivated	suspect

agreement	flexible
cancel	odor
curious	prepare
fact	suggest

Learning Eight New Words

In the space at the left, write the letter of the meaning closest to that of each **boldfaced** word. Use the other words (the *context*) in each sentence to help you figure out the word's meaning.

1 agreement
(uh-**gree**-muhnt)
– noun

- After fighting for hours, the little girls made an **agreement** to share their toys.
- Len is angry because Anita broke their **agreement** to take turns doing the dishes.

___*Agreement* means   a. fight   b. question   c. promise

2 cancel
(**kan**-suhl)
– verb

- I had planned to see the doctor today, but I feel so much better that I think I will **cancel** my visit there.
- The teacher **canceled** the test because so many students were absent.

___*Cancel* means   a. remember   b. not do as planned   c. get ready for

3 curious
(**kyoor**-ee-uhss)
– adjective

- My son is so **curious** about what I got him for his birthday that he asks me questions about it all day long.
- Scientists are **curious** people—they want to know how nature works.

___*Curious* means   a. not interested   b. angry   c. full of questions

4 fact
(**fakt**)
– noun

- It is a strange **fact** that the male sea horse, not the female, gives birth.
- After the robbery, the police asked us many questions. They wanted to get as many **facts** as they could about what had happened.

___*Fact* means   a. rule   b. something true   c. long story

5 flexible
(**flek**-suh-buhl)
– adjective

- The new lamp next to my bed has a long neck that is so **flexible** it can be moved any way I want.
- Karen is so **flexible** that she can sit down and lift her ankle over her head.

___*Flexible* means   a. able to bend   b. real   c. heavy

6 **odor**
  (**oh**-duhr)
  – noun

- If you think there is an **odor** of gas in your home, you should call the gas company right away.
- As I painted the room, the **odor** of the paint began to give me a headache.

___*Odor* means   ⓐ smell   b. cost   c. warm feeling

7 **prepare**
  (pree-**pair**)
  – verb

- To **prepare** for the difficult test, Jeff decided to stay up all night and study.
- Last year, I **prepared** all kinds of interesting dishes for our holiday dinner. But this year, I'm going to relax and let someone else make the meal.

___*Prepare* means   ⓐ get ready   b. watch   c. leave

8 **suggest**
  (suhg-**jest**)
  – verb

- When my son gets bored, I often **suggest** that he call his friends or go outside.
- My cousin **suggested** that we have Thanksgiving dinner at her house. She loves to cook for company.

___*Suggest* means   a. fear   b. forget   ⓒ offer an idea

Matching Words with Meanings

Here are the meanings, or *definitions*, of the eight new words. Write each word next to its meaning. The sentences above and on the facing page will help you decide on the meaning of each word.

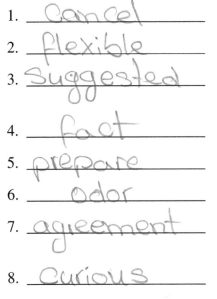

1. ___Cancel___   To stop something that was planned; to call something off

2. ___Flexible___   Able to bend

3. ___Suggested___   To give someone an idea about something; to offer a thought for others to think about

4. ___Fact___   Something true; something that can be proved

5. ___prepare___   To get ready

6. ___Odor___   A smell

7. ___agreement___   Wanting to know more about something; having questions about someone or something

8. ___Curious___   A promise people make to one another; an understanding between people

BE CAREFUL: Don't go any further until you know the answers above are correct. Then you can use the meanings to help you in the following activities. After a while, you will know the words so well that you won't need to check the definitions at all.

Adding One Word to an Item

Complete each item below by writing one word from the box on the answer line at the left. Use each word once.

a. **agreement**	c. **curious**	e. **flexible**	g. **prepare**
b. **cancel**	d. **fact**	f. **odor**	h. **suggests**

fact 1. Diane came to an . . ? . . with her parents that she would get home before midnight on weekends.

cancel 2. During heavy snowstorms, airlines often . . ? . . flights because it is too dangerous to fly.

curious 3. I was . . ? . . about the two new students. They arrived in class carrying briefcases and laptop computers.

flexible 4. I . . ? . . for a visit from my two-year-old niece by hiding all the glass objects so she can't break them.

prepare 5. A fishing rod must be . . ? . . so that it does not break when a fish pulls on the line.

odor 6. The . . ? . . of dirty socks and old sneakers filled the boys' bedroom.

agreement 7. It is a . . ? . . that the world is round.

suggest 8. Before I hand in a paper, I read it out loud to my sister, and she . . ? . . ways to make it better.

Adding Two Words to an Item

Complete each item below by writing **two** words from the box on the answer lines at the left. Use each word once.

a. **agreement**	c. **curious**	e. **flexible**	g. **prepares**
b. **canceled**	d. **facts**	f. **odor**	h. **suggest**

prepares *flexible* 1–2. My muscles get stiff when I run, so I asked the coach to . . ? . . some exercises to make me more . . ? . . .

suggest *agreement* 3–4. Before you make an . . ? . . to buy a used car, learn all the . . ? . . — such as how many miles it has gone and what needs to be fixed.

facts *cancel* 5–6. Julia is . . ? . . about her new neighbors. When they invited her to lunch, she . . ? . . another lunch date so that she could pay them a visit.

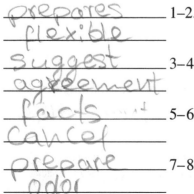

prepare *odor* 7–8. When Jack cleans the smelly old barn, he . . ? . . by putting a handkerchief over his nose to keep out the . . ? . . .

Showing You Understand the Words

PART A

In the space at the left, write the letter of the choice that best completes the sentence or answers the question.

___ 1. If you called to **cancel** a visit to the dentist, you might say,
    a. "Where's the office?"
    b. "I'd like to come in as soon as possible."
    c. "Sorry. I won't be able to come after all."

___ 2. Which of the following would you expect to have a bad **odor**?
    a. An old garbage bag
    b. A broken piano
    c. A rusty bike

___ 3. To **prepare** for a party, you
    a. clean up after the guests leave.
    b. buy food and drinks.
    c. refill your guests' empty plates.

___ 4. If you **suggest** going to a movie with someone, you probably
    a. have other plans that night.
    b. enjoy being with the person.
    c. do not like the person.

PART B

In the space at the left, write the letter of the choice that best completes the sentence or answers the question.

___ 5. People are likely to have an **agreement** with
    a. a stranger.
    b. the owner of the building their apartment is in.
    c. their supermarket.

___ 6. If parents are **curious** about how their kids are doing in school, they will probably
    a. ask the kids questions about teachers, classes, and homework.
    b. ask no questions about teachers, classes, and homework.
    c. sign report cards without looking at the grades given.

___ 7. Which of the following is a **fact**?
    a. "What is your name?"
    b. "Canada is north of the United States."
    c. "I wonder what we are having for lunch."

___ 8. Which of the following is **flexible**?
    a. A bowling ball
    b. A rubber band
    c. A pencil

Adding Words to a Reading

A. The Nose Knows

Read the following paragraphs carefully. Then fill in each blank with a word from the box. Use each word once.

a. **curious**	b. **fact**	c. **odors**	d. **suggest**

Have you ever been (1)___*curious*___ about what life would be like if you couldn't smell anything? Maybe you think, "That wouldn't be so bad." After all, you wouldn't miss some (2)___*fact*___, like the smell coming from the guy sitting next to you who hasn't taken a bath in several weeks. But think about it again. All day, every day, our noses pass along information to us. We walk by the kitchen, pick up the smell of apple pie in the oven, and know that we will enjoy a tasty slice later on. Or we go outside on a warm spring day and pick up the clean smell of freshly cut grass. Other smells that aren't so nice, like those of spilled gasoline or burning wood, may protect us by warning of danger.

It is a (3)___*suggest*___ that smells make us remember the past. For instance, the smell of the outdoors after a rainstorm may remind us of an early-morning hike in the woods we took years ago. Scientists are not sure why smells remind us of the past, but they know it is so. Indeed, scientists (4)___*odor*___ that smell may be the most powerful of all our senses.

B. Barbie: A Bad Example?

Read the following paragraph carefully. Then fill in each blank with a word from the box. Use each word once.

a. **agreement**	b. **cancel**	c. **flexible**	d. **prepare**

"I want a Barbie. I want a Barbie." Most parents have heard that cry. Lots of little girls love Barbie. Barbie has been around for many years, and she will probably be around for many more. But some parents worry about Barbie. They worry that as their daughters (5)___*cancel*___ to grow up, they will look at Barbie and think, "She's so pretty. I want to be like her." The problem is that no healthy, normal woman looks like Barbie. If Barbie were full-sized, she would be more than six feet tall and weigh about one hundred pounds. Little girls may get the idea that in order to be pretty, they must have a very thin body. Parents need to tell their daughters that it is more important to have a strong, (6)___*flexible*___ body—one that can run and jump, twist and turn. Of course, it's hard to tell a little girl that she can't have a Barbie if all her friends do. So some parents get together and, among themselves, make an (7)___*agreement*___ not to buy Barbie dolls. The parents (8)___*prepare*___ their plans to buy Barbie and buy dolls that have more healthy-looking bodies.

Using the Words When Writing and Talking

Now that you understand the meanings of the eight new words in the chapter, you are ready to use them on paper and in speaking. Complete each sentence below in a way that shows you really know what each **boldfaced** word means. Take a few minutes to think about your answer before writing it down and saying it out loud.

1. People sharing an apartment often make an **agreement** to ___eche other___

2. The school had to **cancel** the trip because ___The bass drive she sek___

3. Small children are very **curious**. They ___Ask adult so mony question about Life.___

4. It is a **fact** that a good education will ___be talk all of the world.___

5. To stay **flexible**, many people _____

6. As I passed by the kitchen, I picked up the **odor** of ___The stove.___

7. To **prepare** the store for the holiday season, the workers _____

8. If a young married couple is having money problems. I might **suggest** that the couple ___of the month.___

Scores	Adding One Word to an Item	_75_%	Showing You Understand the Words	_100_%
	Adding Two Words to an Item	_50_%	Adding Words to a Reading	_13_%

Number right: 8 = 100%, 7 = 88%, 6 = 75%, 5 = 63%, 4 = 50%, 3 = 38%, 2 = 25%, 1 = 13%
Enter your scores above and in the vocabulary performance chart on the inside back cover of the book.

daily	negative
entertain	original
experience	produce
identify	tension

Learning Eight New Words

In the space at the left, write the letter of the meaning closest to that of each **boldfaced** word. Use the other words (the *context*) in each sentence to help you figure out the word's meaning.

1 daily
(**day**-lee)
– adjective

- Noah goes to the gym seven days a week. He says **daily** exercise keeps him healthy and happy.
- Washing the dishes is one of my sister's **daily** jobs.

___*Daily* means

   a. happening   b. happening   c. happening
      each year   each week   each day

2 entertain
(en-tur-**tayn**)
– verb

- Cristine thought the novel would **entertain** her, but instead it put her to sleep.
- While we were stuck at home during the snowstorm, my brother **entertained** us with ghost stories.

___*Entertain* means

   a. change   b. make sleepy   c. interest greatly

3 experience
(ek-**spihr**-ee-uhnss)
– noun

- Having my car break down on a busy highway was one **experience** I don't want to have again.
- I'm happy to say that working at the day care center turned out to be a wonderful **experience**.

___*Experience* means

   a. difficult question   b. something that a   c. good reason
                        person lives through

4 identify
(ii-**den**-tuh-fii)
– verb

- Palm readers say they can **identify** many things about a person by looking at the lines of the hand.
- The police used the fingerprints they found to **identify** who the bank robbers were.

___*Identify* means

   a. dislike   b. make   c. find out

5 negative
(**neg**-uh-tiv)
– adjective

- People who feel **negative** about themselves often have trouble making friends.
- I turned off the TV because I didn't want to hear another **negative** story about crime and violence.

___*Negative* means

   a. nice   b. bad   c. interesting

6 original
(uh-**rij**-uh-nuhl)
– adjective

- My ideas for the baby shower were boring and unexciting, but Carla's were interesting and **original**.
- All the students in the class thought that the ending of my short story was **original** and very different from anything they had ever read.

___*Original* means   a. quiet   b. weak   (c.) fresh

7 produce
(pruh-**dooss**)
– verb

- The new factory in town can **produce** millions of bottles a year.
- My little nephew **produces** the loudest snores I have ever heard.

___*Produce* means   (a.) make   b. break   c. take

8 tension
(**ten**-shuhn)
– noun

- Whenever she gets upset or feels **tension**, Jane takes a hot bath.
- When I feel **tension**, I relax by going for a long, quiet walk.

___*Tension* means   a. rest   b. happiness   (c.) worry

Matching Words with Meanings

Here are the meanings, or *definitions*, of the eight new words. Write each word next to its meaning. The sentences above and on the facing page will help you decide on the meaning of each word.

1. ___Negative___   Bad; without anything good; not positive

2. ___experience___   Anything someone has seen or lived through; what happens to someone

3. ___indentify___   To find out exactly who someone is or what something is

4. ___daily___   Done every day; happening or appearing every day

5. 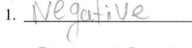___produce___   To make; to bring about

6. ___fresh___   New; not like everything else

7. ___Tension___   A nervous feeling; unrest caused by worry

8. ___entertain___   To keep people's interest with something happy or enjoyable

BE CAREFUL: Don't go any further until you know the answers above are correct. Then you can use the meanings to help you in the following activities. After a while, you will know the words so well that you won't need to check the definitions at all.

Adding One Word to an Item

Complete each item below by writing one word from the box on the answer line at the left. Use each word once.

a. **daily**	c. **experience**	e. **negative**	g. **produced**
b. **entertained**	d. **identify**	f. **original**	h. **tension**

Tension   1. Many students feel . . ? . . before they take a test.

produced   2. After months of cutting and sewing, the group . . ? . . a beautiful quilt.

daily   3. My neighbor, Mrs. Yoo, likes to read the . . ? . . newspaper on her porch.

experience   4. My husband's high-school graduation was an . . ? . . we will never forget.

original   5. I was happy when my boss told me I had some helpful and . . ? . . ideas for improving business.

Indentify   6. My blind date said I could . . ? . . him at the coffee shop by his red hair and beard.

negative   7. Gina doesn't seem to like her relatives. She's always saying . . ? . . things about them.

entertained   8. My three-year-old nephew . . ? . . us by singing a little song about a spider in the rain.

Adding Two Words to an Item

Complete each item below by writing **two** words from the box on the answer lines at the left. Use each word once.

a. **daily**	c. **experience**	e. **negative**	g. **produced**
b. **entertaining**	d. **identify**	f. **original**	h. **tension**

entertaining
daily   1–2. Chandra takes a . . ? . . walk right after work because it helps her calm down after a long day filled with . . ? . . .

experience
negative   3–4. My . . ? . . with dates has often been good, but my brother's has always been . . ? . . .

Identify
Tension   5–6. We could not . . ? . . the rock star who was . . ? . . the crowd, but we knew we had seen him somewhere else.

original
produced   7–8. Years ago, the Coca-Cola Company came up with a completely . . ? . . recipe for a new drink. Today that drink is called "Coke," and millions of gallons of it are . . ? . . each year.

Showing You Understand the Words

PART A

In the space at the left, write the letter of the choice that best completes the sentence.

_____ 1. It's a good idea for you to make a **daily** habit of
    a. going to a doctor.
    b. brushing your teeth.
    c. taking a vacation.

_____ 2. If you want to **entertain** friends who are sick, you might
    a. bring them their homework from school.
    b. bring them several of their favorite movies to play on the VCR.
    c. let them sleep.

_____ 3. You would probably have **negative** feelings about
    a. friends who were nice to you.
    b. a neighbor who visited you in the hospital.
    c. a dog that bit you.

_____ 4. At school, you would probably feel **tension** if your teacher
    a. gave a surprise test.
    b. gave you an "A" on a paper.
    c. said, "Class is over now."

PART B

In the space at the left, write the letter of the choice that best completes the sentence or answers the question.

_____ 5. Which of the following would be a scary driving **experience**?
    a. Listening to the car radio
    b. Rolling down the car window
    c. Sliding on an icy road

_____ 6. To **identify** a patient's problem, a doctor may
    a. do some tests.
    b. send a bill.
    c. give the patient some pills.

_____ 7. If students have an **original** idea for a play, they will
    a. write the play themselves.
    b. copy someone else's play.
    c. listen to a tape of another play.

_____ 8. The milk from cows is used to **produce**
    a. meat.
    b. leather.
    c. cheese.

Adding Words to a Reading

A. Feeling Blue

Read the following paragraph carefully. Then fill in each blank with a word from the box. Use each word once.

a. **entertain**	b. **experience**	c. **produce**	d. **tension**

At some point or another, every one of us has gotten up in the morning feeling a lot of (1) *Tension*. Problems at work, difficulties at home, and too many bills to pay can make us feel down. Studies show that these bad moods can make a real difference in how we feel about ourselves and our lives. For example, bad moods often lead to or (2) *entertain* sad, gloomy thoughts. We may get down on ourselves and think we're not worth much. Thinking that life will always be this way, we may decide that nothing in the world can possibly (3) *produce* us or make us feel better. These beliefs are false, but they seem true at the time. Also, when we are in a bad mood, even a good (4) *experience* —like an excellent meal or a wonderful evening with friends—usually isn't enough to raise our spirits. The only bright spot about bad moods is this fact°—they always pass. When they do, the bad thoughts and feelings pass too.

B. A Late Love Letter

Read the following paragraphs carefully. Then fill in each blank with a word from the box. Use each word once.

a. **daily**	b. **identified**	c. **negative**	d. **original**

Years ago, a man working in Hawaii wrote a love letter to his wife in Seattle. He put the letter in a bottle and threw the bottle into the Pacific Ocean. He hoped the bottle would end up on a beach near Seattle. However, the bottle washed up on a beach thousands of miles away, where it was picked up by Chris Willie. Willie, of course, was curious° about the letter. He took it out of the bottle and read what the man had written. Smiling, Willie thought to himself, "There are so many sad, (5) *identified* things in the world. It's wonderful that the writer has found such a surprising and (6) *original* way to show his love." Then Willie put the letter and the bottle in a package, which he mailed to Seattle. Soon, though, the package was returned, with the message "No longer at this address."

Next, Willie mailed the package to a Seattle (7)___daily___ newspaper. The paper printed the letter, but no one called to say she was the woman to whom the letter was addressed. Six years later, a newspaper reporter finally (8)___Negative___ the woman and read her the letter over the phone. The letter began, "If by the time this letter reaches you I am old and gray, I know that our love will be as great as it is today." When the reporter finished reading, he heard the woman laughing. "Well," she said, "I hate to tell you, but we got divorced." Then she hung up.

Using the Words When Writing and Talking

Now that you understand the meanings of the eight new words in the chapter, you are ready to use them on paper and in speaking. Complete each sentence below in a way that shows you really know what each **boldfaced** word means. Take a few minutes to think about your answer before writing it down and saying it out loud.

1. Many older people like to take a **daily** nap because ___thy taerd___

2. To **entertain** young children, teachers often _____

3. Riding a roller coaster is an **experience** that _____

4. If you want to **identify** your car easily in a parking lot, you _____

5. People who say **negative** things about others often _____

6. I came up with an **original** way to _____

7. In order to **produce** a nice dinner, you will need _____

8. When I feel **tension**, I _____

Scores	Adding One Word to an Item	_____%	Showing You Understand the Words	_____%
	Adding Two Words to an Item	_____%	Adding Words to a Reading	_____%

Number right: 8 = 100%, 7 = 88%, 6 = 75%, 5 = 63%, 4 = 50%, 3 = 38%, 2 = 25%, 1 = 13%
Enter your scores above and in the vocabulary performance chart on the inside back cover of the book.

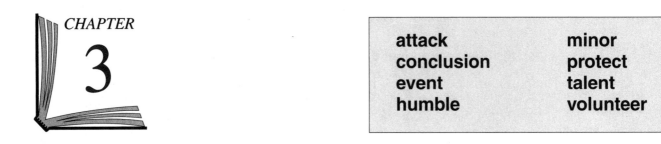

attack   minor
conclusion   protect
event   talent
humble   volunteer

Learning Eight New Words

In the space at the left, write the letter of the meaning closest to that of each **boldfaced** word. Use the other words (the *context*) in each sentence to help you figure out the word's meaning.

1 attack
(uh-**tak**)
– verb

• Army ants **attack** and often destroy other insects in their path.
• The soldiers **attacked** the sleeping village without any warning.

___ *Attack* means   a. run away   b. hurt   c. keep safe

2 conclusion
(kuhn-**kloo**-shuhn)
– noun

• In most action movies, the **conclusion** is always the same—the hero beats the bad guy and wins the heart of the beautiful girl.
• My first date started out well but came to a poor **conclusion**. My car broke down and had to be towed to a garage.

___ *Conclusion* means   a. last part   b. best part   c. first part

3 event
(i-**vent**)
– noun

• Our family party is an **event** that I look forward to each year.
• The first day of school is a big **event** for most children.

___ *Event* means   a. important happening   b. problem   c. special skill

4 humble
(**huhm**-buhl)
– adjective

• Jack always brags about himself, but Kathy is **humble** even when she has reason to be proud.
• Even though his home run won the game, Ali was so **humble** that he just said, "I was lucky" when we thanked him.

___ *Humble* means   a. loud   b. afraid   c. not bragging

5 minor
(**mii**-nor)
– adjective

• Although Tanya's car was badly hurt in the crash, Tanya had only **minor** cuts and bruises.
• The teacher must have liked my paper because she made only a few **minor** changes.

___ *Minor* means   a. dangerous   b. small   c. important

6 protect
(pruh-**tekt**)
– verb

- Before putting the glass candlesticks in a bag, the salesperson wrapped them in newspaper to **protect** them.
- The mother turtle **protects** her eggs by burying them in the sand.

___ *Protect* means   a. hurt   b. look at   c. keep safe

7 talent
(tal-**uhnt**)
– noun

- Some lucky people are born with a **talent** for making friends easily.
- Lian was happy when her uncle told her she had a **talent** for singing.

___ *Talent* means   a. dislike   b. skill   c. fear

8 volunteer
(*vol*-uhn-**teer**)
– noun

- Mrs. Jackson has been a **volunteer** at the hospital for so many years that many people think she is a paid worker.
- My son's teacher sent a note home that said, "I need parent **volunteers** to help when we take trips away from school."

___ *Volunteer* means   a. bad worker   b. paid worker   c. worker who is not paid

Matching Words with Meanings

Here are the meanings, or *definitions*, of the eight new words. Write each word next to its meaning. The sentences above and on the facing page will help you decide on the meaning of each word.

1. ___protect___   To keep safe

2. ___worker who is not paid___ Someone who works or helps for no pay

3. ___Talent___   A special skill, often one that someone is born with

4. ___Humble___   Not important

5. ___Volunteer___   Not thinking too highly of oneself

6. ___Attack___   To hurt; to begin to harm

7. ___Event___   Something that happens, often an important happening

8. ___Minor___   The ending of something

BE CAREFUL: Don't go any further until you know the answers above are correct. Then you can use the meanings to help you in the following activities. After a while, you will know the words so well that you won't need to check the definitions at all.

Adding One Word to an Item

Complete each item below by writing one word from the box on the answer line at the left. Use each word once.

a. **attack**	c. **event**	e. **minor**	g. **talent**
b. **conclusion**	d. **humble**	f. **protects**	h. **volunteers**

Minor _____ 1. Although my VCR had only a . . ? . . problem, it still cost me a lot of money to get it fixed.

Event _____ 2. The first day of school is an important . . ? . . in a child's life.

Protects _____ 3. At the . . ? . . of the school play, the parents and teachers stood up and cheered the kids.

Attack _____ 4. If you tease an animal, you may cause it to . . ? . . you.

Talent _____ 5. I can't draw a straight line, but my son has so much . . ? . . in art that he can draw anything.

Volunteers _____ 6. Since the city did not have money to pay for more police, the mayor asked for . . ? . . to help keep the streets safe.

Conclusion _____ 7. My neighbor is so . . ? . . that he didn't want to accept an award for all the work he has done with the elderly.

Humble _____ 8. Even a gentle animal can be dangerous when it . . ? . . its young.

Adding Two Words to an Item

Complete each item below by writing **two** words from the box on the answer lines at the left. Use each word once.

a. **attacks**	c. **event**	e. **minor**	g. **talent**
b. **conclusion**	d. **humble**	f. **protect**	h. **volunteers**

Talent _____
Event _____ 1–2. Many famous athletes have lots of . . ? . . but few of these "heroes" seem like nice, . . ? . . people.

Protect _____
attack _____ 3–4. Some people think owning a gun is a good way to . . ? . . themselves in case a burglar . . ? . . , but I think having a gun is dangerous.

Conclusion _____
minor _____ 5–6. The main . . ? . . at the picnic was a bicycle race. It went well except for a . . ? . . problem—one of the bikes got a flat tire.

Conclusion _____
volunteers _____ 7–8. At the . . ? . . of Jim's birthday party, everybody left so quickly that we could not find any . . ? . . to help clean up the mess.

Showing You Understand the Words

PART A

In the space at the left, write the letter of the choice that best completes the sentence or answers the question.

____ 1. Bees would **attack** you if you
   a. poked their nest with your finger.
   b. had someone carefully remove their nest.
   c. stayed away from their nest.

____ 2. At the **conclusion** of a movie, you would probably
   a. sit down and look at the screen.
   b. leave the theater.
   c. look around for a better seat.

____ 3. Which of the following would you think of as a real **event** in your life?
   a. Getting married
   b. Taking a trip to the supermarket
   c. Eating dinner at a fast-food restaurant

____ 4. You would probably think skaters had **talent** if they
   a. skated slowly around the rink.
   b. fell down several times.
   c. spun four times in the air before landing.

PART B

In the space at the left, write the letter of the choice that best completes the sentence or answers the question.

____ 5. After winning a game of basketball, **humble** players might
   a. brag that they are better than everyone else.
   b. dance around and shout that they had won.
   c. say that the losers had played well.

____ 6. Which of the following is a **minor** problem that might slow people on their way to work?
   a. A short rain shower
   b. A big flood
   c. A bad snowstorm

____ 7. A good watchdog can **protect** its owner from
   a. spending too much money on pet tags.
   b. strange calls on the phone.
   c. someone trying to break into the house.

____ 8. The **volunteers** at the zoo probably
   a. love working with animals.
   b. are paid for the work they do.
   c. don't like animals.

Adding Words to a Reading

A. Ads That Lie

Read the following paragraphs carefully. Then fill in each blank with a word from the box. Use each word once.

a. **conclusion**	b. **events**	c. **protect**	d. **talent**

Every day of our lives, ads send messages about drinking and smoking that just are not true. It's time we learned how to (1)___*protect*___ ourselves and our kids from these dangerous lies. At the (2)___*conclusion*___ of a long day at work or school, many of us come home and flip on the television. What do we see? We will probably see a TV ad showing healthy young people drinking beer and enjoying life. Maybe they are at the beach, on the ski slopes, or at a party. By the time we are old enough to vote, we will have seen this kind of TV commercial more than 75,000 times. These ads suggest° that drinking is part of a fun-filled life. Is that really true? Not at all. Studies show that drinking leads to car accidents, fighting, loss of memory, birth defects, and more.

Ads for smoking are no better. In magazines and on signs, beautiful young people puff on cigarettes as they enjoy fun-filled (3)___*events*___ like games of volleyball or tennis. But by now, we know that smoking is not part of a healthy life. In real life, top athletes—those who have real (4)___*Talent*___—don't reach for a cigarette at game time. They know that smoking will harm their bodies and can lead to cancer, heart disease, and lung problems.

If you are an adult and you drink and smoke, that's your choice. But to young children who don't know the truth, these ads are dangerous. Cigarettes and beer won't give them strength, good looks, or lots of friends. They will just make them sick. And that's the truth.

B. Horrible Hiccups!

Read the following paragraph carefully. Then fill in each blank with a word from the box. Use each word once.

a. **attacked**	b. **humble**	c. **minor**	d. **volunteer**

Everyone gets the hiccups. To most people, they are just a (5)___*minor*___ problem. But for some people, hiccups can cause real trouble. Between 1948 and 1956, one man hiccupped 160 million times! He tried everything to stop them—drinking a cold glass of water, getting scared by one of his friends, holding his breath. They still came back. Then one day, the hiccups simply stopped. Heinz Isecke, a plumber from England, had an even worse experience.° Starting in 1973, Isecke was (6)_Attacked_ by a fit of hiccups that lasted eight years. Isecke hiccuped so many times that he was unable to sleep. He even had an operation to get rid of the hiccups, but it didn't work. Isecke was a quiet, (7)_Humble_ man who hated to trouble others. But he was so bothered by his hiccups that he asked for help from all over the world. After a few weeks, an unknown (8)_Volunteer_ sent Isecke, free of charge, a "secret" herbal drink. The day after he tried it, Isecke's hiccups were gone. What was in the drink? No one is sure. So the next time you have the hiccups, just be glad you are not Isecke.

Using the Words When Writing and Talking

Now that you understand the meanings of the eight new words in the chapter, you are ready to use them on paper and in speaking. Complete each sentence below in a way that shows you really know what each **boldfaced** word means. Take a few minutes to think about your answer before writing it down and saying it out loud.

1. One reason why someone's dog might **attack** is _____

   _____

2. At the **conclusion** of the horror movie, the monster _____

   _____

3. One of the most important **events** in my life was _____

   _____

4. One of the most **humble** people I know _____

   _____

5. My neighbors have a **minor** problem with their new apartment. It _____

   _____

6. To **protect** your family and home from fire, you should _____

   _____

7. I wish I had a **talent** for _____

   _____

8. One way to keep a park clean is to ask **volunteers** to _____

   _____

Scores	Adding One Word to an Item	_____%	Showing You Understand the Words	_____%
	Adding Two Words to an Item	_____%	Adding Words to a Reading	_____%

Number right: 8 = 100%, 7 = 88%, 6 = 75%, 5 = 63%, 4 = 50%, 3 = 38%, 2 = 25%, 1 = 13%
Enter your scores above and in the vocabulary performance chart on the inside back cover of the book.

accuse	pleasant
claim	precious
embarrassed	public
inspire	unusual

Learning Eight New Words

In the space at the left, write the letter of the meaning closest to that of each **boldfaced** word. Use the other words (the *context*) in each sentence to help you figure out the word's meaning.

1 accuse
(uh-**kyooz**)
– verb

something wrong

• My roommates often **accuse** me of eating food they had bought for themselves.

• My mother asked my little brother if he had spread jam all over the wall. He said "no" and **accused** his teddy bear of being the guilty one.

___*Accuse* means   a. ask   b. blame   c. thank

2 claim
(**klaym**)
– verb

• The ads **claim** that the new diet pills melt away fat while you sleep.

• Car dealers often **claim** that their prices are the lowest in town.

___*Claim* means   a. say that it is true   b. hide   c. forget to say

3 embarrassed
(em-**ba**-ruhsst)
– adjective

nervoso

• Teenage boys often feel **embarrassed** when their voices sound deep one minute and squeaky the next.

• Suki felt **embarrassed** when she dropped a tray loaded with food on the floor of the cafeteria.

___*Embarrassed* means   a. proud   b. easy to like   c. silly and ashamed

4 inspire
(in-**spiir**)
– verb

• Cool fall days **inspire** me to take long walks in the woods.

• The movie *Rocky* **inspired** Stan to become a boxer.

___*Inspire* means   a. stop someone from doing something   b. make someone afraid to do something   c. make someone want to do something

5 pleasant
(**plez**-uhnt)
– adjective

• Let's invite the new neighbors to our party. They seem **pleasant**.

• Rosa smiled at the **pleasant** sound of her children laughing and playing outside.

___*Pleasant* means   a. sleepy   b. mean   c. nice

6 precious
(**presh**-uhss)
– adjective

- Lawrence is so careful with his children that it is plain they are **precious** to him.
- The painting is so **precious** that the museum will never sell it.

___*Precious* means   a. great in value   b. not important   c. funny

7 public
(**puhb**-lik)
– adjective

- Thousands of people enjoyed the city's **public** pools last summer.
- Anyone who lives in the city can use the **public** library without paying.

___*Public* means   a. secret   b. not crowded   c. open to all

8 unusual
(uhn-**yoo**-zhoo-uhl)
– adjective

- Most lions have a golden-brown color, but the **unusual** lion we saw at the zoo was white.
- It is **unusual** to have snow in June, but sometimes it happens.

___*Unusual* means   a. surprising   b. helpful   c. boring

Matching Words with Meanings

Here are the meanings, or *definitions*, of the eight new words. Write each word next to its meaning. The sentences above and on the facing page will help you decide on the meaning of each word.

1. _great in value_ Easy to like; enjoyable; lovely

2. _public_ Open to everyone; not private

3. _unusual_ Not often happening or seen; strange; not usual

4. _blame_ To say someone has done something wrong; to charge someone with a fault or crime

5. _nice_ Worth a lot; having great value

6. _inspire_ To get someone to want to do something; to move someone to take action

7. _Embarrassed_ Feeling silly and ashamed

8. _claim_ To say that something is true, often without being able to show that it is so

BE CAREFUL: Don't go any further until you know the answers above are correct. Then you can use the meanings to help you in the following activities. After a while, you will know the words so well that you won't need to check the definitions at all.

Adding One Word to an Item

Complete each item below by writing one word from the box on the answer line at the left. Use each word once.

a. accused	c. embarrassed	e. pleasant	g. public
b. claims	d. inspires	f. precious	h. unusual

(handwritten notes: wrong, nervoso, nice, greatvalue, open all, tall thru, do something, surprising)

___Inspires___ 1. The teacher . . ? . . Sandra of cheating on the test.

_____ 2. The queen of England owns many famous and . . ? . . jewels.

___Embarrassed___ 3. Many people get red-faced and . . ? . . when given a compliment.

___Pleasant___ 4. One reason people love spring and fall is that the weather then is often so . . ? . . .

___unusual___ 5. Ms. Lennox is a great teacher. She . . ? . . students to do their best.

___public___ 6. I go to a private school, but all my friends go to . . ? . . school.

___precious___ 7. It is . . ? . . for my kids not to be hungry. If they don't want to eat, they must be sick.

___claims___ 8. Jerry . . ? . . that he told his friends he would be late, but no one remembers hearing him say that.

Adding Two Words to an Item

Complete each item below by writing **two** words from the box on the answer lines at the left. Use each word once.

a. accused	c. embarrassed	e. pleasant	g. public
b. claim	d. inspired	f. precious	h. unusual

_____
_____ 1–2. A man at the hotel . . ? . . the person who cleaned his room of stealing a . . ? . . ring.

___Embarrassed___
___public___ 3–4. At home, Troy's wife calls him "Sweetie Pie," but he would be . . ? . . if she used that name in a . . ? . . place, where many other people are around.

___pleasant___
_____ 5–6. It's hard work to be a Santa Claus in a department store. You have to act . . ? . . for hours while children . . ? . . that they have been good all year long.

_____
_____ 7–8. An old girlfriend who liked birds . . ? . . Robert to take up the . . ? . . hobby of finding and saving bird feathers.

Showing You Understand the Words

PART A

In the space at the left, write the letter of the choice that best completes the sentence or answers the question.

___ 1. You would probably feel **embarrassed** if you
   a. cleaned your home well.
   b. forgot your neighbor's name.
   c. finished a good book.

___ 2. To **inspire** a friend to begin an exercise program, you might tell him or her
   a. how much better you feel since you started exercising.
   b. how difficult it is to find the time to exercise.
   c. how expensive it can be to start an exercise program.

___ 3. Which of these would you find a **pleasant** greeting?
   a. "What are *you* doing here?"
   b. "Hi, how are you? You look great!"
   c. "I'm too busy to see you right now."

___ 4. Which of the following would be an **unusual** way for you to get to work in the morning?
   a. Driving a car
   b. Taking a bus
   c. Hopping on one foot

PART B

In the space at the left, write the letter of the choice that best completes the sentence or answers the question.

___ 5. If several store owners **accuse** a person of stealing, they have to
   a. show that the person took things without paying.
   b. show that the person paid for what was taken.
   c. forgive the person.

___ 6. The police **claim** that they will make an arrest soon. The guilty person probably feels
   a. happy.
   b. nervous.
   c. bored.

___ 7. How do most people treat a **precious** watch?
   a. They step all over it.
   b. They take good care of it.
   c. They trade it for something better.

___ 8. Who can go to a **public** meeting of the town council?
   a. Only the mayor
   b. Only members of the town council
   c. Anyone

Adding Words to a Reading

A. An Upsetting Dream

Read the following paragraphs carefully. Then fill in each blank with a word from the box. Use each word once.

a. **claimed**	b. **embarrassed**	c. **inspired**	d. **unusual**

When I was in high school, I had an upsetting dream. It was about a science teacher that I really liked. Her name was Mrs. Kahn. She was kind and friendly and (1)_____ me to work hard. Mrs. Kahn had a ring that I liked a lot. It was made of gold bands that were braided together. One day after school, she told me that her husband had given the ring to her on their first anniversary and that it meant a great deal to her.

In my dream, I was inside Mrs. Kahn's house. She had gone into the kitchen to get us cold drinks. While she was gone, I saw she had left her ring on the table. Before I thought about it, I did something strange and (2)_____. I picked up the ring and started putting it in my pocket. Just at that moment, I looked up and saw Mrs. Kahn standing at the door watching me. Although we both knew I was lying, I (3)_____ that I was only looking at the ring closely because I liked it so much. Mrs. Kahn didn't say anything, but at the conclusion° of the dream, her face showed that she knew what had really happened. Then I woke up. Even though it was just a dream, I felt (4)_____ about stealing the ring. I didn't get over that feeling until I saw Mrs. Kahn the next day and made sure the ring was safe on her finger.

B. A King's Mistake

Read the following paragraphs carefully. Then fill in each blank with a word from the box. Use each word once.

a. **accusing**	b. **pleasant**	c. **precious**	d. **public**

For centuries, people have said that the dog is man's best friend. The following story, for example, is more than a thousand years old. A king had a strong, beautiful dog that he loved greatly. When the king went to war, the dog went with him. When the weather was warm and sunny, the dog joined the king on nice, (5)_____ walks in the countryside. Whenever the king went to the (6)_____ hall, where anyone could talk to him, the dog lay at his feet. If the king felt sad or troubled, he talked to the dog. The dog always listened.

After the king had his first son, he often let the dog watch the baby. He trusted the dog to take care of and protect° this special, (7)_____ child. One day, after being away for an hour or so, the king returned to the baby's room. He saw something terrible. The baby was nowhere in sight. His bed was turned over, and there was blood all over the dog's mouth. (8)_____ the dog, the king shouted, "You killed my son!" He grabbed his knife and stabbed the dog in the heart several times. Then he heard a soft cry. Looking under the baby's bed, he found his baby son, safe and sound. Looking further, he saw the body of a large wolf. Its body was bloody and covered with deep bites. At that moment, the king understood that he had killed the dog that had saved his son's life.

Using the Words When Writing and Talking

Now that you understand the meanings of the eight new words in the chapter, you are ready to use them on paper and in speaking. Complete each sentence below in a way that shows you really know what each **boldfaced** word means. Take a few minutes to think about your answer before writing it down and saying it out loud.

1. Parents may **accuse** a child of _____

   _____

2. Ads for lipstick often **claim** that it _____

   _____

3. I was **embarrassed** when _____

   _____

4. Parents can **inspire** their children to do their best by _____

   _____

5. My idea of a **pleasant** vacation is _____

   _____

6. One very **precious** thing in my life is _____

   _____

7. In good weather, **public** parks become _____

   _____

8. It's **unusual** for teachers to let students _____

   _____

Scores	Adding One Word to an Item	_____%	Showing You Understand the Words	_____%
	Adding Two Words to an Item	_____%	Adding Words to a Reading	_____%

Number right: 8 = 100%, 7 = 88%, 6 = 75%, 5 = 63%, 4 = 50%, 3 = 38%, 2 = 25%, 1 = 13%
Enter your scores above and in the vocabulary performance chart on the inside back cover of the book.

benefit	rival
delay	satisfy
emphasize	tempt
logical	vacant

Learning Eight New Words

In the space at the left, write the letter of the meaning closest to that of each **boldfaced** word. Use the other words (the *context*) in each sentence to help you figure out the word's meaning.

1 **benefit**
(**ben**-uh-fit)
– verb

- People who lost their homes in the flood will **benefit** greatly from the food and clothes that others give them.
- John's grades have **benefited** from the studying he now does after school.

___*Benefit* means
   a. be helped   b. be harmed   c. be told

2 **delay**
(di-**lay**)
– verb

- When Mom and Dad work late, we **delay** dinner until they get home.
- Tony **delayed** doing his homework for an hour because he wanted to watch his favorite TV show.

___*Delay* means
   a. enjoy   b. hurry   c. wait until later

3 **emphasize**
(**em**-fuh-siiz)
– verb

- Sarah uses yellow markers to **emphasize** the important points in her textbooks.
- The speaker **emphasized** his main points by pounding on the table as he spoke.

___*Emphasize* means
   a. show to be important   b. cover up   c. turn around

4 **logical**
(**loj**-ik-uhl)
– adjective

- Juan really likes his science class because his teacher can make the most difficult ideas seem clear and **logical**.
- Your apartment is so small that it does not seem **logical** to invite forty people to the party.

___*Logical* means
   a. empty   b. making sense   c. lucky

5 **rival**
(**rii**-vuhl)
– noun

- I am Yolanda's good friend, but when we face each other on the tennis court, she is my biggest **rival**.
- Kevin and Ted were **rivals**—they each wanted to go on a date with Monica.

___*Rival* means
   a. partner   b. student   c. enemy

6 **satisfy**
(sat-iss-*fii*)
– verb

• I'm not very hungry. Just a sandwich will **satisfy** me.

• My little girl likes me to read to her. A few pages **satisfy** her and then she goes off to play.

___*Satisfy* means a. surprise b. make unhappy c. be enough for

7 **tempt**
(**tempt**)
– verb

• Pies, cakes, candy bars, and ice cream **tempt** many people to go off their diets.

• I don't go to my favorite clothing store often because it **tempts** me to spend too much money.

___*Tempt* means

a. invite someone to do something bad

b. warn someone against doing something bad

c. stop someone from doing something bad

8 **vacant**
(**vay**-kuhnt)
– adjective

• The Committee for a Beautiful City is going to plant a garden in that ugly **vacant** lot.

• Too tired to drive any further, we stopped at a motel and asked if there was a **vacant** room.

___*Vacant* means a. helpful b. crowded c. not in use

Matching Words with Meanings

Here are the meanings, or *definitions*, of the eight new words. Write each word next to its meaning. The sentences above and on the facing page will help you decide on the meaning of each word.

1. _____ Someone that another person tries to beat in a contest of some kind

2. _____ Empty; not being used by anyone

3. _____ To wait until later to do something; to postpone

4. _____ To show that something is important

5. _____ To be helped by something

6. _____ To make someone want to do something that isn't good or right

7. _____ Making sense; using or showing reason

8. _____ To be enough for someone; to fill someone's need or wish

BE CAREFUL: Don't go any further until you know the answers above are correct. Then you can use the meanings to help you in the following activities. After a while, you will know the words so well that you won't need to check the definitions at all.

Adding One Word to an Item

Complete each item below by writing one word from the box on the answer line at the left. Use each word once.

a. **benefited**	c. **emphasize**	e. **rivals**	g. **tempted**
b. **delayed**	d. **logical**	f. **satisfy**	h. **vacant**

_____ 1. Many drivers get lost in our town because the streets often curve sharply, rather than going in . . ? . . directions.

_____ 2. The dry lawn . . ? . . from the heavy rain.

_____ 3. Children often think of their brothers and sisters as . . ? . . for their parents' love.

_____ 4. Tara was so afraid of the dentist that she . . ? . . going to visit him until her tooth really hurt.

_____ 5. The weather reporter raised her voice to . . ? . . that no one should drive during the dangerous ice storm.

_____ 6. Since Doris went off to college, her bedroom at home has been . . ? . .

_____ 7. My brother . . ? . . me to skip school today. He said, "Instead of going to school, come to the park with me."

_____ 8. I can't go to the beach today, but an hour in the swimming pool should . . ? . . me.

Adding Two Words to an Item

Complete each item below by writing **two** words from the box on the answer lines at the left. Use each word once.

a. **benefit**	c. **emphasize**	e. **rival**	g. **tempts**
b. **delay**	d. **logical**	f. **satisfy**	h. **vacant**

_____
_____ 1–2. I'm so tired that I would . . ? . . from a long vacation. It would . . ? . . my need to do nothing but relax.

_____
_____ 3–4. Juan plays poker with his . . ? . . Mark. The desire to win . . ? . . Juan to cheat, but he never does.

_____
_____ 5–6. The . . ? . . lot on the corner is filled with rusty auto parts and old refrigerators. Parents . . ? . . to their children that they should never play there.

_____
_____ 7–8. Since it is raining heavily, it would be . . ? . . for us to . . ? . . our picnic until tomorrow.

Showing You Understand the Words

PART A

In the space at the left, write the letter of the choice that best completes the sentence or answers the question.

___ 1. If you **benefit** from going to bed early, you probably
   a. feel rested when it's time to get up.
   b. feel tired when it's time to get up.
   c. are unhappy with the way you look and feel.

___ 2. If you **delayed** having lunch yesterday, you
   a. never had any lunch at all.
   b. had lunch earlier that usual.
   c. had lunch later than usual.

___ 3. It is noon. The sky turns dark, and you see a flash of lightning. It is **logical** to think that
   a. a thunderstorm is on its way.
   b. a snowstorm is coming.
   c. the weather will be perfect.

___ 4. If you play basketball, who are your **rivals**?
   a. The other people on your team
   b. The people who watch from the sidelines
   c. The people on the other team

PART B

In the space at the left, write the letter of the choice that best completes the sentence or answers the question.

___ 5. When people want to **emphasize** a point, they often
   a. go away without saying anything.
   b. talk so softly that no one can hear them.
   c. speak loudly and clearly.

___ 6. Which of these would **satisfy** a hungry child?
   a. Giving the child a snack
   b. Scolding the child for wanting to eat before dinner
   c. Saying to the child, "Wait until supper time."

___ 7. Which is these might **tempt** a person who is trying to stop smoking?
   a. An article on how smoking causes lung cancer
   b. An open pack of cigarettes
   c. A friend who is also trying to quit smoking

___ 8. If a hotel always has a lot of **vacant** rooms, it
   a. may go out of business.
   b. is always packed with customers.
   c. probably makes all its customers very happy.

Adding Words to a Reading

A. Be Proud of Your Age!

Read the following paragraph carefully. Then fill in each blank with a word from the box. Use each word once.

a. **benefit**	b. **delay**	c. **emphasize**	d. **logical**

    "Young, wrinkle-free skin in two weeks!" "Cover up that gray hair!" "Keep your body fit and young!" Everywhere we look, ads claim° that it is best to do everything we can to stay young. Loudly, the ads (1)_____ one idea over and over: Young is good and old is bad. The message is that we must (2)_____ getting older as long as possible. Sadly, what happens is that as people age, they become unhappy because they don't look twenty anymore. But does this make sense? Wouldn't it be more (3)_____ if we liked ourselves, no matter what our age? Wouldn't we all (4)_____ if we could accept our wrinkles, gray hair, and middle-age bodies? After all, life is meant to be enjoyed, no matter how old we are. Why should we feel bad about looking the age we really are? If we keep seeing life as a race against time, we will end up feeling like losers.

B. Making Anger Work for You

Read the following paragraphs carefully. Then fill in each blank with a word from the box. Use each word once.

a. **rival**	b. **satisfy**	c. **tempted**	d. **vacant**

    Everyone has felt angry at one time or another. Maybe you felt angry when a (5)_____ at school teased you, when a boss treated you unfairly, or when a family member said something mean. If you are like most people, your anger may have (6)_____ you to get back at those who made you feel bad. Maybe you wanted to shout at them or even hit them. But this is not a good way to (7)_____ the need to let people know how you feel.

    Anger is powerful and can be helpful. However, it must be used in a healthy way. If someone makes you angry, you shouldn't yell and accuse° the person of hurting you, nor should you give the person the silent treatment. Instead, tell the person exactly what it is that upsets you. Once you do that, you and the person can work together to change things so you both feel better.

    Here is a real-life example showing how people used their anger in a good way to make their lives better. People living in a city neighborhood were angry. Why? For over a year, they had been promised that a (8)_____ building on their street would be torn down. However, the building was still there and had become home to drug dealers. Instead of sitting around, complaining, and doing nothing but getting even angrier, a group from the neighborhood went to see their mayor. They explained to the mayor how upset they were and how they feared for their children's safety. The mayor listened. And guess what happened! The building was torn down. The neighbors had made good use of their anger and put it to work in the best way possible.

So the next time someone makes you angry, don't strike out against or stop talking to the person. Instead, stay calm and explain why you are angry. You may be surprised by how well things turn out.

Using the Words When Writing and Talking

Now that you understand the meanings of the eight new words in the chapter, you are ready to use them on paper and in speaking. Complete each sentence below in a way that shows you really know what each **boldfaced** word means. Take a few minutes to think about your answer before writing it down and saying it out loud.

1. People's health would **benefit** greatly from _____

   _____

2. Children often **delay** going to bed by _____

   _____

3. In class, teachers often **emphasize** important ideas by _____

   _____

4. If the directions for putting the bike together were not **logical**, then _____

   _____

5. Although the girls are good friends, they are **rivals** in the classroom. They _____

   _____

6. To **satisfy** their hunger, teenage boys _____

   _____

7. A beautiful summer day may **tempt** some people to _____

   _____

8. Shopping centers often have **vacant** stores because _____

   _____

Scores	Adding One Word to an Item	____%	Showing You Understand the Words	____%
	Adding Two Words to an Item	____%	Adding Words to a Reading	____%

Number right: 8 = 100%, 7 = 88%, 6 = 75%, 5 = 63%, 4 = 50%, 3 = 38%, 2 = 25%, 1 = 13%
Enter your scores above and in the vocabulary performance chart on the inside back cover of the book.

definite	oppose
fortunate	refer
leisure	specific
motivated	suspect

Learning Eight New Words

In the space at the left, write the letter of the meaning closest to that of each **boldfaced** word. Use the other words (the *context*) in each sentence to help you figure out the word's meaning.

1 definite
(**def**-uh-nit)
– adjective

____*Definite* means

- Roger did not know his sister's plan to take a vacation was **definite** until he saw a plane ticket on the table.
- With our team ahead by three runs in the final inning, it seemed **definite** that we would win the game.

    a. certain   b. not fair   c. wrong

2 fortunate
(**for**-chuh-nit)
– adjective

____*Fortunate* means

- Steve's grandmother is a **fortunate** person. She won the lottery two times in one year.
- I feel **fortunate** to have a comfortable place to live and plenty of food, when so many people in the world have so little.

    a. sorry   b. scared   c. lucky

3 leisure
(**lee**-zhur)
– noun

____*Leisure* means

- When you finally have some **leisure**, you should come to my house and relax with me over a steaming cup of coffee.
- Our boss doesn't like us to have any **leisure** on the job. If there is a second or two when we are not working, she rushes over and asks, "Don't you have anything to do?"

    a. hard work   b. time off   c. deep sleep

4 motivated
(**moh**-tuh-vay-tid)
– adjective

____*Motivated* means

- A teacher's job is to get students **motivated** so they want to learn.
- Needing money to pay her bills made Maria a **motivated** worker.

    a. interested and excited   b. well-known   c. good-looking

5 oppose
(uh-**pohz**)
– verb

____*Oppose* means

- My parents **oppose** my plan to hitchhike across the country. They say hitchhiking would be dangerous.
- I think school uniforms would be a good idea, but the student council **opposes** them.

    a. are happy about   b. are against   c. speak about

6 refer
(ri-**fur**)
– verb

- My brothers and sisters get angry when my relatives **refer** to me as "the smart one in the family."
- My grandfather **refers** to World War I as "The Great War."

___*Refer to* means   a. put a stop to   b. be unable to remember   c. talk about

7 specific
(spi-**sif**-ik)
– adjective

- The record-store clerk asked if I needed help finding a **specific** title.
- Of all the conversations I ever had with my father, there was one **specific** talk I will never forget.

___*Specific* means   a. special   b. boring   c. future

8 suspect
(suh-**spekt**)
– verb

- Some scientists **suspect** that there is life on many planets other than Earth.
- Mr. Bosshart **suspects** that the clothes missing from his store were stolen by an employee.

___*Suspect* means   a. hope   b. do not think   c. believe

Matching Words with Meanings

Here are the meanings, or *definitions*, of the eight new words. Write each word next to its meaning. The sentences above and on the facing page will help you decide on the meaning of each word.

1. _____   To speak briefly about someone or something

2. _____   Interested and excited about doing something

3. _____   To be against something

4. _____   Lucky

5. _____   Free time (for rest or fun)

6. _____   To think that something is true or likely to be true

7. _____   Limited to just one; exact; particular

8. _____   Sure; without doubt; certain

BE CAREFUL: Don't go any further until you know the answers above are correct. Then you can use the meanings to help you in the following activities. After a while, you will know the words so well that you won't need to check the definitions at all.

Adding One Word to an Item

Complete each item below by writing one word from the box on the answer line at the left. Use each word once.

a. **definite**	c. **leisure**	e. **opposes**	g. **specific**
b. **fortunate**	d. **motivated**	f. **refers**	h. **suspect**

_____ 1. Working in a hospital, I see many very sick people, which makes me feel . . ? . . that my family and I are well.

_____ 2. Mrs. Soma knew little English when class started. But because she is smart and very . . ? . ., she learned fast.

_____ 3. Aunt Ida thinks her new boyfriend loves her, but I . . ? . . he is interested only in her money.

_____ 4. Because she works at two jobs and goes to school at night, Nilsa has very little . . ? . . .

_____ 5. The mayor . . ? . . raising taxes—she feels we already pay too many taxes.

_____ 6. It is . . ? . . that Lena is getting married—today I saw an engagement ring on her hand.

_____ 7. Our history teacher always . . ? . . to the country's "good old days."

_____ 8. I am looking for a . . ? . . recipe for chocolate cake, the one my mother used to make with chocolate chips and sour cream.

Adding Two Words to an Item

Complete each item below by writing **two** words from the box on the answer lines at the left. Use each word once.

a. **definite**	c. **leisure**	e. **oppose**	g. **specific**
b. **fortunate**	d. **motivated**	f. **refer**	h. **suspected**

_____
_____ 1–2. Linda went to school to meet her son's teacher. At the meeting, she was happy to hear the teacher . . ? . . to the boy as a . . ? . ., hardworking student.

_____
_____ 3–4. It is . . ? . . that I have health insurance, because my doctor says it is . . ? . . that I will need an operation.

_____
_____ 5–6. Ana . . ? . . that her family might do something special for her birthday, but she did not know their . . ? . . plan—to have a surprise party for her.

_____
_____ 7–8. The employees . . ? . . the company's plan to get rid of coffee breaks. Because they work so hard, they feel they need some . . ? . . on the job.

Showing You Understand the Words

PART A

In the space at the left, write the letter of the choice that best completes the sentence or answers the question.

___ 1. Which of these would make you feel **fortunate**?
    a. Taking the bus to work
    b. Having your TV set break in the middle of an important soccer game
    c. Jumping out of the way of a truck just before it hit you

___ 2. Which of these might you do if you were **motivated** to save money?
    a. Buy everything you want without thinking about the price.
    b. Make a budget and cut out grocery coupons.
    c. Give a few dollars to your little cousin.

___ 3. Which law might you **oppose**?
    a. One that you think is harmful
    b. One that you believe is needed
    c. One that was passed years ago and works well

___ 4. If police **suspected** that you had done something against the law, they would probably
    a. leave you alone.
    b. ask you many questions.
    c. say, "We're sorry."

PART B

In the space at the left, write the letter of the choice that best completes the sentence or answers the question.

___ 5. If it is **definite** that a company is going to close forever, the employees will probably
    a. spend all their savings.
    b. start looking for other jobs.
    c. be happy that their jobs are safe.

___ 6. Most people use their **leisure** to
    a. do more work.
    b. relax and rest.
    c. clean the house.

___ 7. If friends **refer** to a difficulty they are having with their landlord, they probably
    a. are happy with the way things are in their apartment.
    b. are not happy with the way things are in their apartment.
    c. feel good that the problem in their apartment has been solved.

___ 8. Which of these is a **specific** place to go on vacation?
    a. A place far away
    b. The ocean
    c. Hawaii

Adding Words to a Reading

A. How Not to Treat Customers

Read the following paragraphs carefully. Then fill in each blank with a word from the box. Use each word once.

a. **definite**	b. **motivated**	c. **specific**	d. **suspect**

There are two department stores in my town. I will call them Store "A" and Store "B." They carry many of the same items. They are about the same size. They look very much the same. But oh, how different they are to shop in. At Store "A," employees are (1) _____ to keep customers happy. They help customers find things; they carry packages; they hand out lollipops to children. They will even guide a customer away from a (2)_____ brand item to something that costs less but is just as good. Customers find that shopping in Store "A" is a very pleasant° experience. The rule in this store seems to be "The customer is always right."

I don't know this for sure, but I (3)_____ that the rule in Store "B" is "The customer is a big bother." Clerks just stare at customers who ask for help. They talk with fellow employees while customers wait in long lines at the checkout counters. When a customer asks a clerk for information, the clerk often answers, "I don't know," and walks away. Several months ago, I heard that Store "B" might go out of business. Now it is (4)_____. The store will close by the end of the month. Are you surprised? I'm not!

B. Stuck in the Middle

Read the following paragraph carefully. Then fill in each blank with a word from the box. Use each word once.

a. **fortunate**	b. **leisure**	c. **oppose**	d. **referring**

Have you ever heard anyone use the term "sandwich generation"? It doesn't have anything to do with eating sandwiches. Instead, when people talk about the "sandwich generation," they are (5)_____ to adults who are caring for their own children and their aging parents at the same time. People in the sandwich generation are "caught in the middle," like the filling of a sandwich. As people live longer, more and more adults end up taking care of their elderly parents. They may feel torn between giving time to their kids and their parents, all of whom need daily° help. The sandwich generation is so busy that it has very little (6)_____. If they are lucky, members of the sandwich generation will have relatives who help them with their heavy load. If they are not so (7)_____, they will have nobody to help them out. They may even have relatives who (8)_____ everything they try to do. For example, sometimes several members of a family feel strongly that Mom or Dad should never be placed in a nursing home. However, they don't do anything to help the family member who is trying to care for an elderly parent at home. Members of the sandwich generation can easily get overworked and overtired because of everything that is expected of them.

Using the Words When Writing and Talking

Now that you understand the meanings of the eight new words in the chapter, you are ready to use them on paper and in speaking. Complete each sentence below in a way that shows you really know what each **boldfaced** word means. Take a few minutes to think about your answer before writing it down and saying it out loud.

1. You would feel **definite** about your vacation plans when _____

   _____

2. I am **fortunate** to have _____

   _____

3. Some people have trouble relaxing. Even during their **leisure**, they _____

   _____

4. Students feel **motivated** when _____

   _____

5. One reason why people are **opposed** to smoking is _____

   _____

6. My family or friends sometimes **refer** to me as _____

   _____

7. One **specific** way to make your boss happy is to _____

   _____

8. The police **suspected** the man wasn't telling the truth because _____

   _____

Scores	Adding One Word to an Item	_____%	Showing You Understand the Words	_____%
	Adding Two Words to an Item	_____%	Adding Words to a Reading	_____%

Number right: 8 = 100%, 7 = 88%, 6 = 75%, 5 = 63%, 4 = 50%, 3 = 38%, 2 = 25%, 1 = 13%
Enter your scores above and in the vocabulary performance chart on the inside back cover of the book.

UNIT

1

Review Activities

On the next ten pages are activities to help you review the words you learned in Unit One. You may do these activities in any order.

• Completing a Crossword Puzzle #1

• Completing a Crossword Puzzle #2

• Choosing the Best Word to Complete an Item

• Adding a Word to an Item, Parts A and B

• Finding the Same or the Opposite Meaning

• Using the Words When Writing and Talking

Completing a Crossword Puzzle #1

The box at the right lists twenty-four words from Unit One. Using the meanings at the bottom of the page, fill in these words to complete the puzzle that follows.

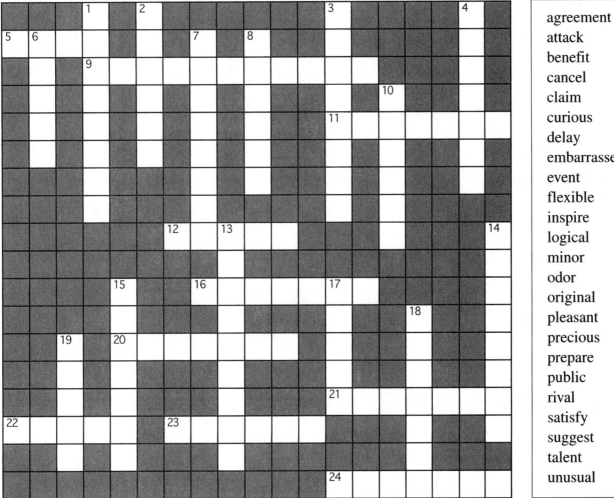

agreement
attack
benefit
cancel
claim
curious
delay
embarrassed
event
flexible
inspire
logical
minor
odor
original
pleasant
precious
prepare
public
rival
satisfy
suggest
talent
unusual

ACROSS

5. A smell
9. Feeling silly and ashamed
11. To be enough for someone; to fill someone's need or wish
12. To say something is true, often without being able to show that it is so
16. To get ready
20. To offer a thought for others to think about
21. Making sense; using or showing reason
22. Not important
23. To stop something that was planned
24. Not often happening or seen; strange; not usual

DOWN

1. Worth a lot; having great value
2. Open to everyone
3. Easy to like; enjoyable
4. To be helped by something
6. To wait until later to do something; to postpone
7. New; fresh; not like anything else

8. A special skill, often one that someone is born with
10. To hurt; to begin to harm
13. A promise people make to one another
14. Able to bend
15. To get someone to want to do something; to move someone to take action
17. Someone that another person tries to beat in a contest of some kind
18. Wanting to know more about something
19. An important happening

Completing a Crossword Puzzle #2

The box at the right lists twenty-four words from Unit One. Using the meanings at the bottom of the page, fill in these words to complete the puzzle that follows.

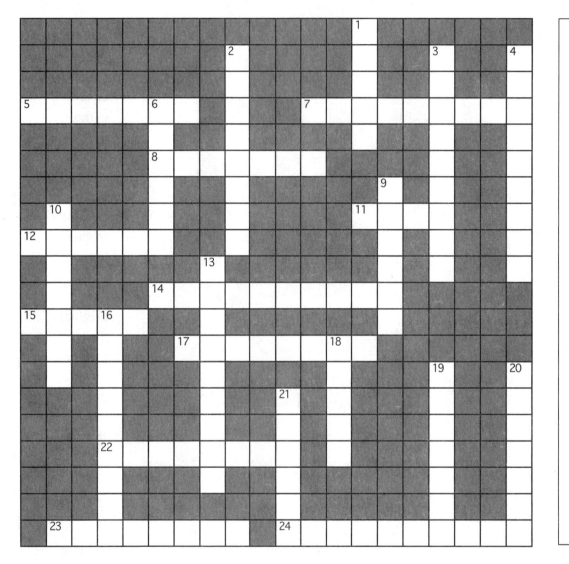

accuse
conclusion
daily
definite
emphasize
entertain
experience
fact
fortunate
humble
identify
leisure
motivated
negative
oppose
produce
protect
refer
specific
suspect
tempt
tension
vacant
volunteer

ACROSS

5. A nervous feeling
7. Someone who works or helps for no pay
8. To keep safe
11. Something true; something that can be proved
12. Not thinking too highly of oneself
14. The ending of something
15. To speak briefly about someone or something
17. Sure; without doubt
22. Limited to just one; exact; particular

23. To find out exactly who someone is or what something is
24. Anything someone has seen or lived through

DOWN

1. Done every day; happening or appearing every day
2. Bad; without anything good; not positive
3. Interested and excited about doing something
4. Lucky
6. To be against something

9. Empty; not being used
10. To think that something is true or likely to be true
13. To keep people's interest with something happy or enjoyable
16. To show that something is important
18. To make people want to do something that is not good or right
19. Free time (for rest or fun)
20. To make; to bring about
21. To say someone has done something wrong

Choosing the Best Word to Complete an Item

On the answer line at the left, write the word that best completes each item.

_____ 1. The TV show . . ? . . that a photo of Elvis had been found on the moon.

a. delayed   b. claimed   c. prepared

_____ 2. My wife and I cannot come to an . . ? . . about whether to spend the holidays with her parents or mine.

a. agreement   b. experience   c. event

_____ 3. The promise of money can . . ? . . people to do things they know are not right.

a. tempt   b. emphasize   c. oppose

_____ 4. I cannot remember the . . ? . . time that the train will arrive, but I know it will be in the afternoon.

a. humble   b. specific   c. motivated

_____ 5. The people in town . . ? . . the government's plan to build a garbage dump near their homes.

a. opposed   b. satisfied   c. protected

_____ 6. Unless they are angry or afraid, wolves will not . . ? . . a human being.

a. cancel   b. emphasize   c. attack

_____ 7. In movies made years ago, there was always a handsome hero in love with a beautiful young woman. But the hero had a . . ? . .—a bad guy who wanted the young woman for himself.

a. leisure   b. rival   c. fact

_____ 8. Jeanne was . . ? . . when she learned she had fallen asleep in class and had snored loudly.

a. precious   b. embarrassed   c. curious

_____ 9. The most important . . ? . . in our family this year was my grandmother's wedding.

a. talent   b. event   c. conclusion

_____ 10. Elena's new vocabulary skills have . . ? . . her to read more and to be less shy about talking in class.

a. protected   b. inspired   c. claimed

_____ 11. To keep up with the news, I read the . . ? . . newspaper. But my husband sticks to *Time* magazine, which comes out only once a week.

a. daily   b. humble   c. negative

_____ 12. My son seems to have a real . . ? . . for the trumpet. Just two weeks after he started lessons, he could play several songs very well.

a. conclusion   b. talent   c. rival

(Continues on next page)

_____ 13. I keep coming up with boring ideas for decorating the apartment, but my roommate has several . . ? . . thoughts about what we can do.

a. original   b. negative   c. public

_____ 14. To . . ? . . for an exam, don't wait until the last minute. Start studying well ahead of time.

a. accuse   b. prepare   c. identify

_____ 15. To deal with . . ? . ., you may find it helpful to exercise. A long walk can make you feel less worried and less nervous.

a. tension   b. fact   c. agreement

_____ 16. Brenda didn't find the movie at all interesting, but it . . ? . . Omar greatly. He thought it was really funny.

a. entertained   b. emphasized   c. protected

_____ 17. Small children are . . ? . . about everything. They are always asking questions like "Why is the sky blue?" and "Why can't dogs talk?"

a. pleasant   b. flexible   c. curious

_____ 18. The people waiting for the subway started to groan when they heard that bad weather had . . ? . . all the trains for at least thirty minutes.

a. motivated   b. delayed   c. attacked

_____ 19. The . . ? . . of garbage rotting in the hot sun makes me sick to my stomach.

a. odor   b. talent   c. tension

_____ 20. Skydiving is said to be an exciting . . ? . ., but I am in no hurry to try it.

a. experience   b. agreement   c. conclusion

_____ 21. When your teacher . . ? . . something by writing it on the board, be sure to get the point down in your notebook.

a. protects   b. cancels   c. emphasizes

_____ 22. Even though his car was destroyed in the accident, James felt . . ? . . because he was able to walk away without a scratch.

a. fortunate   b. specific   c. negative

_____ 23. People who win awards often say they feel "proud but . . ? . . ." They want to get across the idea that winning hasn't made them feel like big shots.

a. humble   b. flexible   c. logical

_____ 24. Tony likes to read. Whenever he has a moment of . . ? . ., he grabs a book and finds a nice, quiet spot to read.

a. leisure   b. conclusion   c. talent

| _Score_ | Choosing the Best Word to Complete an Item | _____% |

Number right: 24 = 100%, 23 = 96%, 22 = 92%, 21 = 88%, 20 = 83%; 19 = 79%, 18 = 75%, 17 = 71%; 16 = 67%, 15 = 63%. 14 = 58%, 13 = 54%,
12 = 50%, 11 = 46%, 10 = 42%, 9 - 38%, 8 = 33%, 7 = 29%, 6 = 25%, 5 - 21%, 4 = 17%, 3 = 13%, 2 = 8%, 1 = 4%
Enter your scores above and in the vocabulary performance chart on the inside back cover of the book.

Adding a Word to an Item

PART A

Complete each item below by writing one word from the box on the answer line at the left. Use each word once.

a. **accuse**	d. **identify**	g. **produces**	j. **satisfy**
b. **cancel**	e. **negative**	h. **protect**	k. **suggest**
c. **fact**	f. **precious**	i. **referred**	l. **volunteer**

_____ 1. The factory where my wife works . . ? . . vacuum cleaners.

_____ 2. I have a tune running through my head, but I cannot . . ? . . it. I don't know what it's from.

_____ 3. When I was growing up, my mother ran our house like the army. Looking me squarely in the eye one day, she said, "I want a . . ? . . to clean the kitchen—you."

_____ 4. "I really hate to . . ? . . my appointment," Mimi told the dentist. "But I just cannot come. I cannot find a baby sitter."

_____ 5. I felt angry and hurt when my teachers . . ? . . to my older sister as the best student they had ever had.

_____ 6. To . . ? . . the furniture while the living room was being painted, we covered everything with sheets.

_____ 7. When the toaster did not work, my daughter said, "Dad, I . . ? . . you try plugging it in."

_____ 8. Of all the things you own, what is the most . . ? . . to you? What is so important to you that you would be very upset if you lost it?

_____ 9. Do not . . ? . . me of forgetting the tickets! You were the one who was going to bring them!

_____ 10. It is a . . ? . . that February is the shortest month of the year; no one can argue about that.

_____ 11. Gordon's feelings about his new job are very . . ? . . . Even though he hasn't started working yet, he expects to dislike the job, to be bored, and to do badly.

_____ 12. One sandwich did not . . ? . . Li's hunger, so he ate two more. Then he felt full.

(Continues on next page)

PART B

Complete each item below by writing one word from the box on the answer line at the left. Use each word once.

a. **benefit**	d. **flexible**	g. **motivated**	j. **suspected**
b. **conclusion**	e. **logical**	h. **pleasant**	k. **unusual**
c. **definite**	f. **minor**	i. **public**	l. **vacant**

_____ 13. The . . ? . . of the movie was terrible. At the end, the good guys died and the bad guys went free.

_____ 14. A good fishing pole must be strong but . . ? . . . It has to be able to bend without breaking.

_____ 15. One apartment on our floor has been . . ? . . for months. No one wants to rent it because it's too noisy. It's right next to the elevators.

_____ 16. The new restaurant is very . . ? . . . It has good food, soft lights, and friendly service.

_____ 17. Because my brother found cake crumbs outside my bedroom door, he . . ? . . that I was the one who had eaten the last of his birthday cake.

_____ 18. When Janice has a problem, she doesn't make decisions based on her feelings. Instead, she is highly . . ? . . and thinks carefully about what she should do.

_____ 19. After listening to the coach's pep talk, the players were so . . ? . . that they felt they could beat the best team in the state.

_____ 20. As a rule, I go to bed at 10:00 p.m. It is . . ? . . for me to be up for the 11:00 news.

_____ 21. It is . . ? . . . My insurance _will_ cover my hospital stay.

_____ 22. When you are studying a textbook chapter, underline the most important ideas but not the . . ? . . points.

_____ 23. Our school would . . ? . . from two things: a new gym and a better library.

_____ 24. The garden behind the bank is a . . ? . . area. It's open to everyone, not just to people who work at the bank.

Scores	Part A (Adding a Word) _____%	Part B (Adding a Word) _____%

Number right in each part: 12 = 100%, 11 = 92%, 10 = 83%, 9 = 75%, 8 = 67%; 7 = 58%, 6 = 50%, 5 = 42%; 4 = 33%, 3 = 25%. 2 = 17%, 1 = 8%
Enter your scores above and in the vocabulary performance chart on the inside back cover of the book.

Finding the Same or the Opposite Meaning

PART A

In the space at the left, write the letter of the choice that correctly completes each sentence. In most cases, the correct answer will have the **same** or **almost the same** meaning as the **boldfaced** word.

___ 1. A young man **accused** two teenagers of stealing. That means the young man
    a. joined the two teenagers in stealing.   b. told the two teenagers about the stealing.
    c. said the two teenagers had stolen something.

___ 2. If a teacher **cancels** a class, that means the class
    a. will cover important material.   b. is called off.
    c. will meet as always.

___ 3. If friends say that their plans to move to a new home are **definite**, that means
    a. the plans are not clear yet.   b. the plans will change.
    c. the plans will not change.

___ 4. If a history teacher tests you on the **facts** of the Second World War, you need to know
    a. what actually happened during the war.   b. why your teacher is so interested in the war.
    c. what might have happened if the fighting had ended earlier.

___ 5. I would like to **identify** the beautiful flowers in my neighbor's garden. In other words, I would like to
    a. find out what kind of flowers they are.   b. plant the flowers.
    c. take the flowers.

___ 6. If a company **produces** candy, that means it
    a. buys candy and then sells it to people.   b. makes the candy.
    c. wraps the candy for the candymaker.

___ 7. If my boots **protect** me from the rain and snow, they
    a. keep out the wet and cold.   b. leak, so that my feet get wet and cold.
    c. need to be replaced.

___ 8. If you **refer** to a trip you took, you
    a. speak of the trip.   b. tell your friends not to take the same trip.
    c. say you will go someplace else next time.

___ 9. If I say that one scoop of ice cream **satisfies** me, I mean that
    a. one scoop is enough for me.   b. having one scoop will not be enough for me.
    c. I would rather have a doughnut.

___10. If I **suggest** a school project to my children, I
    a. give them some ideas to help them get started.   b. do much of the project for them.
    c. tell them they should not come to me for help.

___11. If you **suspect** that two relatives sometimes lie, you
    a. know for sure that they lie.   b. know for sure that they never lie.
    c. think that they lie.

(Continues on next page)

___12. When people work as **volunteers**, they
    a. receive a large paycheck.   b. work without pay.
    c. get a paid two-week vacation.

PART B
In the space at the left, write the letter of the choice that is the **opposite** of the **boldfaced** word.

 _c_   **Example:** The opposite of **up** is
    a. before   b. under   c. down

___13. The opposite of **benefit** is
    a. hurt   b. try   c. laugh

___14. The opposite of **conclusion** is
    a. work   b. end   c. beginning

___15. The opposite of **flexible** is
    a. funny   b. sunny   c. stiff

___16. The opposite of **logical** is
    a. not feeling sad   b. not fattening   c. not making sense

___17. The opposite of **minor** is
    a. very dry   b. very important   c. very dirty

___18. The opposite of **motivated** is
    a. bored   b. hungry   c. happy

___19. The opposite of **negative** is
    a. pretty   b. good   c. bad

___20. The opposite of **pleasant** is
    a. warm   b. quiet   c. not nice

___21. The opposite of **precious** is
    a. not worth much   b. not friendly   c. not smart

___22. The opposite of **public** is
    a. straight   b. private   c. sweet

___23. The opposite of **tension** is
    a. relaxation   b. noise   c. unhappiness

___24. The opposite of **vacant** is
    a. cheap   b. in use   c. falling apart

Scores	Part A (Same Meanings) _____ %	Part B (Opposite Meanings) _____ %

Number right in each part: 12 = 100%, 11 = 92%, 10 = 83%, 9 = 75%, 8 = 67%; 7 = 58%, 6 = 50%, 5 = 42%; 4 = 33%, 3 = 25%. 2 = 17%, 1 = 8%
Enter your scores above and in the vocabulary performance chart on the inside back cover of the book.

Using the Words When Writing and Talking

The items below will help you use many of the words in this unit on paper and in conversation. Feel free to use **any tense of a boldfaced verb** and to make a **boldfaced noun plural**. (See pages 249–251 and 252.)

1. Using the word **agreement**, write or talk about a time that you and someone you know solved a problem by making a promise to one another. For example, you and your roommate might have promised to split up household jobs, or you and a neighbor might have promised not to play your radios late at night.

2. Using the word **attack**, write or talk about a time when someone or something tried to harm you. It could be that a neighbor's dog tried to bite you, a schoolyard bully wanted to beat you up, or some angry bees tried to sting you.

3. Using the word **claim**, write or talk about a time you heard someone say something was true but you know the person could not prove it. Perhaps you heard someone making big promises on a TV commercial or during an election.

4. Using the word **curious**, write or talk about someone who wants to learn more about things. It might be a child who asks lots of questions or an adult who has returned to school to get more education.

5. Using the word **daily**, write or talk about something you do every day that makes you feel good. It might be drinking a cold glass of orange juice every morning or taking a warm shower before going to bed.

6. Using the word **delay**, write or talk about something you will do—but not right away. Tell why you are waiting until later to do it. It might be cleaning your closet, taking a course, changing your job, or ending a relationship.

7. Using the word **embarrassed**, write or talk about a time when you or someone you know felt silly because of something that happened in front of other people. Maybe you tripped when you walked into a fancy restaurant or your closest friend forgot to invite you to your own surprise birthday party.

8. Using the word **emphasize**, write or talk about one thing that parents should tell their children is important. Perhaps you think parents should tell kids it is important to have good manners, stay away from drugs, do well in school, or be kind to others.

9. Using the word **entertain**, write or talk about a movie, play, concert, or TV show that you have enjoyed.

10. Using the word **event**, write or talk about a special happening that you look forward to. It might be a a company picnic, a trip to an amusement park, or a visit from a favorite relative.

11. Using the word **experience**, write or talk about a time in your life that you will always remember. Maybe it was your first day of school, a stay in the hospital, a wonderful vacation, or a scary plane ride.

12. Using the word **fortunate**, describe something in your life that makes you feel thankful. You might feel lucky to have a special friend, a job you like, or a home that brings you happiness.

(Continues on next page)

13. Using the word **humble**, write or talk about one person you know who doesn't brag and doesn't think highly of himself or herself, even though that person has good reason to be proud. The person could be a relative, friend, neighbor, classmate, or teacher.

14. Using the word **inspire**, write or talk about a time that someone got you interested in doing something you had never tried before. Maybe a relative got you excited about camping, or a person on a TV show gave you the idea to try oil painting.

15. Using the word **leisure**, write or talk about how you like to relax during your free time. Perhaps you like to walk, read, or take naps.

16. Using the word **odor**, write or talk about a place you try to stay away from because it smells bad. You might describe a garbage dump or a kitchen where food you do not like is being cooked.

17. Using the word **oppose**, write or talk about a time you were against what someone was doing. You might have been against your best friend's leaving a job or against a relative's speaking unkindly of a neighbor.

18. Using the word **original**, write or talk about a time you came up with an idea that no one else had thought of before. Maybe you came up with a new recipe for chili or a new way of getting a job done at work.

19. Using the word **prepare**, write or talk about something you do to get ready for class. Perhaps you sharpen your pencil, read your notes, or study your homework.

20. Using the word **rival**, describe two people who feel they have to beat each other in some sort of contest. You might have two friends who always try to get better grades than each other, or maybe you have two relatives who always try to beat each other in games.

21. Using the word **specific**, write or talk about a certain kind of music, TV show, or movie that you dislike a great deal.

22. Using the word **talent**, write or talk about someone who has a special skill. The person might dance beautifully, play a sport well, or tell good jokes.

23. Using the word **tempt**, think of a magazine advertisement or TV commercial that makes you want to do something you know you should not do. Maybe an ad makes you want to buy a car that costs too much or eat something that isn't good for you.

24. Using the word **unusual**, write or talk about something that would be strange if it happened in the middle of the summer—for example, the temperature dropping below zero or snow falling heavily.

Unit Two

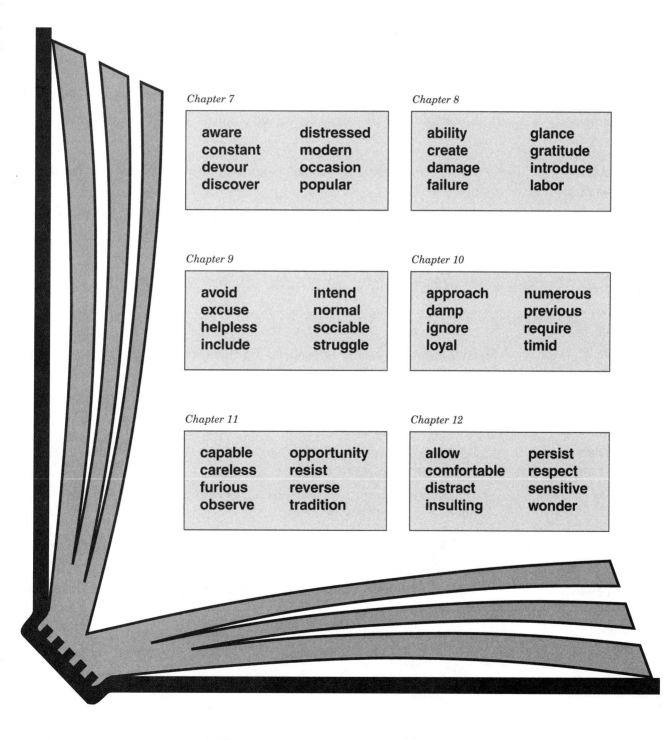

aware	distressed
constant	modern
devour	occasion
discover	popular

Learning Eight New Words

In the space at the left, write the letter of the meaning closest to that of each **boldfaced** word. Use the other words (the *context*) in each sentence to help you figure out the word's meaning.

1 **aware**
(uh-**wair**)
– adjective

___*Aware* means

• The warnings on the radio made everyone **aware** of the dangerous icy roads.
• Even though Mr. and Mrs. Patel were **aware** that their children were planning an anniversary party, they acted as if they knew nothing about it.

    a. sad   b. ashamed   c. knowing

2 **constant**
(**kon**-stuhnt)
– adjective

___*Constant* means

• Because there are three teenagers in our family, the phone is in **constant** use.
• All night long, I hear the **constant** sound of a dog barking outside my window.

    a. never-ending   b. quiet   c. sad

3 **devour**
(di-**vou**-ur)
– verb

___*Devour* means

• I want to **devour** the last piece of chocolate fudge cake myself before anyone else has a chance to eat it.
• By accident, my family **devoured** the cherry cheesecake that I had made for my girlfriend's graduation.

    a. make   b. eat quickly   c. save for later

4 **discover**
(diss-**kuh**-vur)
– verb

___*Discover* means

• It took my four-year old sister only minutes to **discover** a secret hiding place in my new apartment.
• Not long ago, scientists **discovered** a two-thousand-year-old ship sitting on the bottom of the ocean.

    a. lose   b. sell   c. find

5 **distressed**
(diss-**trest**)
– adjective

___*Distressed* means

• The kitten, crying loudly from the top of the tree, was too **distressed** to move.
• The workers were **distressed** after hearing that the factory would close and they would lose their jobs.

    a. full of energy   b. upset   c. up-to-date

6 modern
(**mod**-urn)
– adjective

- Instead of using **modern** machines, the Amish prefer old-fashioned machines pulled by horses.
- Dad doesn't like **modern** music. He would rather listen to music written thirty years ago.

___*Modern* means   a. up-to-date   b. broken down   c. strong

7 occasion
(uh-**kay**-zhuhn)
– noun

- Halloween is a great **occasion** for most children.
- Tom hates to dress up. Even on special **occasions** like birthdays and anniversaries, he wears jeans and sneakers.

___*Occasion* means   a. regular day   b. special time   c. boring time

8 popular
(**pop**-yuh-lur)
– adjective

- The Beatles and Elvis Presley are among the most **popular** performers of all time.
- Eva is liked by her teachers and is also **popular** with her classmates.

___*Popular* means   a. healthy   b. not known   c. well-liked

Matching Words with Meanings

Here are the meanings, or *definitions*, of the eight new words. Write each word next to its meaning. The sentences above and on the facing page will help you decide on the meaning of each word.

1. _____   To find something for the first time; to come upon something

2. _____   A time when something takes place, often something special; an event

3. _____   Knowing about something; having knowledge

4. _____   Never stopping; always happening; happening again and again

5. _____   To eat quickly and hungrily

6. _____   Of the present time; up-to-date; not old-fashioned

7. _____   Liked by many people

8. _____   Very upset; troubled

BE CAREFUL: Don't go any further until you know the answers above are correct. Then you can use the meanings to help you in the following activities. After a while, you will know the words so well that you won't need to check the definitions at all.

Adding One Word to an Item

Complete each item below by writing one word from the box on the answer line at the left. Use each word once.

a. **aware**	c. **devour**	e. **distressed**	g. **occasion**
b. **constant**	d. **discovered**	f. **modern**	h. **popular**

_____ 1. It took Greg's dog only thirty seconds to . . ? . . a full bowl of food.

_____ 2. Sara's little sister was . . ? . . when her pet snake died.

_____ 3. To look up the meanings of new words like "software" and "hard drive," you need a good . . ? . . dictionary.

_____ 4. The last time I saw Aunt Bonita was at a very special . . ? . . —her daughter's wedding.

_____ 5. Phil was happy the day he . . ? . . a shortcut to work.

_____ 6. Since Steve had missed class, he was not . . ? . . that his teacher had changed the day for the final exam.

_____ 7. Small children can tire a parent with their . . ? . . questions—like "Why doesn't the sky fall down?" and "Why does it get dark when I close my eyes?"

_____ 8. The restaurant runs out of taco salad almost every day. It's the most . . ? . . dish on the menu.

Adding Two Words to an Item

Complete each item below by writing **two** words from the box on the answer lines at the left. Use each word once.

a. **aware**	c. **devour**	e. **distressed**	g. **occasions**
b. **constant**	d. **discovered**	f. **modern**	h. **popular**

_____
_____ 1–2. The World Series and Super Bowl have become so . . ? . . that many Americans watch them together as if they were important family . . ? . . .

_____
_____ 3–4. Because of my . . ? . . hunger for sweets, I can quickly . . ? . . a whole box of chocolate-chip cookies.

_____
_____ 5–6. . . ? . . medicine has . . ? . . cures for many diseases that used to kill people.

_____
_____ 7–8. Because we hid in the trees, the animals were not . . ? . . of us and never got frightened or . . ? . . .

Showing You Understand the Words

PART A

In the space at the left, write the letter of the choice that best completes the sentence or answers the question.

____ 1. Which of the following should you be **aware** of before diving into a swimming pool?
   a. How much the pool cost
   b. What the pool is made of
   c. How deep the pool is

____ 2. Which of the following would you want to **discover** in your living room?
   a. A bag of trash
   b. A fifty-dollar bill
   c. A roll of bathroom tissue

____ 3. You would probably be **distressed** if someone told you that
   a. you had won the lottery.
   b. your neighbor has two sisters.
   c. you did not do well on a test.

____ 4. If you are using a **modern** tool to add up numbers, you probably are using
   a. pencil and paper.
   b. a computer.
   c. your fingers.

PART B

In the space at the left, write the letter of the choice that best completes the sentence or answers the question.

____ 5. One thing that is **constant** in everyone's life is
   a. going to sleep and waking up.
   b. making a lot of money.
   c. doing well in school.

____ 6. A cat would probably **devour**
   a. a ball of string.
   b. a large dog.
   c. a juicy mouse.

____ 7. Most people think it is a special **occasion** when
   a. they drive to work every morning.
   b. they get a bad cold.
   c. they turn twenty-one.

____ 8. Which of the following foods is the most **popular** with children?
   a. Spinach
   b. Pizza
   c. Coffee

Adding Words to a Reading

A. The Joy of Ice Cream

Read the following paragraph carefully. Then fill in each blank with a word from the box. Use each word once.

a. **devour**	b. **modern**	c. **occasions**	d. **popular**

For hundreds of years, people have enjoyed ice cream. No one is sure when people first started to (1)_____ the frozen treat. But paintings show an icy dessert being enjoyed as far back as the twelfth century. Ice cream as we know it became (2)_____ among the rich and powerful in Europe during the 1500s. King Charles I of England liked ice cream so much he made a law which said that it could be served only at his table. He even said that he would have his chef's head cut off if the chef gave his secret ice-cream recipe to anyone. To Charles, the food was much too precious° to share. In the United States, too, ice cream was eaten on special (3)_____ by the country's richest people. George Washington, Thomas Jefferson, and James Madison were all big fans of the frozen dessert. However, ice cream did not reach the rest of the nation until 1845. At that time, a New Jersey woman made a hand-held ice-cream maker. Thanks to that machine, ice cream in the (4)_____ world is not just for kings and presidents. Now it's for all of us!

B. A Noisy Apartment

Read the following paragraph carefully. Then fill in each blank with a word from the box. Use each word once.

a. **aware**	b. **constant**	c. **discover**	d. **distressed**

When Carla decided to move out of her parents' house, she thought it might be hard to find a nice apartment for a low rent. So she felt fortunate° to (5)_____ a clean and pretty little apartment that was not too expensive. Within a week of moving in, though, she was not so happy. When she had rented the place, she had not seen how close it was to the train tracks. Soon she became very (6)_____ of the noise from the trains. In fact, the noise was almost (7)_____ because trains went roaring past several times every hour, day and night. At first, Carla was really (8)_____. She even thought about moving. But she decided to stay six weeks to see if she could get used to the noise. Little by little, she did. Now the noise does not bother her at all. When friends ask, "How can you bear that noise?" she answers, "What noise?"

Using the Words When Writing and Talking

Now that you understand the meanings of the eight new words in the chapter, you are ready to use them on paper and in speaking. Complete each sentence below in a way that shows you really know what each **boldfaced** word means. Take a few minutes to think about your answer before writing it down and saying it out loud.

1. I became **aware** that I had overslept when _____

   _____

2. Throughout the two-hour class, I heard the **constant** sound of _____

   _____

3. From the way most people **devour** ice cream, it is clear that _____

   _____

4. After I moved into my new home, I **discovered** that _____

   _____

5. At the zoo, animals become so **distressed** in their cages that _____

   _____

6. I like the **modern** look of _____

   _____

7. A family **occasion** I will never forget was _____

   _____

8. If you go into a school playground, you can usually tell right away who the most **popular** kids

   are. All the other children _____

   _____

Scores	Adding One Word to an Item	_____%	Showing You Understand the Words	_____%
	Adding Two Words to an Item	_____%	Adding Words to a Reading	_____%

Number right: 8 = 100%, 7 = 88%, 6 = 75%, 5 = 63%, 4 = 50%, 3 = 38%, 2 = 25%, 1 = 13%
Enter your scores above and in the vocabulary performance chart on the inside back cover of the book.

ability	glance
create	gratitude
damage	introduce
failure	labor

Learning Eight New Words

In the space at the left, write the letter of the meaning closest to that of each **boldfaced** word. Use the other words (the *context*) in each sentence to help you figure out the word's meaning.

1 ability
(uh-**bil**-i-tee)
– noun

___*Ability* means

- Many animals, such as cats and deer, have the **ability** to see at night.
- When my teacher saw me in the school play, she said I had the **ability** to be a good actor.

  a. feeling of thanks   b. special power   c. wish

2 create
(kree-**ayt**)
– verb

___*Create* means

- Children like to **create** drawings that their parents can put up on the refrigerator.
- Starting with a ball of gray clay, I **created** a small bowl that I liked a lot.

  a. study   b. make   c. look at quickly

3 damage
(**dam**-ij)
– noun

___*Damage* means

- Even though the accident was not bad, there was a lot of **damage** to Julia's car.
- **Damage** caused by the hurricane was so great that many people could not find their homes.

  a. hard work   b. danger   c. harm

4 failure
(**fayl**-yur)
– noun

___*Failure* means

- The dinner that Rashid cooked for Janelle was a **failure**. Everything was burned to a crisp.
- When she was turned down for the job she wanted badly, Betsy felt like a **failure**.

  a. something that   b. something that   c. something that doesn't
     works easily   works well   turn out well

5 glance
(glanss)
– verb

___*Glance* means

- The sun is so bright that if you just **glance** at it, you can hurt your eyes.
- Instead of reading the directions carefully, Leon simply **glanced** at the box before trying to put the toy together.

  a. look quickly   b. listen carefully   c. keep from looking

6 gratitude
(**grat**-uh-tood)
– noun

- Because of his **gratitude** for my working overtime, the boss gave me an extra day of vacation.
- When friends help you or do you a favor, it's good to show them **gratitude** for what they did.

___*Gratitude* means   a. anger   b. thanks   c. worry

7 introduce
(in-truh-**dooss**)
– verb

- As soon as the moving van leaves, we will go next door and **introduce** ourselves to our new neighbors.
- Someonee **introduced** Jenna to me in kindergarten, and we have been friends ever since.

___*Introduce* means   a. sell something   b. not agree   c. meet someone for
                          to someone   with someone   the first time

8 labor
(**lay**-bur)
– noun

- The beautiful tablecloth is the result of months of my grandmother's **labor**.
- It will take a full day of **labor** to clean out the garage.

___*Labor* means   a. space   b. quiet   c. hard work

Matching Words with Meanings

Here are the meanings, or *definitions*, of the eight new words. Write each word next to its meaning. The sentences above and on the facing page will help you decide on the meaning of each word.

1. _____ A feeling or showing of thanks; thankfulness

2. _____ Harm; injury

3. _____ The skill or power to do something

4. _____ Hard work

5. _____ To make one person known to another for the first time

6. _____ To make something; to bring something into being

7. _____ To look at something quickly; to take a fast look at something

8. _____ Someone or something that does not turn out well; someone or
                               something that fails

BE CAREFUL: Don't go any further until you know the answers above are correct. Then you can use the meanings to help you in the following activities. After a while, you will know the words so well that you won't need to check the definitions at all.

Adding One Word to an Item

Complete each item below by writing one word from the box on the answer line at the left. Use each word once.

| a. **ability** | c. **damage** | e. **glanced** | g. **introduce** |
| b. **create** | d. **failure** | f. **gratitude** | h. **labor** |

_____ 1. After I shoveled her walkway, my neighbor was so happy she gave me a hug to show her . . ? . . .

_____ 2. On TV and in the movies, Superman has the . . ? . . to fly.

_____ 3. Even though we only . . ? . . at the bedroom set in the store window, we knew right away that it was the one we wanted.

_____ 4. Every year, insects that eat wood cause millions of dollars of . . ? . . in homes across the country.

_____ 5. As a dancer, I am a . . ? . . because I can't move my arms and legs at the same time.

_____ 6. At the party, I will . . ? . . you to my cousin. I think you will like her.

_____ 7. It took thousands of workers and many years of hard . . ? . . to build the Pyramids in Egypt.

_____ 8. Chang used several boards to . . ? . . a desk.

Adding Two Words to an Item

Complete each item below by writing **two** words from the box on the answer lines at the left. Use each word once.

| a. **ability** | c. **damage** | e. **glance** | g. **introduced** |
| b. **created** | d. **failure** | f. **gratitude** | h. **labor** |

_____
_____ 1–2. After many hours of . . ? . . in the kitchen, Paul's sister . . ? . . some wonderful cookies—and a big mess.

_____
_____ 3–4. Because of his doctor's great . . ? . . , the . . ? . . to my father's heart could be repaired.

_____
_____ 5–6. When Jamal . . ? . . his parents to his teacher, they told her how much . . ? . . they had for the extra help she had given their son.

_____
_____ 7–8. I had only to . . ? . . at the bookcase I had made to know that it was a . . ? . . . Not one of the shelves was straight.

Showing You Understand the Words

PART A

In the space at the left, write the letter of the choice that best completes the sentence or answers the question.

___ 1. Which of the following might you **glance** at?
   a. A song on the radio
   b. Your watch to see the time
   c. A movie you want to see

___ 2. You would probably feel **gratitude** if someone
   a. smashed your new car.
   b. bought you a nice present.
   c. gave you a bad haircut.

___ 3. You might need to be **introduced** to
   a. your brother and sister.
   b. the parents of a new friend.
   c. your old boss.

___ 4. Which of the following would take a lot of **labor**?
   a. Watching TV
   b. Picking up a pencil
   c. Moving a heavy couch

PART B

In the space at the left, write the letter of the choice that best completes the sentence or answers the question.

___ 5. Someone who writes children's books must have the **ability** to
   a. sew quickly.
   b. tell a good story.
   c. get along with people.

___ 6. Which of the following is needed to **create** a sandwich?
   a. A glass of milk
   b. A napkin
   c. Two slices of bread

___ 7. On farms, insects cause crop **damage** by
   a. eating plants that grow in the field.
   b. crawling into living rooms.
   c. buzzing loudly.

___ 8. Which of the following would make many people feel like a **failure**?
   a. Winning the lottery
   b. Moving to a beautiful new apartment
   c. Getting fired

Adding Words to a Reading

A. Nuts in the Senate

Read the following paragraph carefully. Then fill in each blank with a word from the box. Use each word once.

a. **created**	b. **failure**	c. **glanced**	d. **introduced**

On a cold winter day in 1921, an interesting event° took place. A man spoke to the United States Senate about something he thought was very important: peanuts. The man's name was George Washington Carver. When the senators found out what he came to talk about, at first they laughed. But that did not stop Carver or make him feel like a (1)_____. Carver, an African-American scientist, believed so much in peanuts that he wanted the Senate to pass laws to help farmers who grew them. After someone (2)_____ him to the senators, Carver showed them many interesting things. He began with several items that he had (3)_____ out of peanuts—dye, soap, wood stain, and gravy. Next, he handed out paper made from peanut shells, shaving cream made from peanut oil, and rubber made from the nut itself. But he saved the best for last. Just as Carver's time was almost up, one of the senators asked, "What is the brown stuff in the jar you are holding?" Carver (4)_____ at the man and smiled. Opening the jar, he let the senators smell and then taste what was inside. Much to their surprise, the "brown stuff" smelled good and tasted even better. By the end of the day, the Senate had passed the law Carver wanted, and the nation had begun its love affair with—you guessed it—peanut butter!

B. Calling Dr. Leech

Read the following paragraph carefully. Then fill in each blank with a word from the box. Use each word once.

a. **ability**	b. **damage**	c. **gratitude**	d. **labor**

When the ear of seven-year-old Jimmy Taylor was nearly torn off by a dog, the doctors didn't know if they could help. They spent hours trying to repair the (5)_____. But after all their (6)_____, Jimmy's ear was not getting better. Instead, the blood in his ear began to dry up, and the ear puffed up and turned blue. The doctors knew that Jimmy would lose his ear unless they acted quickly. So they decided on an unusual° treatment that is not often followed today but was widely used hundreds of years ago. They decided to use leeches, bloodsucking worms that live in ponds and lakes. In the mouth of a leech are juices that have the (7)_____ to break up dried-up blood, letting the blood flow freely again. The blood then helps the problem area get better. Six leeches were rushed to the hospital to feed on the dried-up blood in Jimmy's ear. The doctors made small holes in the skin of Jimmy's ear and placed the hungry leeches at the holes. After just a few hours, the ear turned a pink, healthy color. It was clear that Jimmy's ear would be saved. Did Jimmy show any (8)_____ to his wormy helpers? Not really. When he found out that it was leeches that had saved his ear, all he could do was make a face and say, "Yuck!"

Using the Words When Writing and Talking

Now that you understand the meanings of the eight new words in the chapter, you are ready to use them on paper and in speaking. Complete each sentence below in a way that shows you really know what each **boldfaced** word means. Take a few minutes to think about your answer before writing it down and saying it out loud.

1. I wish I had the **ability** to _____

   _____

2. Children often **create** a mess in the house by _____

   _____

3. After the flood, **damage** was so widespread that _____

   _____

4. Parents can help their children not feel like **failures** by _____

   _____

5. In a restaurant, if you **glance** many times at the food that people at the next table are eating, they

   _____

   _____

6. One way to show **gratitude** to others is _____

   _____

7. To **introduce** two people to each other, all you have to do is say something like, " _____

   _____."

8. It took days of **labor** to _____

   _____

Scores	Adding One Word to an Item	_____%	Showing You Understand the Words	_____%
	Adding Two Words to an Item	_____%	Adding Words to a Reading	_____%

Number right: 8 = 100%, 7 = 88%, 6 = 75%, 5 = 63%, 4 = 50%, 3 = 38%, 2 = 25%, 1 = 13%
Enter your scores above and in the vocabulary performance chart on the inside back cover of the book.

avoid	intend
excuse	normal
helpless	sociable
include	struggle

Learning Eight New Words

In the space at the left, write the letter of the meaning closest to that of each **boldfaced** word. Use the other words (the *context*) in each sentence to help you figure out the word's meaning.

1 avoid
(uh-**void**)
– verb

____*Avoid* means

- One way to stay healthy is to **avoid** foods with a lot of sugar and fat.
- Steven **avoided** getting stuck in a traffic jam by taking another road to get to work.

    a. get closer to   b. keep away from   c. enjoy

2 excuse
(eks-**kyooss**)
– noun

____*Excuse* means

- Cora's **excuse** for not handing in her homework was that it had gotten wet in the rain.
- Instead of saying that he did not want to go to the party, Bill made up an **excuse** about having a bad cold.

    a. reason   b. happy time   c. question

3 helpless
(**help**-liss)
– adjective

____*Helpless* means

- Newborn babies are completely **helpless**. They need adults to do everything for them.
- When I broke my hip, I was **helpless** for six weeks. I could not even get myself something to eat.

    a. not able to   b. not able to take   c. not very
       see well   care of oneself   well known

4 include
(in-**klood**)
– verb

____*Include* means

- The new band will **include** a drummer, a singer, and a guitar player.
- Pedro's costume for the Halloween party **includes** a rubber mask, a purple wig, and a long black cape.

    a. be without   b. stay away from   c. be made up of

5 intend
(in-**tend**)
– verb

____*Intend* means

- After working outside in the hot sun for hours, I **intend** to go home and take a cold shower.
- Greg **intended** to spend his paycheck on a nice vacation, but then his car broke down.

    a. forget   b. hate   c. plan

6 **normal**
(**nor**-muhl)
– adjective

• The parents were happy to learn that their little boy's fear of the dark was **normal**.

• The **normal** time for the class to begin is 9 a.m., but today we will meet at 11 a.m.

___*Normal* means   a. usual   b. strange   c. easily hurt

7 **sociable**
(**soh**-shuh-buhl)
– adjective

• Eric is shy and doesn't like parties, but his sister is very **sociable**.

• The store wants to hire a **sociable** person to say hello to customers as they walk through the door.

___*Sociable* means   a. quiet   b. friendly   c. angry

8 **struggle**
(**struhg**-uhl)
– noun

• Rita did well in her English course, but the class was a real **struggle** for her at first.

• It is a **struggle** to work and go to school at the same time.

___*Struggle* means   a. boring time   b. easy time   c. difficult time

Matching Words with Meanings

Here are the meanings, or *definitions*, of the eight new words. Write each word next to its meaning. The sentences above and on the facing page will help you decide on the meaning of each word.

1. _____   A reason, often not true, why something happened

2. _____   To plan to do something

3. _____   To stay away from someone or something

4. _____   Friendly; enjoying the company of others

5. _____   A hard and difficult time

6. _____   Unable to take care of oneself

7. _____   Usual; regular

8. _____   To be made up of; to have within itself

BE CAREFUL: Don't go any further until you know the answers above are correct. Then you can use the meanings to help you in the following activities. After a while, you will know the words so well that you won't need to check the definitions at all.

Adding One Word to an Item

Complete each item below by writing one word from the box on the answer line at the left. Use each word once.

a. **avoided**	c. **helpless**	e. **intended**	g. **sociable**
b. **excuse**	d. **includes**	f. **normal**	h. **struggle**

_____ 1. The teacher had . . ? . . to give a test on Friday, but then she saw that half the class was absent.

_____ 2. Many people feel . . ? . . at fancy restaurants. They always need to ask their friends what they should order and how much they should tip.

_____ 3. When Bill caught the flu, his friends . . ? . . him so they wouldn't get sick, too.

_____ 4. Because Eva is so . . ? . ., she wants a job where she will work with people.

_____ 5. Sira's . . ? . . for not going to basketball practice was that she couldn't find her sneakers.

_____ 6. A . . ? . . . workday runs from about 9 a.m. to 5 p.m.

_____ 7. To Joanne, a weekend is not perfect unless it . . ? . . sleeping late, seeing friends, and going to a movie.

_____ 8. It was a . . ? . . for Thien to save enough money to bring his parents to this country.

Adding Two Words to an Item

Complete each item below by writing **two** words from the box on the answer lines at the left. Use each word once.

a. **avoid**	c. **helpless**	e. **intend**	g. **sociable**
b. **excuse**	d. **includes**	f. **normal**	h. **struggle**

_____ 1–2. In order to . . ? . . hurting Bruno's feelings, Rosa made up an . . ? . . to
_____   explain why she was not able to go to the movies with him.

_____ 3–4. A . . ? . . day at a fast-food restaurant . . ? . . getting covered in grease,
_____   getting burned by hot ovens, and being yelled at by customers.

_____ 5–6. Before going to the city next weekend, I . . ? . . to buy a map and a
_____   guidebook. Without them, I would feel lost and . . ? . . .

_____ 7–8. For . . ? . . people, speaking in front of crowds is often easy. But for
_____   shy folks, talking to large groups can be a real . . ? . . .

Showing You Understand the Words

PART A

In the space at the left, write the letter of the choice that best completes the sentence or answers the question.

_____ 1. If you were really tired, you would probably want to **avoid**
   a. relaxing in front of the TV.
   b. going to bed early.
   c. going out to a party.

_____ 2. You might try to find an **excuse** if you
   a. forgot your best friend's birthday.
   b. fixed your neighbor's roof.
   c. came to work on time.

_____ 3. You would probably feel **helpless** if you were
   a. at home with your family.
   b. at a party with friends.
   c. lost in a strange city.

_____ 4. Which of the following would it be **normal** for you to see in a grocery store?
   a. People playing basketball
   b. Bananas on a shelf
   c. A can of soup stuck to the ceiling

PART B

In the space at the left, write the letter of the choice that best completes the sentence or answers the question.

_____ 5. Which of the following should a good winter outfit **include**?
   a. Sandals, a bathing suit, and sunglasses
   b. Warm boots, a thick jacket, and a wool hat
   c. Sneakers, a pair of jeans, and a T-shirt

_____ 6. If two people **intend** to make up after a fight, they will
   a. continue to find fault with each other.
   b. never speak to each other again.
   c. say they are sorry.

_____ 7. A **sociable** person would probably
   a. have trouble making friends.
   b. look forward to a neighborhood party.
   c. be nervous about talking to an old friend.

_____ 8. It would be a **struggle** for people who love chocolate to
   a. turn down a slice of chocolate cake.
   b. eat all of a chocolate candy bar by themselves.
   c. enjoy a hot fudge sundae.

Adding Words to a Reading

A. TV and Violence

Read the following paragraph carefully. Then fill in each blank with a word from the box. Use each word once.

a. **avoid**	b. **excuse**	c. **includes**	d. **normal**

Would you want someone teaching your kids how to be mean and hurtful? That is often what happens when kids watch television. Today's most-watched TV shows are filled with violence and crime. And no one watches more of these shows than America's kids. In a (1)_____ week, many children sit in front of the TV set for more than twenty-seven hours. By the time kids finish grade school, they have seen over 100,000 acts of people using force to cause harm. This number (2)_____ more than 8,000 killings. By the time kids graduate from high school, they will have spent more time watching TV than sitting in the classroom or talking with their families. The effects of watching this much TV are scary. Studies show that when kids watch people fighting and shooting each other, they are more likely to be violent themselves. True, in the modern° world, it is hard for kids to (3)_____ watching TV. But that is no (4)_____ for parents to let their kids watch whatever they want. If parents find that their kids are watching one violent show after another, the adults must act. What should they do? They should get up, turn off the TV, and help the kids find better ways to spend their time.

B. Are You Ready for a Pet?

Read the following paragraph carefully. Then fill in each blank with a word from the box. Use each word once.

a. **helpless**	b. **intend**	c. **sociable**	d. **struggle**

If you (5)_____ to get a pet, make sure you know what you are doing. A new pet may be cute, but it also means lots of work. Puppies, for example, are friendly, (6)_____ animals. They like to be around people, but they also like to chew things. And to them, it does not matter whether they are chewing your kitchen table or your leather jacket. Teaching puppies not to destroy things and be housetrained can be a long, hard (7)_____ that lasts for months. Kittens also can make life difficult. Those sweet little animals scratch everything in sight.

In no time, a kitten's sharp claws can rip a new sofa apart, causing damage° that cannot be fixed. What about smaller pets such as goldfish? They may not take as much everyday work as dogs and cats. However, fish often get sick, and they are completely (8)_____ if they jump out of their tank. The time and money you spend at the vet's office can really add up. For all the fun and friendship pets give, they are also a lot of work and expense. Keep that in mind before you bring one home.

Using the Words When Writing and Talking

Now that you understand the meanings of the eight new words in the chapter, you are ready to use them on paper and in speaking. Complete each sentence below in a way that shows you really know what each **boldfaced** word means. Take a few minutes to think about your answer before writing it down and saying it out loud.

1. People often **avoid** the supermarket on weekends because _____

2. Most children are good at finding **excuses** for _____

3. I used to feel **helpless** when _____

4. My favorite singers **include** _____

5. In a few years, I **intend** to _____

6. It is **normal** for teenagers to _____

7. The monkeys at the zoo are so **sociable** that _____

8. It was a **struggle** for me to learn how to _____

Scores	Adding One Word to an Item	_____%	Showing You Understand the Words	_____%
	Adding Two Words to an Item	_____%	Adding Words to a Reading	_____%

Number right: 8 = 100%, 7 = 88%, 6 = 75%, 5 = 63%, 4 = 50%, 3 = 38%, 2 = 25%, 1 = 13%
Enter your scores above and in the vocabulary performance chart on the inside back cover of the book.

approach	numerous
damp	previous
ignore	require
loyal	timid

Learning Eight New Words

In the space at the left, write the letter of the meaning closest to that of each **boldfaced** word. Use the other words (the *context*) in each sentence to help you figure out the word's meaning.

1 approach
(uh-**prohch**)
– verb

• As you **approach** a stop sign, slow your car down and get ready to stop.
• The man on the corner **approached** us and said, "Do you have any extra change?"

___*Approach* means   a. go away from   b. need   c. come near

2 damp
(**damp**)
– adjective

• At the ocean, clothes often feel sticky and **damp**.
• I got angry when I saw my roommate's **damp**, dirty socks on the table.

___*Damp* means   a. clean   b. a bit wet   c. good-smelling

3 ignore
(ig-**nor**)
– verb

• It is hard to **ignore** the smell of delicious food when you are really hungry.
• When Ruby **ignored** her little girl's question, the child shouted it loudly.

___*Ignore* means   a. know   b. pay no attention to   c. need

4 loyal
(**loi**-uhl)
– adjective

• I read about a dog in England who was so **loyal** to his owner that after the man died, the dog went to his grave every day.
• No matter how many games they lose, Connie is **loyal** to her favorite baseball team.

___*Loyal* means   a. faithful   b. mean   c. helpful

5 numerous
(**noo**-mur-uhss)
– adjective

• On a clear evening, you can see **numerous** stars in the night sky.
• Although Mr. Colon has **numerous** reasons why he has not stopped smoking, none of them is a good one.

___*Numerous* means   a. a few   b. ugly   c. lots of

6 previous
(**pree**-vee-uhss)
– adjective

- It's hard to understand what's going on in a TV soap opera if you haven't seen the show the **previous** day.
- Robert married a woman who had two children from a **previous** marriage.

___*Previous* means   a. next   b. earlier   c. favorite

7 require
(ri-**kwii**-ur)
– verb

- Many jobs today **require** employees who know how to use a computer.
- When we went camping, we couldn't take our three dogs with us in the van. They **require** too much space.

___*Require* means   a. send away   b. do without   c. need

8 timid
(**tim**-id)
– adjective

- On the first day of kindergarten, most children in the class were too **timid** to speak.
- It is hard for a **timid** person to talk in front of a group.

___*Timid* means   a. fearful   b. noisy   c. old

Matching Words with Meanings

Here are the meanings, or *definitions*, of the eight new words. Write each word next to its meaning. The sentences above and on the facing page will help you decide on the meaning of each word.

1. _____   Ready to stand by or stand up for someone; faithful

2. _____   Many

3. _____   Earlier; happening before something else

4. _____   A little wet; moist

5. _____   To need something

6. _____   To come close or closer to someone or something

7. _____   To pay no attention to something

8. _____   Shy

BE CAREFUL: Don't go any further until you know the answers above are correct. Then you can use the meanings to help you in the following activities. After a while, you will know the words so well that you won't need to check the definitions at all.

Adding One Word to an Item

Complete each item below by writing one word from the box on the answer line at the left. Use each word once.

a. **approached**	c. **ignored**	e. **numerous**	g. **require**
b. **damp**	d. **loyal**	f. **previous**	h. **timid**

_____ 1. Steve is a truck driver now. In his . . ? . . job, he was a cook in a restaurant.

_____ 2. After Mona played basketball, her clothes were . . ? . . with sweat.

_____ 3. Although he was born in another country, Akira is so . . ? . . to the United States that he joined the Army.

_____ 4. The Halloween trick-or-treaters put on their masks as they . . ? . . each house.

_____ 5. The school offers . . ? . . art classes, including watercolor painting and cartoon drawing.

_____ 6. Betty . . ? . . what the doctor told her to do and ended up so sick that she missed work for a week.

_____ 7. To feel rested, I . . ? . . seven or eight hours of sleep each night.

_____ 8. Most people feel a bit . . ? . . at parties where they don't know anyone.

Adding Two Words to an Item

Complete each item below by writing **two** words from the box on the answer lines at the left. Use each word once.

a. **approached**	c. **ignores**	e. **numerous**	g. **requires**
b. **damp**	d. **loyal**	f. **previous**	h. **timid**

_____ 1–2. Lawrence is always . . ? . . to his friends. He . . ? . . anything bad he
_____ hears about them and pays attention only to the good things.

_____ 3–4. Tonya's new hairstyle . . ? . . a lot of work. The hair has to be set on
_____ big rollers while it is still . . ? . . from being washed.

_____ 5–6. I gave . . ? . . reasons why I couldn't sing in the choir, but the real
_____ reason was that I was too . . ? . . to try out.

_____ 7–8. When I was out in the yard, my new neighbor . . ? . . me to ask if I
_____ knew the . . ? . . owner of her house well.

Showing You Understand the Words

PART A

In the space at the left, write the letter of the choice that best completes the sentence or answers the question.

___ 1. Which of the following might feel **damp** against your bare feet?
   a. Grass in the early morning
   b. A bath towel that was never used
   c. A sidewalk on a sunny day

___ 2. If you plan to get **numerous** things done this weekend, you will probably be
   a. sleeping all weekend.
   b. busy all weekend.
   c. lazy all weekend.

___ 3. If you used to be a waiter, now are a painter, and plan to become a circus clown, which is your **previous** job?
   a. A waiter
   b. A painter
   c. A clown

___ 4. If you are **timid**, which of these would be hard for you to do?
   a. Wash the dishes
   b. Give a speech in front of strangers
   c. Carry a heavy package

PART B

In the space at the left, write the letter of the choice that best completes the sentence or answers the question.

___ 5. When people **approach** the ticket booth at a movie theater, they probably
   a. have just arrived at the theater.
   b. have already seen the movie.
   c. are ready to leave the theater.

___ 6. A man on the corner asked people for some money. Which of the following people **ignored** him?
   a. A woman who gave him fifty cents
   b. A couple who walked past without looking at him
   c. A teenager who said "Get a job!"

___ 7. When a football team does badly, a **loyal** fan
   a. boos them and says, "Get off the field, you jerks."
   b. hopes they lose games.
   c. keeps cheering for them.

___ 8. If a newspaper ad says a job "**requires** heavy lifting," anyone applying for the job
   a. will not be asked to do any lifting.
   b. needs to be strong.
   c. doesn't need to be strong.

Adding Words to a Reading

A. Help for Shy People

Read the following paragraphs carefully. Then fill in each blank with a word from the box. Use each word once.

a. **damp**	b. **numerous**	c. **require**	d. **timid**

Many people are a little shy. In fact, probably everyone feels shy once in a while. But some people are so (1)_____ that it makes their lives difficult. For them, making everyday conversation—even with people they know—can be a struggle°. And the thought of speaking to a stranger makes their hands (2)_____ with sweat. Being so shy gets in the way of having friends or doing well at school or on the job.

Many adult-education schools offer courses to help shy people. Shy people (3)_____ practice in talking to strangers. So the teacher of such a course may ask students to speak to class members they don't know. Students are also given (4)_____ tricks for getting over their shyness. For example, they might be told to think about a friend who is outgoing and friendly; then they make believe they are that person and try to act as he or she would. Students also are given interesting assignments to do at home. One assignment might be for students to start a conversation with someone they don't know but have always wanted to meet. After a while, the students in these classes learn to relax, make friends, and enjoy life more.

B. Not a Laughing Matter

Read the following paragraph carefully. Then fill in each blank with a word from the box. Use each word once.

a. **approached**	b. **ignored**	c. **loyal**	d. **previous**

The other day, I had lunch with a group of friends from work. My friend Patty, who recently remarried and has two children, was in the group. While we were eating, one of the men said something mean about his ex-wife. Some people laughed, but Patty (5)_____ what he said. A little later, he made another mean joke about his ex-wife. Then he (6)_____ Patty and said, "What about you? Tell us about your (7)_____ husband. What kind of jerk was he?" Patty replied, "My ex-husband and I had our problems. But I am not going to make fun of him just so you can have a laugh. I married him because he's a good guy in many ways. We had a couple of wonderful kids together. Our marriage is over, but I still feel (8)_____ to him. I don't want him laughing about me with his friends. And I do not intend° to laugh at him either." Everybody at the table was quiet. We quickly started talking about something else. There were no more dumb jokes that day about an ex-husband or an ex-wife.

Using the Words When Writing and Talking

Now that you understand the meanings of the eight new words in the chapter, you are ready to use them on paper and in speaking. Complete each sentence below in a way that shows you really know what each **boldfaced** word means. Take a few minutes to think about your answer before writing it down and saying it out loud.

1. I would not like to **approach** _____
   _____

2. When it is **damp** outside, older folks often feel _____
   _____

3. When children **ignore** what their parents tell them, _____
   _____

4. When people are hospitalized, a visit from a **loyal** friend makes them _____
   _____

5. Students give **numerous** reasons why _____
   _____

6. One of the vocabulary words in the **previous** chapter was _____
   _____

7. For me, a good party **requires** _____
   _____

8. I sometimes feel **timid** when _____
   _____

| *Scores* | Adding One Word to an Item | _____% | Showing You Understand the Words | _____% |
| | Adding Two Words to an Item | _____% | Adding Words to a Reading | _____% |

Number right: 8 = 100%, 7 = 88%, 6 = 75%, 5 = 63%, 4 = 50%, 3 = 38%, 2 = 25%, 1 = 13%
Enter your scores above and in the vocabulary performance chart on the inside back cover of the book.

capable	opportunity
careless	resist
furious	reverse
observe	tradition

Learning Eight New Words

In the space at the left, write the letter of the meaning closest to that of each **boldfaced** word. Use the other words (the *context*) in each sentence to help you figure out the word's meaning.

1 capable
(**kay**-puh-buhl)
– adjective

____ *Capable* means

- Only the most **capable** runners should try a twenty-six-mile race.
- Of all the people who applied for the job, Maya was the most **capable**, so she was hired.

    a. having skill   b. not ready   c. not careful

2 careless
(**kair**-luhss)
– adjective

____ *Careless* means

- Each year hundreds of fires are started by **careless** smokers.
- The **careless** painter splashed drops of paint all over the carpet.

    a. intelligent   b. not careful   c. cheerful

3 furious
(**fyoo**-ree-uhss)
– adjective

____ *Furious* means

- People who cannot control their tempers often become **furious** over small problems.
- My parents were **furious** when I tracked mud all over the clean kitchen floor just before their guests arrived.

    a. helpful   b. quiet   c. angry

4 observe
(uhb-**zurv**)
– verb

____ *Observe* means

- Mirrors hanging high in the corners of the store let the owner **observe** people who might be stealing.
- The lifeguards at the pool closely **observed** the kids in the water.

    a. miss   b. copy   c. watch

5 opportunity
(op-ur-**too**-nuh-tee)
– noun

____ *Opportunity* means

- Because of his excellent grades, Kevin has the **opportunity** to go to a top-rated college.
- Sheila's job gives her the **opportunity** to meet many interesting people.

    a. problem   b. habit   c. chance

6 resist
(ri-**zist**)
– verb

- Many people are strong and can **resist** a hot fudge sundae topped with whipped cream, nuts, and a cherry. I'm not one of those people.
- The children **resisted** sleep as long as they could. Then they went to bed.

___*Resist* means   a. answer   b. say no to   c. invite

7 reverse
(ri-**vurss**)
– verb

- As a little girl, I liked to **reverse** the order of dinner and start with dessert.
- My father likes to **reverse** our home movies so that it looks as if everyone is walking backward.

___*Reverse* means   a. say loudly   b. keep   c. turn around

8 tradition
(truh-**dish**-uhn)
– noun

- It is a Latin American **tradition** to have a special party on a girl's fifteenth birthday.
- Two **traditions** in the United States are watching fireworks on the Fourth of July and eating turkey on Thanksgiving.

___*Tradition* means   a. handed-down way   b. law   c. difficult time
of doing something

Matching Words with Meanings

Here are the meanings, or *definitions*, of the eight new words. Write each word next to its meaning. The sentences above and on the facing page will help you decide on the meaning of each word.

1. _____ A chance to do something that will probably lead to good things

2. _____ Paying little or no attention; not careful

3. _____ Very angry

4. _____ To keep from doing something

5. _____ To see and pay attention to something

6. _____ A special way of doing something that is passed down from older to younger people; a custom

7. _____ Having the skill to do something; able

8. _____ To turn something around; to go in the opposite direction

BE CAREFUL: Don't go any further until you know the answers above are correct. Then you can use the meanings to help you in the following activities. After a while, you will know the words so well that you won't need to check the definitions at all.

Adding One Word to an Item

Complete each item below by writing one word from the box on the answer line at the left. Use each word once.

a. **capable**	c. **furious**	e. **opportunity**	g. **reversed**
b. **careless**	d. **observes**	f. **resist**	h. **tradition**

_____ 1. Research shows that people who often become . . ? . . have more heart problems than those who are slow to anger.

_____ 2. At first, Mom said I could not borrow the car, but then she . . ? . . her decision and gave me the keys.

_____ 3. Even good students can become . . ? . . if they rush to get their work done.

_____ 4. Dolphins and bats are . . ? . . of hearing sounds that people cannot hear.

_____ 5. For many children throughout the world, Halloween is a day to wear masks and tell ghost stories. This scary . . ? . . is believed to be hundreds of years old.

_____ 6. The school principal . . ? . . a different classroom every day, just to see how students and teachers are doing.

_____ 7. Since I don't really love candy, I can easily . . ? . . it.

_____ 8. Hector takes every . . ? . . to spend time with his children. He tries to get them up every morning and to put them to bed every night.

Adding Two Words to an Item

Complete each item below by writing **two** words from the box on the answer lines at the left. Use each word once.

a. **capable**	c. **furious**	e. **opportunity**	g. **reverses**
b. **careless**	d. **observe**	f. **resist**	h. **tradition**

_____ 1–2. Although she doesn't eat meat, Donna . . ? . . her position every
_____   Thanksgiving. Following . . ? . ., she has turkey with stuffing.

_____ 3–4. Without thinking, Andrew turned down an . . ? . . to see the President
_____   of the United States in person. Now he is . . ? . . at himself.

_____ 5–6. Most people are . . ? . . of keeping their weight down if they exercise
_____   often and . . ? . . fatty foods.

_____ 7–8. When you are driving on the highway, you must . . ? . . everything
_____   around you. It takes only one . . ? . . mistake to cause an accident.

Showing You Understand the Words

PART A

In the space at the left, write the letter of the choice that best completes the sentence or answers the question.

___ 1. Which of the following behaviors would make you **furious**?
   a. Someone breaking into your mailbox
   b. Someone enjoying a meal that you cooked
   c. Someone walking down your street

___ 2. If you are baby-sitting, it would be your job to **observe**
   a. the children you are taking care of.
   b. the food in the refrigerator.
   c. the neighbors next door.

___ 3. If you are looking for a job **opportunity**, you probably
   a. will not look at the "Help Wanted" ads in the newspaper.
   b. are happy with the job you have now.
   c. are not happy with the job you have now.

___ 4. If you want to save money, which of these activities should you **resist**?
   a. Working overtime
   b. Going shopping at the mall
   c. Playing basketball

PART B

In the space at the left, write the letter of the choice that best completes the sentence.

___ 5. **Capable** students usually
   a. live one block from school.
   b. are good-looking.
   c. do well in school.

___ 6. A person who is **careless** might
   a. spill some coffee.
   b. drink some water.
   c. share a lunch.

___ 7. A fifteen-year old girl was upset because her parents said she couldn't date until she was 16. However, her parents just **reversed** what they said earlier. This means that the girl
   a. still can't date until age 16.
   b. can date now.
   c. can date only boys who are sixteen years old.

___ 8. In the United States, it is a **tradition** on birthdays to
   a. paint eggs different colors and put them in baskets.
   b. have a cake with candles on it.
   c. eat fish for dinner.

Adding Words to a Reading

A. Taking Risks

Read the following paragraphs carefully. Then fill in each blank with a word from the box. Use each word once.

a. **capable**	b. **observe**	c. **opportunities**	d. **resist**

Taking risks in life can make us feel good about ourselves. All of us should try something new—even something scary—every once in a while. Each of us is (1)_____ of taking chances, but we often don't. Instead, we sometimes let good (2)_____ pass us by because they seem a bit too risky. Maybe we don't apply for an exciting new job because we are not sure we can handle it. Perhaps we delay° returning to school because we are afraid that the work will be too hard. Maybe we walk away from a relationship because it is becoming more important than we had planned.

If you (3)_____ yourself getting frightened by something new and different, that is all the more reason to face it head-on and not run away. Finding that you have the strength inside to overcome your fears will make you feel proud of yourself. You will begin to feel that you have what it takes to get through even the difficult times. So if you want to move ahead in life, with your head held high, don't (4)_____ making a change or taking a chance. Go for it.

B. Bad Manners Hurt Everyone

Read the following paragraph carefully. Then fill in each blank with a word from the box. Use each word once.

a. **careless**	b. **furious**	c. **reverse**	d. **tradition**

Many people these days don't have good manners. Acting as though they are the only people in the world, they are (5)_____ about the feelings of others. These selfish people ignore° other people's feelings—they pay attention only to their own wishes. They push their way into lines, blast their horns at other drivers, and play loud music late at night when their neighbors are trying to sleep. Such rude behavior makes most of us (6)_____. Sadly, though, it has gotten to the point where nicely asking people to act more politely can be dangerous. You never know if someone will turn against you violently. It is time to turn things around. It is time to

(7)_____ all this bad behavior. We need to go back to the

(8)_____ of caring about our fellow human beings. Paying

attention to our manners is a good place to start.

Using the Words When Writing and Talking

Now that you understand the meanings of the eight new words in the chapter, you are ready to use them on paper and in speaking. Complete each sentence below in a way that shows you really know what each **boldfaced** word means. Take a few minutes to think about your answer before writing it down and saying it out loud.

1. Only the most **capable** students will _____

_____

2. **Careless** driving leads to _____

_____

3. Many people get **furious** when _____

_____

4. I was lucky that my neighbor **observed** our house when _____

_____

5. I would like the **opportunity** to _____

_____

6. In the grocery store, I try to **resist** _____

_____

7. I used to think that spring was the best time of year. But then I **reversed** myself, and now I think

   that _____

_____

8. One of my favorite family **traditions** is _____

_____

Scores	Adding One Word to an Item	_____%	Showing You Understand the Words	_____%
	Adding Two Words to an Item	_____%	Adding Words to a Reading	_____%

Number right: 8 = 100%, 7 = 88%, 6 = 75%, 5 = 63%, 4 = 50%, 3 = 38%, 2 = 25%, 1 = 13%
Enter your scores above and in the vocabulary performance chart on the inside back cover of the book.

allow	persist
comfortable	respect
distract	sensitive
insulting	wonder

Learning Eight New Words

In the space at the left, write the letter of the meaning closest to that of each **boldfaced** word. Use the other words (the *context*) in each sentence to help you figure out the word's meaning.

1 allow
(uh-**low**)
– verb

___*Allow* means

- Some schools will **allow** students to wear shorts on days when the weather is very hot.
- Jay's parents **allowed** him to go to the mall after he did his homework.

    a. hate   b. let   c. stop

2 comfortable
(**kuhm**-fur-tuh-buhl)
– adjective

___*Comfortable* means

- When Brian first met his girlfriend's parents, he was nervous, but now he is **comfortable** with them.
- The burning sun and the ants made it hard to get **comfortable** at the picnic.

    a. relaxed   b. mean   c. thirsty

3 distract
(diss-**trakt**)
– verb

___*Distract* means

- When babies want something they can't have, it's a good idea to **distract** them by handing them a favorite toy.
- None of us can study with Julie in the room. The loud way she chews gum **distracts** us.

    a. have questions   b. make clean   c. take away
        about   attention

4 insulting
(in-**suhlt**-ing)
– adjective

___*Insulting* means

- Rafael is angry because someone wrote an **insulting** message about him on the sidewalk.
- Our boss calls his workers **insulting** names, such as "stupid" and "lazy."

    a. kind   b. easy to understand   c. hurtful

5 persist
(pur-**sist**)
– verb

___*Persist* means

- To reach a goal, you must **persist** rather than giving up at the first sign of a problem.
- The salesperson **persisted** in trying to sell me a car, even after I said I wasn't interested.

    a. give up easily   b. keep doing something   c. forget

6 respect
(ri-**spekt**)
– noun

- I have **respect** for my aunt because every day she works hard to take care of her young kids and her older parents.
- Because she has so much **respect** for her grandmother, Mona changed out of her torn jeans before visiting her.

___*Respect* means

a. great fear   b. great liking   c. great anger

7 sensitive
(**sen**-suh-tiv)
– adjective

- My dog is **sensitive.** When I am sad, she sits down gently beside me and puts her paw in my lap.
- Pablo is a **sensitive** person. At parties, he always spends time talking to anyone who looks nervous and out of place.

___*Sensitive* means

a. not caring   b. happy   c. caring

8 wonder
(**wuhn**-dur)
– verb

- Don't you **wonder** why the dinosaurs died out millions of years ago?
- Everyone **wonders** why Hector and Andrew are angry at one another, but neither of them will talk about it.

___*Wonder* means

a. want to know   b. answer   c. blame

Matching Words with Meanings

Here are the meanings, or *definitions*, of the eight new words. Write each word next to its meaning. The sentences above and on the facing page will help you decide on the meaning of each word.

1. _____ A feeling of great liking and honor for someone or something; looking up to someone or something

2. _____ To want to know or learn about something

3. _____ To let someone do something

4. _____ Mean; nasty; rude

5. _____ To keep doing something, especially when faced with difficulties; to not give up

6. _____ To weaken someone's attention

7. _____ Relaxed; at ease; in a state of comfort

8. _____ Understanding the feelings and needs of others; caring

BE CAREFUL: Don't go any further until you know the answers above are correct. Then you can use the meanings to help you in the following activities. After a while, you will know the words so well that you won't need to check the definitions at all.

Adding One Word to an Item

Complete each item below by writing one word from the box on the answer line at the left. Use each word once.

| a. **allow** | c. **distracted** | e. **persists** | g. **sensitive** |
| b. **comfortable** | d. **insulting** | f. **respect** | h. **wondered** |

_____ 1. Whenever my new kitten sits on my lap, she feels so . . ? . . that she falls asleep.

_____ 2. Joseph hasn't found work yet. But he will because he . . ? . . in looking for a job.

_____ 3. Because cigarettes are so dangerous, not many parents . . ? . . their children to smoke.

_____ 4. The children's fight . . ? . . the bus driver so much that he almost crashed into a tree.

_____ 5. My parents taught me to have . . ? . . for education and learning. That's why I have always done well in school.

_____ 6. I won't answer Vera when she speaks to me in that . . ? . . tone of voice.

_____ 7. We send our children to a . . ? . . doctor. Whenever they are scared, she uses smiles and kind words to take away their fears.

_____ 8. We . . ? . . who the man sitting in the back of the class was until the teacher said, "Ladies and gentlemen, I'd like you to meet my brother."

Adding Two Words to an Item

Complete each item below by writing **two** words from the box on the answer lines at the left. Use each word once.

| a. **allow** | c. **distract** | e. **persisted** | g. **sensitive** |
| b. **comfortable** | d. **insulting** | f. **respect** | h. **wonder** |

_____
_____ 1–2. At the movies, we asked the man next to us to stop saying rude, . . ? . . things to us. When he . . ? . ., we got the manager to throw him out.

_____
_____ 3–4. Jim is an excellent student and doesn't . . ? . . anyone to . . ? . . him from his homework.

_____
_____ 5–6. Mr. Brown is a caring, . . ? . . teacher who goes out of his way to make shy students feel . . ? . . in class.

_____
_____ 7–8. I feel great . . ? . . for my parents. I often . . ? . . how they raised such a large family without losing their tempers.

Showing You Understand the Words

PART A

In the space at the left, write the letter of the choice that best completes the sentence or answers the question.

____ 1. If you feel **comfortable** at a family party, you will probably
  a. sit sadly in the corner.
  b. leave as soon as possible.
  c. stay for a long while.

____ 2. If you are writing a paper for school, which of the following would be likely to **distract** you?
  a. Loud music outside your window
  b. A gentle breeze coming in the window
  c. A dictionary sitting on a shelf

____ 3. If you **persist** in trying to learn to swim, you would probably
  a. stop going to the swimming pool.
  b. decide to start running instead.
  c. go to the swimming pool as often as you can.

____ 4. If you **wonder** how big the raise you are getting at work will be, you
  a. know how much you will receive.
  b. do not know how much you will receive.
  c. spend the money before you get it.

PART B

In the space at the left, write the letter of the choice that best completes the sentence.

____ 5. The new town rule doesn't **allow** dogs to run free in the neighborhood. From now on, people will have to
  a. put their dogs on a leash.
  b. give away their dogs.
  c. get indoor cats instead.

____ 6. When people are called an **insulting** name, they often
  a. seem happy.
  b. feel hurt.
  c. look silly.

____ 7. Workers who have **respect** for their boss
  a. look up to and learn from the boss.
  b. argue with the boss.
  c. don't listen to what the boss says.

____ 8. People who are **sensitive**
  a. don't like to hurt or upset others.
  b. don't care how others feel.
  c. laugh at others who feel sad.

Adding Words to a Reading

A. Two Different Sisters

Read the following paragraph carefully. Then fill in each blank with a word from the box. Use each word once.

a. **comfortable**	b. **distract**	c. **insulting**	d. **sensitive**

Carla and Luisa are sisters. They are both smart young women who work at the same company. But Carla gets along better with others than Luisa. One difference is that Carla is a (1)_____ person who cares about people and how they feel. If someone looks unhappy, she will always stop and ask if she can help in any way. Luisa, though, never takes the time to see what's bothering a coworker. Because she thinks only of her job, she will not let anything (2)_____ her from doing her work. However, Carla is sociable° and enjoys joking and having fun with the other workers. If people say to her, "Carla, you are as slow as molasses in January!" she knows they are not serious. But if a coworker makes a gentle joke about Luisa, Luisa gets upset and finds the joke (3)_____. It's not surprising that many people at work do not feel relaxed or (4)_____ around Luisa.

B. How "Honest Abe" Earned His Name

Read the following paragraph carefully. Then fill in each blank with a word from the box. Use each word once.

a. **allow**	b. **persisted**	c. **respect**	d. **wonder**

When Abraham Lincoln was a young man, he worked as a clerk in a general store. One day a woman came in and bought some things. She paid and went away. But after she left the store, Lincoln began to (5)_____ if he had added up the bill correctly. Had he been careless°? He looked at the bill again and saw that he had charged the woman six cents too much. It was only a few cents. But Lincoln would not (6)_____ himself to keep the woman's money. That night, he closed up the store and began walking toward the woman's house, which was several miles away. Although it grew dark, Lincoln (7)_____ until he reached the woman's home and returned her six cents. After Lincoln became President, even those who disliked him had to give him (8)_____ for his honesty.

Using the Words When Writing and Talking

Now that you understand the meanings of the eight new words in the chapter, you are ready to use them on paper and in speaking. Complete each sentence below in a way that shows you really know what each **boldfaced** word means. Take a few minutes to think about your answer before writing it down and saying it out loud.

1. Most parents do not **allow** their very young children to watch movies that _____

_____

2. To get **comfortable** at the end of the day, I _____

_____

3. One thing that **distracts** me when I am trying to study is _____

_____

4. If someone says something **insulting** to me, the best thing to do is _____

_____

5. When learning how to drive a car, most people **persist**, even though they _____

_____

6. Children should show their **respect** for older people by _____

_____

7. A **sensitive** person will _____

_____

8. I have always **wondered** if _____

_____

Scores	Adding One Word to an Item	_____%	Showing You Understand the Words	_____%
	Adding Two Words to an Item	_____%	Adding Words to a Reading	_____%

Number right: 8 = 100%, 7 = 88%, 6 = 75%, 5 = 63%, 4 = 50%, 3 = 38%, 2 = 25%, 1 = 13%
Enter your scores above and in the vocabulary performance chart on the inside back cover of the book.

Review Activities

On the next ten pages are activities to help you review the words you learned in Unit Two. You may do these activities in any order.

- Completing a Crossword Puzzle #1

- Completing a Crossword Puzzle #2

- Choosing the Best Word to Complete an Item

- Adding a Word to an Item, Parts A and B

- Finding the Same or the Opposite Meaning

- Using the Words When Writing and Talking

Completing a Crossword Puzzle #1

The box at the right lists twenty-four words from Unit Two. Using the meanings at the bottom of the page, fill in these words to complete the puzzle that follows.

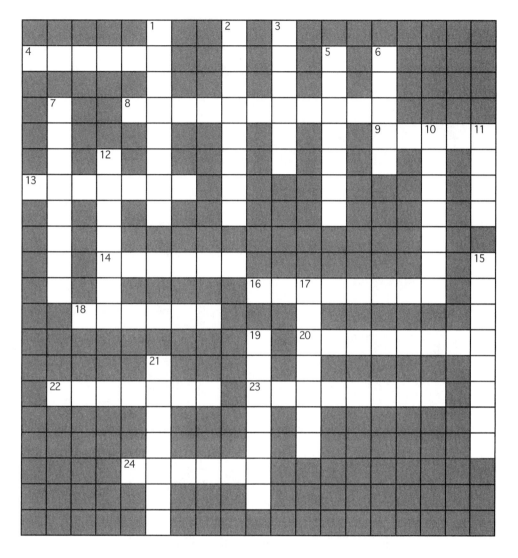

ability
approach
avoid
capable
careless
damp
excuse
furious
helpless
ignore
include
intend
loyal
normal
numerous
observe
opportunity
previous
require
resist
respect
reverse
sociable
struggle

ACROSS

4. To pay no attention
8. A chance to do something that will probably lead to good things
9. To stay away from someone or something
13. To go in the opposite direction
14. To plan to do something
16. A hard and difficult time
18. To keep from doing something
20. Friendly; enjoying the company of others
22. To be made up of; to have within itself
23. Earlier; happening before something else
24. Usual; regular

DOWN

1. Unable to take care of oneself
2. To come close or closer to someone or something
3. A reason, often not true, why something happened
5. The skill or power to do something
6. Ready to stand by or stand up for someone; faithful
7. Many
10. To see and pay attention to something
11. A little wet; moist
12. To need something
15. Not careful; paying little attention
17. A feeling of great liking and honor for someone or something
19. Having the skill to do something
21. Very angry

Completing a Crossword Puzzle #2

The box at the right lists twenty-four words from Unit Two. Using the meanings at the bottom of the page, fill in these words to complete the puzzle that follows.

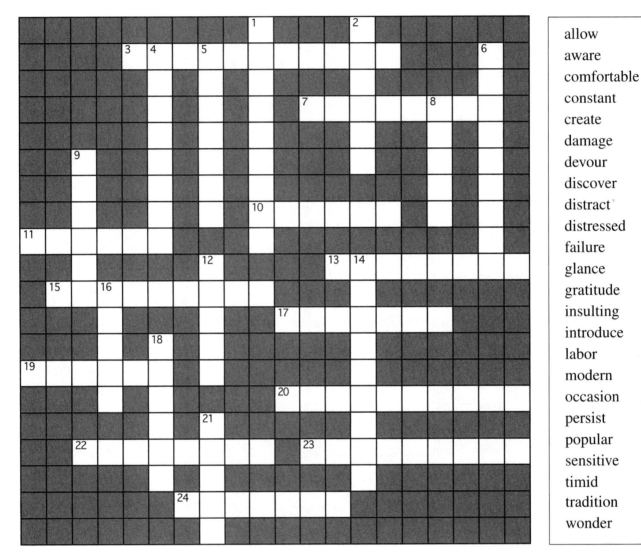

allow
aware
comfortable
constant
create
damage
devour
discover
distract
distressed
failure
glance
gratitude
insulting
introduce
labor
modern
occasion
persist
popular
sensitive
timid
tradition
wonder

ACROSS

3. Relaxed; at ease
7. Never stopping; happening again and again
10. Harm; injury
11. Of the present time; up-to-date; not old-fashioned
13. To find something for the first time
15. A special way of doing something that is passed down; a custom
17. To keep doing something, especially when faced with difficulties
19. To eat quickly and hungrily
20. Very upset; troubled
22. To weaken someone's attention
23. Understanding the feelings and needs of others; caring
24. Liked by many people

DOWN

1. A feeling of thanks
2. To look at something quickly
4. A time when something takes place, often something special
5. Someone or something that does not turn out well
6. To make one person known to another for the first time
8. Knowing about something
9. To want to know or learn about something
12. Shy
14. Mean; nasty; rude
16. To let someone do something
18. To make something; to bring something into being
21. Hard work

Choosing the Best Word to Complete an Item

On the answer line at the left, write the word that best completes each item.

_____ 1. Even a small child is . . ? . . of doing simple jobs around the house, such as clearing the table.
   a. capable   b. damp   c. sociable

_____ 2. Old-fashioned telephones have round dials, but . . ? . . ones have buttons.
   a. helpless   b. modern   c. insulting

_____ 3. The art set Lisa got for her birthday . . ? . . markers, colored pencils, and a set of paints.
   a. ignores   b. devours   c. includes

_____ 4. On the first day of class, the teacher helped the students feel . . ? . . by learning their names and asking friendly questions about their families.
   a. comfortable   b. numerous   c. previous

_____ 5. Because she is . . ? . . , Grandmother likes living with a group of other retired people.
   a. insulting   b. furious   c. sociable

_____ 6. On those . . ? . . when my children don't have school, I need to find a baby sitter for them.
   a. occasions   b. excuses   c. traditions

_____ 7. Although our . . ? . . suppertime is 6:30, we did not eat until 8:00 last night.
   a. normal   b. sensitive   c. popular

_____ 8. When I turned 15, my parents . . ? . . me to wear a little makeup and date.
   a. wondered   b. created   c. allowed

_____ 9. Born in the United States, Paco was happy to have the . . ? . . to visit Mexico, where both his parents had been raised.
   a. respect   b. opportunity   c. labor

_____ 10. Although whales need air, they have the . . ? . . to stay under water for as long as two hours.
   a. gratitude   b. excuse   c. ability

_____ 11. We could tell by the cold weather and shorter days that winter was quickly . . ? . . .
   a. approaching   b. including   c. distracting

_____ 12. When my parents said they wanted to talk to me about the yard work I had not done, I tried to . . ? . . them by telling a joke.
   a. require   b. devour   c. distract

(Continues on next page)

_____ 13. At exactly 6 p.m., the owner of the store went to the sign on the door that said "Open" and . . ? . . it to the other side, which said "Sorry, closed."

   a. glanced   b. introduced   c. reversed

_____ 14. Bad weather can cause a great deal of . . ? . . to a crop of oranges.

   a. damage   b. opportunity   c. excuse

_____ 15. It was a . . ? . . for Greta to stop smoking, but she is proud that she finally did it.

   a. respect   b. gratitude   c. struggle

_____ 16. Although I never buy anything over the phone, there is one telephone salesperson who . . ? . . in calling me at least once a week.

   a. persists   b. creates   c. resists

_____ 17. Are you . . ? . . that you are wearing one black shoe and one brown shoe?

   a. modern   b. aware   c. capable

_____ 18. When the neighbors got together to paint Mrs. Kim's house, she cooked dinner for all of them to show them her . . ? . . .

   a. failure   b. occasion   c. gratitude

_____ 19. It makes me angry when my kids leave . . ? . . towels lying on the bathroom floor.

   a. comfortable   b. damp   c. popular

_____ 20. Sandra is a . . ? . . boss. She always knows when a worker is upset, even if the worker acts as if nothing is wrong.

   a. previous   b. modern   c. sensitive

_____ 21. The hungry teenagers . . ? . . a box of crackers and a jar of peanut butter while putting away the groceries.

   a. devoured   b. introduced   c. created

_____ 22. It took Carla a long time to choose new eyeglass frames because there were . . ? . . styles for her to look at.

   a. helpless   b. numerous   c. furious

_____ 23. Most religions teach that people should . . ? . . speaking unkindly of others.

   a. reverse   b. intend   c. avoid

_____ 24. Joseph's . . ? . . to find work in his hometown has made him think about moving to a larger city where there are more jobs.

   a. tradition   b. occasion   c. failure

Score	Choosing the Best Word to Complete an Item	_____%

Adding a Word to an Item

PART A

Complete each item below by writing one word from the box on the answer line at the left. Use each word once.

a. **create**	d. **insulting**	g. **observed**	j. **popular**
b. **excuse**	e. **introduced**	h. **require**	k. **timid**
c. **furious**	f. **loyal**	i. **resist**	l. **wonder**

_____ 1. TV soap operas often end in a way that makes people . . ? . . what is going to happen next.

_____ 2. Believe it or not, you can . . ? . . a very good candy by mixing only three things: peanut butter, honey, and powdered milk.

_____ 3. Because Meg and Gerald are so happy that they met and fell in love, they wrote a thank-you note to the friend who . . ? . . them.

_____ 4. The pizza restaurant on the corner is so . . ? . . that people often have to wait an hour for a table.

_____ 5. Barry had a good . . ? . . for falling asleep in class—he had been up all night with his sick child.

_____ 6. The store owner called police when she . . ? . . two scary-looking men walking around the building and looking in the windows.

_____ 7. Some brave children run right up to a department-store Santa Claus, but others are so . . ? . . that they won't go near him at all.

_____ 8. When parents say . . ? . . things to their children, such as "You're stupid," the youngsters often begin to think poorly of themselves.

_____ 9. My parents taught me to work hard and . . ? . . doing things the easy way.

_____ 10. Even if the new supermarket has low prices, I am going to be . . ? . . to the neighborhood grocery store where I have shopped for years.

_____ 11. I knew that Dad would be upset that I lost his wallet, but he was more than upset. He was . . ? . . .

_____ 12. "In order to do this trick," said the magician, "I . . ? . . a brave person from the audience to come up on stage with me."

(Continues on next page)

PART B

Complete each item below by writing one word from the box on the answer line at the left. Use each word once.

a. **careless**	d. **distressed**	g. **ignores**	j. **previous**
b. **constant**	e. **glanced**	h. **intend**	k. **respect**
c. **discovered**	f. **helpless**	i. **labor**	l. **tradition**

_____ 13. After their children are grown and leave home, Mr. and Mrs. Siskin . . ? . . to sell their house and move to an apartment.

_____ 14. When I first moved away from home, I felt as . . ? . . as a baby.

_____ 15. Many people lost their . . ? . . for the mayor when they learned he had made up stories about being a war hero.

_____ 16. At first, I only . . ? . . at the couple entering the store. But when I realized they were famous movie actors, I turned around and stared.

_____ 17. The last time I was at the library, I . . ? . . a writer whose books I really like.

_____ 18. My children are so . . ? . . about having to move to another city that they aren't eating or sleeping well.

_____ 19. When the restaurant owners saw the new menus, they were very unhappy. The . . ? . . printer had spelled the name of the restaurant wrong.

_____ 20. The children put many hours of . . ? . . into building their tree house. They often worked from the time they got home from school until it was dark.

_____ 21. The . . ? . . of throwing rice at a wedding is a very old one, going back many hundreds of years.

_____ 22. Mr. and Mrs. Shue called their landlord to complain about the . . ? . . loud music and shouting from their neighbors downstairs.

_____ 23. Most people in my office are bothered by the sounds of heavy traffic outside. But Rhonda . . ? . . the noise and gets her job done.

_____ 24. Last winter was not bad, but the . . ? . . one was the coldest I can remember.

Scores   Part A (Adding a Word) _____%   Part B (Adding a Word) _____%

Number right in each part: 12 = 100%, 11 = 92%, 10 = 83%, 9 = 75%, 8 = 67%; 7 = 58%, 6 = 50%, 5 = 42%; 4 = 33%, 3 = 25%. 2 = 17%, 1 = 8%
Enter your scores above and in the vocabulary performance chart on the inside back cover of the book.

Finding the Same or the Opposite Meaning

PART A

In the space at the left, write the letter of the choice that correctly completes each sentence. In most cases, the correct answer will have the **same** or **almost the same** meaning as the **boldfaced** word.

___ 1. If you see coming toward you a couple you want to **avoid**, you would probably
 a. call out their names.   b. walk the other way.
 c. walk up to them and tell them who you are.

___ 2. If a three-year-old asks **constant** questions, the questions
 a. go on and on and never seem to stop.   b. are hard to understand.
 c. are about private matters.

___ 3. If you **create** a new way of doing a job at work, you
 a. come up with the idea on your own.   b. have trouble finding a way to do the job better.
 c. are happy that other people found a way to do the job better.

___ 4. If insects do a lot of **damage** to a plant, the plant will
 a. grow tall.   b. be healthy and strong.
 c. be harmed badly.

___ 5. If something happens that makes you feel like a **failure**, you might feel as though
 a. nothing works out well for you.   b. everything turns out well for you.
 c. everyone is on your side.

___ 6. If a friend is **furious** with you, the friend would be
 a. really angry with you.   b. relaxed with you.
 c. fearful of you.

___ 7. If a turtle is **helpless** when it is on its back, that means that it
 a. is especially strong.   b. is sleepy.
 c. can't help itself by turning over.

___ 8. If dinner at a restaurant **includes** dessert, this means that
 a. dessert will be a part of the meal. b. dessert will not be a part of the meal.
 c. dessert will be the only thing in the meal.

___ 9. An **insulting** joke is one that is
 a. nice and funny.   b. mean and rude.
 c. hard to remember.

___10. If you **intend** to clean the house on Saturday, you
 a. forget to clean the house on Saturday.   b. plan to clean the house on Saturday.
 c. try hard to keep from cleaning the house on Saturday.

___11. If you **reverse** your car, you
 a. love your car.   b. sell your car.
 c. turn your car in the other direction.

(Continues on next page)

___12. Teenagers who **resist** using drugs
    a. never heard of drugs.   b. use a lot of drugs.
    c. work hard to keep from using drugs.

PART B

In the space at the left, write the letter of the choice that is the **opposite** of the **boldfaced** word.

___13. The opposite of **capable** is
    a. not able   b. painful   c. colorful

___14. The opposite of **careless** is
    a. difficult   b. easy   c. careful

___15. The opposite of **damp** is
    a. ugly   b. cold   c. dry

___16. The opposite of **glance** is
    a. repeat slowly   b. look at carefully   c. give back

___17. The opposite of **ignore** is
    a. pay attention   b. open slowly   c. clean completely

___18. The opposite of **labor** is
    a. truth   b. fault   c. rest

___19. The opposite of **modern** is
    a. straight   b. old-fashioned   c. good-looking

___20. The opposite of **observe** is
    a. not see   b. not try   c. not hurt

___21. The opposite of **persist** is
    a. give up   b. hurry   c. look at

___22. The opposite of **numerous** is
    a. few   b. straight   c. small

___23. The opposite of **sociable** is
    a. perfect   b. unfriendly   c. sharp

___24. The opposite of **timid** is
    a. brave   b. tiny   c. smooth

Scores	Part A (Same Meanings) _____%	Part B (Opposite Meanings) _____%

Number right in each part: 12 = 100%, 11 = 92%, 10 = 83%, 9 = 75%, 8 = 67%; 7 = 58%, 6 = 50%, 5 = 42%; 4 = 33%, 3 = 25%. 2 = 17%, 1 = 8%
Enter your scores above and in the vocabulary performance chart on the inside back cover of the book.

Using the Words When Writing and Talking

The items below will help you use many of the words in this unit on paper and in conversation. Feel free to use **any tense of a boldfaced verb** and to make a **boldfaced noun plural**. (See pages 249–251 and 252.)

1. Using the word **ability**, write or talk about a special skill of someone you know well. The person might be able to fix anything, cook well, or get along with anybody.

2. Using the word **allow**, write or talk about one thing you believe parents should *not* let their children do. Maybe you feel parents should not let their kids smoke, go out on school nights, date before they are 16, or wear certain clothing styles.

3. Using the word **approach**, write or tell about a time that a stranger came up to you and began to talk. It could have been the time your car broke down and a passerby offered to help, or it might have been when you moved into a new home and a neighbor came over to say hello.

4. Using the word **aware**, write or talk about a time when you first came to understand something. It could be the first time you understood that your parents were less than perfect, or the first time you learned of a problem in your school, in your neighborhood, or in the country.

5. Using the word **comfortable**, write or tell about a time you made someone feel relaxed and at ease. Perhaps you invited a new neighbor to dinner, took time to show a coworker around on the first day on the job, or helped a relative feel less nervous about going into the hospital.

6. Using the word **devour**, write or talk about a time when you (or someone else) ate a lot of something really quickly. You might describe the way you ate a hot-fudge sundae or the way friends ate a pizza.

7. Using the word **discover**, write or talk about a time when you found out about or learned something new. Perhaps you came across a shortcut to work or an easy way to do something that used to be difficult.

8. Using the word **distract**, write or talk about something that got your attention when you needed to to take care of another matter. Maybe a classmate kept talking while you were trying to listen to a teacher or the beautiful weather made it difficult for you to stay indoors and study.

9. Using the word **distressed**, write or talk about something that upset you and made you unhappy. Perhaps it was doing poorly on a test, learning that a friend was sick, or having a fight with someone you cared for.

10. Using the word **excuse**, write or talk about a time you made up a reason not to do something—for example, go to a party, visit an elderly relative, or work hard in school or on the job.

11. Using the word **gratitude**, write or talk about a time when you felt thankful to someone. The person might have done you a favor, helped you with something you didn't know how to do, or simply been good to you when you needed a friend.

12. Using the word **introduce**, write or talk about a time you went up to someone you wanted to meet and told the person your name and a little bit about yourself. You might describe the first time you met a neighbor, a coworker, or your closest friend.

(Continues on next page)

13. Using the word **loyal**, write or talk about a person who stood by someone he or she believed in. The person might be a sports fan who kept rooting for a team that always lost, or a friend who said good things about someone whom everyone else hated.

14. Using the word **normal**, write or talk about what your usual weekday is like. You might talk about what you do on a regular morning or what happens in a usual evening at your home.

15. Using the word **occasion**, write or tell about a time in your life that you will never forget—perhaps a vacation, wedding, birth, or holiday.

16. Using the word **opportunity**, write or talk about a time when you had a chance to do something special. Maybe you had the chance to take a wonderful trip, see a famous person, or take a great job.

17. Using the word **popular**, write or talk about someone you know who has many friends and always seems to be at the center of a crowd of people.

18. Using the word **previous**, write or talk about the job you had before this one, the school you attended before the one you go to now, or something new you learned from an earlier chapter of this book.

19. Using the word **require**, write or talk about what you need to do in order to feel wide-awake in the morning. You might need to drink several cups of coffee, take a long shower, or eat a good breakfast.

20. Using the word **respect**, write or talk about a person you think highly of. It could be a relative, teacher, or classmate you look up to.

21. Using the word **sensitive**, write or talk about someone you know (perhaps a grandparent, coworker, or classmate) who always seems to understand how others feel.

22. Using the word **struggle**, write or talk about something that you or someone else did that took a lot of hard work to do. It might be learning how to speak a new language, getting used to being single after being divorced, or living through a hard time such as the loss of a friend or a loved one.

23. Using the word **tradition**, write or talk about something special that you and your family always do, year after year. It might be having a cookout to start the summer season, watching a favorite movie on a certain holiday, or celebrating birthdays in a special way that everyone enjoys.

24. Using the word **wonder**, write or talk about something that you have questions about and would like to learn more about. Perhaps you would like to know more about a certain career, person, or part of the country.

Unit Three

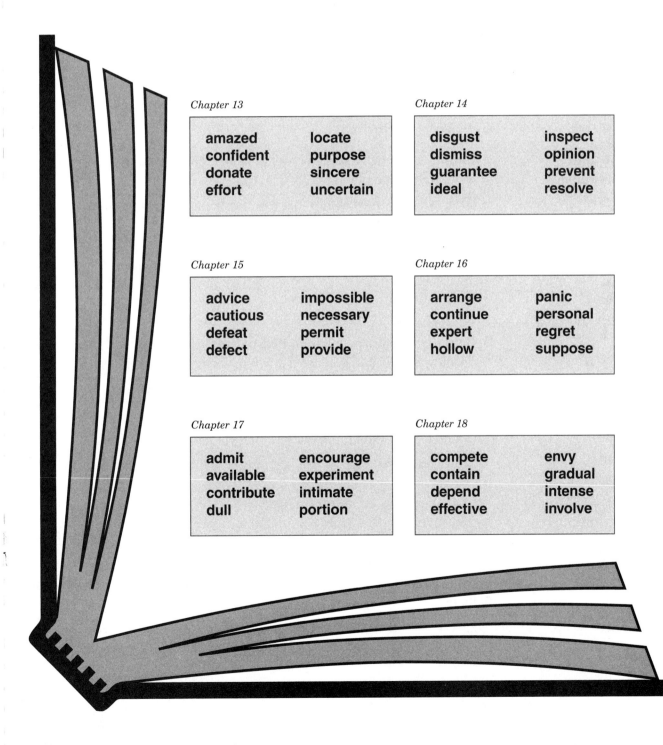

Chapter 13

amazed	locate
confident	purpose
donate	sincere
effort	uncertain

Chapter 14

disgust	inspect
dismiss	opinion
guarantee	prevent
ideal	resolve

Chapter 15

advice	impossible
cautious	necessary
defeat	permit
defect	provide

Chapter 16

arrange	panic
continue	personal
expert	regret
hollow	suppose

Chapter 17

admit	encourage
available	experiment
contribute	intimate
dull	portion

Chapter 18

compete	envy
contain	gradual
depend	intense
effective	involve

amazed	locate
confident	purpose
donate	sincere
effort	uncertain

Learning Eight New Words

In the space at the left, write the letter of the meaning closest to that of each **boldfaced** word. Use the other words (the *context*) in each sentence to help you figure out the word's meaning.

1 amazed
(uh-**mayzd**)
– adjective

- The police were **amazed** that no one was hurt in the bad traffic accident.
- The crowd was **amazed** by the runner's speed.

___*Amazed* means
    a. surprised   b. bored   c. worried

2 confident
(**kon**-fi-duhnt)
– adjective

- Even though Shelly said she was full, we were **confident** she would find room for a piece of cake.
- After winning three games in a row, the team felt **confident** about doing well the rest of the season.

___*Confident* means
    a. sorry   b. honest   c. sure

3 donate
(**doh**-nayt)
– verb

- Instead of throwing out old books, I **donate** them to a library so others can read them.
- Because so many people **donated** money to us when our house burned down, we were able to make a down payment on a new house.

___*Donate* means
    a. show   b. find   c. give

4 effort
(**ef**-urt)
– noun

- It took a lot of **effort** to move the big sofa into the room.
- With great **effort**, the weight lifter raised the barbell above his head.

___*Effort* means
    a. hard work   b. sadness   c. good looks

5 locate
(**loh**-kayt)
– verb

- Can you **locate** Alaska on the map?
- No matter how well I hide the candy bars I buy, my son always **locates** them.

___*Locate* means
    a. lose   b. find   c. forget

6 purpose
(**pur**-puhss)
– noun

- My **purpose** in speaking to the class was to tell everyone about the exciting book I had read.
- What was our **purpose** for buying such an expensive computer? We wanted to get the best possible model.

___*Purpose* means   a. reason   b. problem   c. job

7 sincere
(sin-**sihr**)
– adjective

- Because Dave has a warm smile, he seems like a **sincere** young man, but in fact he is not very honest.
- I voted for Cara Sanchez because she seems **sincere** about wanting to help people.

___*Sincere* means   a. truthful   b. not honest   c. angry

8 uncertain
(uhn-**sur**-tuhn)
– adjective

- The twins look so much alike that I am **uncertain** who is Marco and who is Miguel.
- Verna is **uncertain** whether she should go to college or join the Army.

___*Uncertain* means   a. not interested   b. sure   c. not sure

Matching Words with Meanings

Here are the meanings, or *definitions*, of the eight new words. Write each word next to its meaning. The sentences above and on the facing page will help you decide on the meaning of each word.

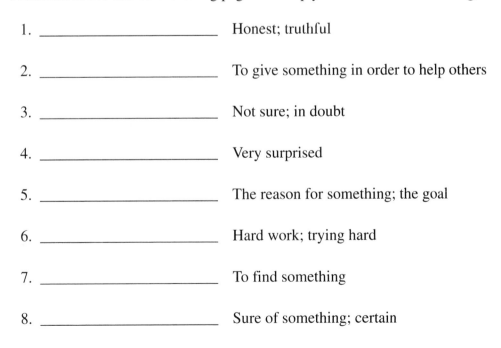

1. _____   Honest; truthful

2. _____   To give something in order to help others

3. _____   Not sure; in doubt

4. _____   Very surprised

5. _____   The reason for something; the goal

6. _____   Hard work; trying hard

7. _____   To find something

8. _____   Sure of something; certain

BE CAREFUL: Don't go any further until you know the answers above are correct. Then you can use the meanings to help you in the following activities. After a while, you will know the words so well that you won't need to check the definitions at all.

Adding One Word to an Item

Complete each item below by writing one word from the box on the answer line at the left. Use each word once.

a. **amazed**	c. **donate**	e. **locate**	g. **sincere**
b. **confident**	d. **effort**	f. **purpose**	h. **uncertain**

_____ 1. After weeks of practice, Beth was not worried—she felt . . ? . . that she would pass her driver's test.

_____ 2. Mrs. Chen could not . . ? . . her keys. She looked everywhere for them.

_____ 3. You should always ask your doctor to explain the . . ? . . of any medicine you take.

_____ 4. The handwriting in the letter is so hard to read that I am . . ? . . what it says.

_____ 5. Looking for a job takes a lot of . . ? . .—it is a job itself.

_____ 6. Each year, thousands of lives are saved by people who . . ? . . their blood.

_____ 7. My teacher was . . ? . . when I got a perfect score on the test because I had never done that well before.

_____ 8. I thought Rita was . . ? . . about being my friend, but now I think she just wanted to meet my good-looking older brother.

Adding Two Words to an Item

Complete each item below by writing **two** words from the box on the answer lines at the left. Use each word once.

a. **amazed**	c. **donate**	e. **locate**	g. **sincere**
b. **confident**	d. **effort**	f. **purpose**	h. **uncertain**

_____
_____ 1–2. Because so many people saw my car being stolen, the police were . . ? . . that they would be able to . . ? . . it soon.

_____
_____ 3–4. Everyone is . . ? . . by all the time and . . ? . . the fifth-graders put into their play; they even wrote their own music for it.

_____
_____ 5–6. The mayor said, "Let's have a party to celebrate the holiday season." But the real . . ? . . of the party was to get people to . . ? . . money to help pay for his re-election.

_____
_____ 7–8. Joe seemed . . ? . . when he said he would meet me at three o'clock. But he often says one thing and does another, so I was . . ? . . that he would show up.

Showing You Understand the Words

PART A

In the space at the left, write the letter of the choice that best completes the sentence or answers the question.

____ 1. You would be **amazed** by which of the following?
   a. A bird flying in the sky
   b. Children playing in a park
   c. A man in a chicken suit walking down the middle of a highway

____ 2. If you **donate** your time to a nursing home, you probably
   a. expect to be paid.
   b. enjoy helping older people.
   c. are too busy to help.

____ 3. It would take a lot of **effort** for you to
   a. pick up a pencil.
   b. pick up a large box filled with bricks.
   c. pick up a pickle.

____ 4. If you are **uncertain** that you have enough food for a party, you would probably
   a. invite more people.
   b. take a nap.
   c. buy more food.

PART B

In the space at the left, write the letter of the choice that best completes the sentence or answers the question.

____ 5. A boxer who is **confident** about winning a fight might say,
   a. "The other guy is so big, he scares me."
   b. "Let's call off the match."
   c. "I'll knock the other guy out in minutes."

____ 6. What might someone do to **locate** a lost dog?
   a. Put a "lost dog" ad in the newspaper.
   b. Get a new dog.
   c. Drive the dog somewhere and leave it there.

____ 7. The main **purpose** of a car is
   a. to store old clothes and books.
   b. to take people from one place to another.
   c. to give people a place to sit.

____ 8. A person who is **sincere**
   a. is never on time.
   b. can be trusted.
   c. likes noise.

Adding Words to a Reading

A. Ready to Do Well

Read the following paragraphs carefully. Then fill in each blank with a word from the box. Use each word once.

a. **amazed**	b. **confident**	c. **effort**	d. **uncertain**

Feeling very nervous, Michelle walked into her English class on the morning of the final exam. She hated tests, and she was (1)_____ that she would pass this one. Just as she sat down, she saw her friend Teresa come into the classroom. Michelle waved to Teresa and was (2)_____ to see that she looked happy and calm. There was even a smile on Teresa's face, and she was humming a song. When Teresa took her seat, Michelle said to her, "You don't look a bit worried! Aren't you scared about the test?"

"No," said Teresa. "I put a lot of (3)_____ into studying for it."

"Are you sure you will pass?" asked Michelle.

"I think I will," said Teresa. "But even if I don't, I know that I did my best to get ready for it. And that is all I can do."

Michelle had also worked hard to prepare for the test, so Teresa's words made her feel a bit more comfortable°. As she relaxed, and her worries went away, she began to feel more (4)_____ that she too would do well on the test.

B. Advertising for a Date

Read the following paragraphs carefully. Then fill in each blank with a word from the box. Use each word once.

a. **donate**	b. **locate**	c. **purpose**	d. **sincere**

Kevin had broken up with his girlfriend, and he was lonely. All the women he knew were married or had boyfriends, so he had no opportunity° to meet someone new to date. He didn't want to go to bars with the (5)_____ of trying to meet women. So how, he asked himself, could he (6)_____ an interesting person to go out with? Finally, he had an idea. He put an ad in the local newspaper. This is how the ad read: "I would like to meet a woman who can be a good friend. Maybe later we will decide we like each other enough to be more than friends. I am a (7)_____ guy. I don't tell lies or play games. Because I like to help others, I (8)_____ a couple of hours each week to a local soup kitchen, for the homeless and poor. I would like to meet someone who enjoys laughing. She should also be kind, honest, and caring. If that sounds like you, I would like to meet you."

Kevin's ad worked. In a short time, he met several nice women. One of them, Hana, has become his steady girlfriend. Now he likes to tell people, "Hana and I found each other in the want ads."

Using the Words When Writing and Talking

Now that you understand the meanings of the eight new words in the chapter, you are ready to use them on paper and in speaking. Complete each sentence below in a way that shows you really know what each **boldfaced** word means. Take a few minutes to think about your answer before writing it down and saying it out loud.

1. I was **amazed** when _____

   _____

2. One thing I am **confident** about is _____

   _____

3. Once I **donated** _____

   _____

4. It took a lot of **effort** for me to _____

   _____

5. Many people have trouble **locating** their cars when _____

   _____

6. Teachers should have a clear **purpose** in mind when _____

   _____

7. You may question whether your friends are **sincere** if _____

   _____

8. With talk of the factory closing down, many workers were **uncertain** whether _____

   _____

Scores	Adding One Word to an Item	_____%	Showing You Understand the Words	_____%
	Adding Two Words to an Item	_____%	Adding Words to a Reading	_____%

Number right: 8 = 100%, 7 = 88%, 6 = 75%, 5 = 63%, 4 = 50%, 3 = 38%, 2 = 25%, 1 = 13%
Enter your scores above and in the vocabulary performance chart on the inside back cover of the book.

disgust	inspect
dismiss	opinion
guarantee	prevent
ideal	resolve

Learning Eight New Words

In the space at the left, write the letter of the meaning closest to that of each **boldfaced** word. Use the other words (the *context*) in each sentence to help you figure out the word's meaning.

1 disgust
(diss-**guhst**)
– verb

___*Disgust* means

• The old cigarettes, sweaty socks, and moldy pizza on the floor of Steve's bedroom **disgust** me.
• Elizabeth likes chicken and beef, but the smell of seafood **disgusts** her.

    a. make happy   b. sicken   c. make busy

2 dismiss
(diss-**miss**)
– verb

___*Dismiss* means

• The principal decided to **dismiss** the students early so they could get home before the storm.
• The judge would not **dismiss** the angry neighbors until they shook hands.

    a. punish   b. forget   c. let leave

3 guarantee
(ga-ruhn-**tee**)
– noun

___*Guarantee* means

• Greg was happy that the used car he bought came with a six-month **guarantee**. He will not have to pay for any repairs during this time.
• It was just bad luck that my stereo stopped working a day after the **guarantee** ran out.

    a. promise to   b. wish to   c. hope to buy
       fix something   go somewhere   something

4 ideal
(ii-**dee**-uhl)
– adjective

___*Ideal* means

• Fall is the **ideal** season because it is not too hot and not too cold.
• The **ideal** meal should taste good, be healthful, and cost very little.

    a. short   b. very bad   c. best

5 inspect
(in-**spekt**)
– verb

___*Inspect* means

• At the factory, workers **inspect** every new car before it is shipped out.
• After the kids clean their room, Mira **inspects** it all over, from the bookshelves to under the beds.

    a. hide carefully   b. look at carefully   c. stop

6 opinion
(uh-**pin**-yuhn)
– noun

• My husband liked the movie we saw last night, but I had a different **opinion**.

• Jamie asked her friends for their **opinion** of her new hair color.

___*Opinion* means

   a. thought   b. fear   c. wish

7 prevent
(pri-**vent**)
– verb

• My sister hid her Halloween candy to **prevent** the rest of us from eating it.

• The high fence and guard dog **prevented** anyone from breaking into the house.

___*Prevent* means

   a. stop   b. help   c. cause

8 resolve
(ri-**zolv**)
– verb

• I was glad to hear Dad say that on New Year's Day he may **resolve** to quit smoking.

• Before Tina went away to college, she and her best friends from high school **resolved** to write to each other once a week.

___*Resolve* means

   a. forget   b. fail   c. decide

Matching Words with Meanings

Here are the meanings, or *definitions*, of the eight new words. Write each word next to its meaning. The sentences above and on the facing page will help you decide on the meaning of each word.

1. _____ A promise (by a seller to a buyer) to fix or replace something that breaks

2. _____ To look at something closely in order to find problems or errors

3. _____ To let someone leave; to send someone away

4. _____ What someone thinks or feels about something

5. _____ To keep someone from doing something; to stop something from happening

6. _____ To cause someone to have a feeling of sickness or strong dislike

7. _____ To make a strong decision to do something

8. _____ Perfect; meeting every need or wish

BE CAREFUL: Don't go any further until you know the answers above are correct. Then you can use the meanings to help you in the following activities. After a while, you will know the words so well that you won't need to check the definitions at all.

Adding One Word to an Item

Complete each item below by writing one word from the box on the answer line at the left. Use each word once.

a. **disgusts**	c. **guarantee**	e. **inspected**	g. **prevent**
b. **dismissed**	d. **ideal**	f. **opinion**	h. **resolves**

_____ 1. Ever since her expensive VCR fell apart, Tisha won't buy anything unless a store will give her a . . ? . . .

_____ 2. Thanks for asking me how I feel about the plans for the party, but my . . ? . . isn't really important.

_____ 3. The way drunk people sometimes act . . ? . . me. I hate to see people make fools of themselves.

_____ 4. We . . ? . . many apartments before choosing the one we wanted.

_____ 5. Every Monday morning, Nora . . ? . . to make the week better than the one before.

_____ 6. When Jon sprained his ankle at work, his boss . . ? . . him so he could go to the doctor.

_____ 7. Warm, sunny days are . . ? . . for going swimming.

_____ 8. To . . ? . . myself from gaining weight, I exercise every night after dinner.

Adding Two Words to an Item

Complete each item below by writing **two** words from the box on the answer lines at the left. Use each word once.

a. **disgusted**	c. **guarantee**	e. **inspected**	g. **prevent**
b. **dismissed**	d. **ideal**	f. **opinion**	h. **resolved**

_____
_____ 1–2. All the blood in the movie sickened and . . ? . . me. In my . . ? . . , the movie would have been better without all the violence.

_____
_____ 3–4. To . . ? . . anyone from getting hurt when the fire broke out, Mrs. Brown . . ? . . her workers and told them to go home.

_____
_____ 5–6. When the computer broke down just two months after he had bought it, Carlo . . ? . . never again to buy anything if it didn't come with a . . ? . . .

_____
_____ 7–8. After my boss . . ? . . my work folder, he said I was an . . ? . . worker and gave me a big raise.

Showing You Understand the Words

PART A

In the space at the left, write the letter of the choice that best completes the sentence.

___ 1. You would probably think that your job is **ideal** if
   a. your boss screams and yells at you all day.
   b. you like your work, and the pay is good.
   c. you don't like your work, and the pay is low.

___ 2. You might want someone to **inspect** your favorite restaurant if you
   a. found broken glass in your food.
   b. had an excellent meal there.
   c. like how clean and neat everything is.

___ 3. If you are known for your strong **opinions**, you probably
   a. can lift furniture easily.
   b. say what you think and feel.
   c. have healthy feet.

___ 4. If you have a high fever, you might **resolve** to
   a. go out into the cold without a jacket
   b. have a party and stay up all night
   c. stay home and get lots of rest

PART B

In the space at the left, write the letter of the choice that best completes the sentence or answers the question.

___ 5. Which of the following would probably **disgust** most people?
   a. Newly cut roses
   b. Freshly baked chocolate chip cookies
   c. A pile of garbage on a hot summer day

___ 6. A boss may **dismiss** workers early if they
   a. have not finished their work.
   b. completed their work way before deadline.
   c. just came back from a long vacation.

___ 7. People should try to get a **guarantee** when they
   a. buy a used car.
   b. buy a candy bar.
   c. borrow a computer from a friend.

___ 8. People can sometimes **prevent** themselves from getting sick if they
   a. smoke a lot of cigarettes and eat a lot of junk food.
   b. share food and drinks with people who are already sick.
   c. get enough rest, food, and exercise.

Adding Words to a Reading

A. The Good and Bad Sides of Malls

Read the following paragraphs carefully. Then fill in each blank with a word from the box. Use each word once.

a. **dismiss**	b. **guarantees**	c. **opinion**	d. **resolve**

Most people think malls are great. But why do so many people share this (1)_____? First of all, malls are easy to use. Before malls, people had to go to many small stores to locate° what they needed. Today's shoppers have to go to only one place to find what they want. Another reason people like malls is cost. A department store in a mall is large enough to be able to offer low prices. Malls can also offer the best (2)_____ in town. For example, if a TV bought in a mall department store breaks down, the store will often fix the TV free of charge, no questions asked.

But not everything about malls is good. Here's why. As malls spread across the country, they put hundreds of small family-owned shops and restaurants out of business. How? When you buy clothes at a mall, you are not spending your money at stores which have been in the area since before the malls were built. The same is true for restaurants. When you buy a taco in the mall food court, that takes business away from the taco restaurant on Main Street in town. Over time, it becomes harder and harder for small businesses to stay open. Their owners may (3)_____ to fight to stay open. But often they are forced to (4)_____ all their workers and close their doors forever. Towns that used to have streets filled with shoppers now have empty stores and lost jobs. That's why malls are not as wonderful as they seem.

B. As Good As It Looks?

Read the following paragraphs carefully. Then fill in each blank with a word from the box. Use each word once.

a. **disgust**	b. **ideal**	c. **inspected**	d. **prevents**

Did you ever want to know why the food in TV ads always looks (5)_____? Did you ever wonder° why it looks so much better on TV than it does in real life? The answer may surprise you. Often the tasty-looking food you see on TV is fake—or at least partly fake. There is no rule that says TV ads must show real food. Advertisers are free to add whatever they want to make what they sell look good. Nothing (6)_____ an advertiser from adding something strange that would (7)_____ people if they knew about it.

To make milk seem creamy and white, advertisers add sticky white glue to each glass! The dark steamy coffee in TV ads is no better. In a few ads, it has soap added to it to make it look bubbly and fresh. One company even made its chicken look good and crispy by spraying it with brown paint. The nice roasted color made it look great. But if you (8)_____ the chicken closely, you would have seen a coat of oily paint all over it. So it's not surprising that the food you make at home never looks as good as the food on TV. Maybe you need to add some paint or glue to your recipes!

Using the Words When Writing and Talking

Now that you understand the meanings of the eight new words in the chapter, you are ready to use them on paper and in speaking. Complete each sentence below in a way that shows you really know what each **boldfaced** word means. Take a few minutes to think about your answer before writing it down and saying it out loud.

1. I once saw something that **disgusted** me. It was _____

   _____

2. A boss might **dismiss** workers early if _____

   _____

3. The store gave me a **guarantee** when _____

   _____

4. My idea of an **ideal** vacation is _____

   _____

5. At the supermarket, I always **inspect** _____

   _____

6. It is my **opinion** that _____

   _____

7. One way to **prevent** a fire at home is to _____

   _____

8. One thing I **resolve** to do over the next year is _____

   _____

Scores	Adding One Word to an Item	_____%	Showing You Understand the Words	_____%
	Adding Two Words to an Item	_____%	Adding Words to a Reading	_____%

Number right: 8 = 100%, 7 = 88%, 6 = 75%, 5 = 63%, 4 = 50%, 3 = 38%, 2 = 25%, 1 = 13%
Enter your scores above and in the vocabulary performance chart on the inside back cover of the book.

CHAPTER

15

advice	impossible
cautious	necessary
defeat	permit
defect	provide

Learning Eight New Words

In the space at the left, write the letter of the meaning closest to that of each **boldfaced** word. Use the other words (the *context*) in each sentence to help you figure out the word's meaning.

1 advice
(ad-**viis**)
– noun

• My mother's **advice** to me whenever I get sick is to stay in bed.

• Friends often give good **advice** when you are trying to make a decision.

___*Advice* means   a. helpful idea   b. friendship   c. mistake

2 cautious
(**kaw**-shuhss)
– adjective

• Ever since he stepped on a bee, Paul has been **cautious** about walking in the grass with bare feet.

• You need to be **cautious** when riding a bike on busy roads.

___*Cautious* means   a. happy   b. tired   c. careful

3 defeat
(di-**feet**)
– verb

• If you can **defeat** your fears, you can do anything.

• Our soccer team played so well that we **defeated** the first-place team.

___*Defeat* means   a. beat   b. keep   c. hide

4 defect
(**dee**-fekt)
– noun

• Martina returned her new jacket to the store because it had a **defect**— the zipper would not close.

• My boss finds **defects** in everyone else's work, but he thinks his own work is perfect.

___*Defect* means   a. cost   b. problem   c. best part

5 impossible
(im-**poss**-uh-buhl)
– adjective

• Mira has to work on Saturday, so it is **impossible** for her to go on the camping trip this weekend.

• Until the 1960s, many people thought it would be **impossible** to travel to the moon.

___*Impossible* means   a. usual   b. not able to happen   c. safe

6 necessary
(**ness**-uh-*ser*-ee)
– adjective

- Before the bank can cash your check, it will be **necessary** for you to show your driver's license.
- You will have to fill out the **necessary** forms before the doctor will see you.

___*Necessary* means   a. not wanted   b. careful   c. needed

7 permit
(pur-**mit**)
– verb

- Most stores don't want customers to bring their pets inside, but they do **permit** people to bring in Seeing-Eye dogs.
- I don't understand why Ralph **permits** his son to speak to him so rudely.

___*Permit* means   a. understand   b. let   c. win

8 provide
(pruh-**viid**)
– verb

- Two soup kitchens in the city **provide** free meals to hungry families.
- Before the test, the instructor **provided** a pencil to every student.

___*Provide* means   a. give   b. take away   c. show

Matching Words with Meanings

Here are the meanings, or *definitions*, of the eight new words. Write each word next to its meaning. The sentences above and on the facing page will help you decide on the meaning of each word.

1. _____   Not taking chances; careful

2. _____   A helpful idea about how to do something

3. _____   A problem or mistake that keeps something from being perfect; a fault

4. _____   To gain a victory over someone or something; to win in a contest of some kind

5. _____   To let someone do something

6. _____   To give something that people need

7. _____   Very important to something else; needed

8. _____   Not possible; not able to be done

BE CAREFUL: Don't go any further until you know the answers above are correct. Then you can use the meanings to help you in the following activities. After a while, you will know the words so well that you won't need to check the definitions at all.

Adding One Word to an Item

Complete each item below by writing one word from the box on the answer line at the left. Use each word once.

a. **advice**	c. **defeated**	e. **impossible**	g. **permits**
b. **cautious**	d. **defects**	f. **necessary**	h. **provide**

_____ 1. The store sells "not quite perfect" clothes that have small . . ? . . you can barely see.

_____ 2. When we saw lightning in the sky, we decided to be . . ? . . and go indoors.

_____ 3. The basketball star's . . ? . . to students was simple: "Stay in school, work hard, and stay off drugs!"

_____ 4. To bake a tall cake, several eggs are . . ? . . .

_____ 5. I know who is bringing hot dogs to the picnic, but who will . . ? . . the soda?

_____ 6. If you water plants only once in a while, it will be . . ? . . for them to grow healthy and strong.

_____ 7. We . . ? . . the ants in our kitchen with a broom and a can of bug spray.

_____ 8. My boss . . ? . . workers to wear jeans on Fridays.

Adding Two Words to an Item

Complete each item below by writing **two** words from the box on the answer lines at the left. Use each word once.

a. **advice**	c. **defeat**	e. **impossible**	g. **permitted**
b. **cautious**	d. **defect**	f. **necessary**	h. **provide**

_____
_____ 1–2. The best piece of . . ? . . my father gave me was this: "Don't be afraid to try." He made me believe that if I worked hard enough, no problem could . . ? . . me.

_____
_____ 3–4. Because Katie was born with a . . ? . . in her heart, it was . . ? . . for her to have an operation when she was just two days old.

_____
_____ 5–6. The landlord told me it was . . ? . . for me to keep a pet, so why has he . . ? . . my neighbors to have two dogs and a cat?

_____
_____ 7–8. . . ? . . parents will . . ? . . a baby sitter with the phone numbers of the police and fire stations.

Showing You Understand the Words

PART A
In the space at the left, write the letter of the choice that best completes the sentence or answers the question.

____ 1. If you are a **cautious** person and someone invites you to go skydiving, you will probably say,
    a. "Let's go!"
    b. "I'm glad you asked."
    c. "No way!"

____ 2. How would you feel if another team **defeated** your favorite team in an important game?
    a. Happy
    b. Upset
    c. Lazy

____ 3. If you found a **defect** in a watch you had just bought, you would probably
    a. be happy.
    b. return the watch.
    c. wear the watch.

____ 4. If it is **impossible** for you to work nights, you
    a. will work nights, not days.
    b. look for a day job.
    c. don't care when you work.

PART B
In the space at the left, write the letter of the choice that best completes the sentence or answers the question.

____ 5. Someone who asks for **advice**
    a. has already decided what to do.
    b. does not have many friends.
    c. is not sure what to do.

____ 6. Which of the following is **necessary** in order to have a baseball game?
    a. Two teams
    b. Hot dogs and a cold drink
    c. Many fans

____ 7. A bar that **permits** smoking probably
    a. has customers that smoke.
    b. throws out anyone who lights up.
    c. has a no-smoking rule.

____ 8. In a restaurant, who **provides** the meal?
    a. The customer
    b. The server
    c. The person at the cash register

Adding Words to a Reading

A. A Belief in Flying

Read the following paragraph carefully. Then fill in each blank with a word from the box. Use each word once.

a. **advice**	b. **defeated**	c. **impossible**	d. **permit**

What do you think life would be like without the telephone? Without the radio, TV, cars, or airplanes? If the people who came up with these wonderful inventions had listened to the (1)_____ they were given, they would have given up. Instead, they were able to remain motivated° to reach their goals. For instance, many people told the Wright brothers, who invented the airplane, that flying was (2)_____. "We would have been born with wings if we were meant to fly!" people said. Sometimes the Wright brothers thought these people were right. After all, there were many times that their "flying machines" crashed to the ground. But these setbacks never (3)_____ the Wright brothers. They would not (4)_____ themselves to give up. Finally, in 1903, they invented a flying machine that really worked. Every airplane in the sky today is there because the Wright brothers believed in what they were doing.

B. She Tries Before She Buys

Read the following paragraphs carefully. Then fill in each blank with a word from the box. Use each word once.

a. **cautious**	b. **defect**	c. **necessary**	d. **provide**

Mr. Henderson works in the vegetable section of the Quick-Mart store. The other day, he saw a customer pick up a tomato and take a big bite of it.

"Wait a minute!" Mr. Henderson said. "What do you think you're doing? You can't eat something you haven't paid for."

The woman looked at him in surprise. "I'm just a (5)_____ shopper," she explained. "I don't buy anything until I inspect° it to be sure that it's really good. And these tomatoes aren't very good."

"What's wrong with them?" asked Mr. Henderson.

"Well, they look good on the outside," said the woman. "But they have a (6)_____ inside. They are hard and sour, not juicy and sweet. Biting into that one was like eating a red tennis ball."

"I'm sorry you don't like the tomatoes," said Mr. Henderson. "But it is still (7)_____ for you to pay for the tomato you ate."

"Oh, all right," said the woman. "Here's fifty cents. But you really should (8)_____ customers with a chance to taste before we buy. Otherwise, how do we know what we are getting?"

Using the Words When Writing and Talking

Now that you understand the meanings of the eight new words in the chapter, you are ready to use them on paper and in speaking. Complete each sentence below in a way that shows you really know what each **boldfaced** word means. Take a few minutes to think about your answer before writing it down and saying it out loud.

1. The best **advice** I ever got was _____

_____

2. People should be extra **cautious** when _____

_____

3. One childhood fear that I **defeated** was _____

_____

4. I once bought something with a **defect**. It was _____

_____

5. As much as I tried, it was **impossible** for me to _____

_____

6. If people want to improve their vocabulary, it will be **necessary** for them to _____

_____

7. On school nights, many parents often do not **permit** their children to _____

_____

8. Most people enjoy watching the evening TV news. It **provides** them with _____

_____

Scores	Adding One Word to an Item	_____%	Showing You Understand the Words	_____%
	Adding Two Words to an Item	_____%	Adding Words to a Reading	_____%

Number right: 8 = 100%, 7 = 88%, 6 = 75%, 5 = 63%, 4 = 50%, 3 = 38%, 2 = 25%, 1 = 13%
Enter your scores above and in the vocabulary performance chart on the inside back cover of the book.

arrange	panic
continue	personal
expert	regret
hollow	suppose

Learning Eight New Words

In the space at the left, write the letter of the meaning closest to that of each **boldfaced** word. Use the other words (the *context*) in each sentence to help you figure out the word's meaning.

1 arrange
(uh-**raynj**)
– verb

• The first thing Chen did in his new apartment was **arrange** his furniture so that each piece was exactly where he wanted it.

• I **arranged** all the books on the shelf in alphabetical order.

___*Arrange* means   a. buy   b. mix up   c. put in order

2 continue
(kuhn-**tin**-yoo)
– verb

• The weather report says that heavy rain will **continue** for several days and cause flooding.

• My neighbors **continued** playing their radio loudly, even though I asked them to turn it down.

___*Continue* means   a. keep quiet   b. keep outside   c. keep going

3 expert
(**ek**-spurt)
– noun

• My little brother is an **expert** on dinosaurs. He knows all their names, what they looked like, what they ate, and where they lived.

• Aunt Sonia likes sweets so much she calls herself a dessert **expert**.

___*Expert* means

    a. someone who does not know much about something

    b. someone who knows a lot about something

    c. someone who is afraid of something

4 hollow
(**hol**-oh)
– adjective

• The pipe used to be **hollow**, but now it is filled with earth and tree roots.

• The bank robbers hid the money in a **hollow** tree.

___*Hollow* means   a. against the law   b. out of shape   c. empty

5 panic
(**pan**-ik)
– noun

• Gary felt **panic** when he saw the large, hairy spider.

• As the fire moved closer and closer to our block, we tried to fight the feeling of **panic** inside us.

___*Panic* means   a. great fear   b. great hunger   c. great love

6 **personal**
(**pur**-suh-nuhl)
– adjective

- For the last five years, Tara has kept a diary so she can write down her **personal** thoughts and feelings.
- With close friends, you can talk about **personal** subjects, such as problems you're having at home or on the job.

___*Personal* means   a. not important   b. close to one's heart   c. not expensive

7 **regret**
(ri-**gret**)
– verb

- Our neighbors thought painting their house purple would be fun, but now they **regret** that they did it.
- Bill **regrets** yelling at his little brother and making him cry.

___*Regret* means   a. feel bad about   b. be thankful   c. be nervous

8 **suppose**
(suh-**pohz**)
– verb

- I **suppose** I will go to the movies tonight, but I won't decide until later.
- We had **supposed** that my brother would bring his new girlfriend home for Thanksgiving, but he visited her family instead.

___*Suppose* means   a. remember   b. see clearly   c. think

Matching Words with Meanings

Here are the meanings, or *definitions*, of the eight new words. Write each word next to its meaning. The sentences above and on the facing page will help you decide on the meaning of each word.

1. _____ Having to do with a person's life and feelings; private

2. _____ A sudden feeling of great fear

3. _____ Being empty inside

4. _____ Someone who knows a lot about a subject

5. _____ To be sorry; to feel bad about something that happened

6. _____ To put something in order

7. _____ To keep on doing something; to not stop

8. _____ To guess that something is true or will happen

BE CAREFUL: Don't go any further until you know the answers above are correct. Then you can use the meanings to help you in the following activities. After a while, you will know the words so well that you won't need to check the definitions at all.

Adding One Word to an Item

Complete each item below by writing one word from the box on the answer line at the left. Use each word once.

a. **arranged**	c. **expert**	e. **panic**	g. **regretted**
b. **continue**	d. **hollow**	f. **personal**	h. **supposed**

_____ 1. When water started leaking into the house, Glenda . . ? . . . that she had not gotten the roof fixed.

_____ 2. Sometimes children ask adults . . ? . . questions like "What scares you?" and "Do you ever cry?"

_____ 3. Raccoons like to build their homes inside . . ? . . places.

_____ 4. Shaking and feeling a great deal of . . ? . . , the man dialed 911 as quickly as he could.

_____ 5. Melissa is an . . ? . . at math, but she does not know much about history.

_____ 6. The way the chef . . ? . . the food on the plate made the meal look better than it tasted.

_____ 7. The man at the gas station told us to . . ? . . driving on Route 95 until the very end.

_____ 8. I . . ? . . you would be hungry after the test, so I bought sandwiches and soft drinks.

Adding Two Words to an Item

Complete each item below by writing **two** words from the box on the answer lines at the left. Use each word once.

a. **arrange**	c. **expert**	e. **panic**	g. **regrets**
b. **continue**	d. **hollow**	f. **personal**	h. **suppose**

_____ 1–2. I don't know how to . . ? . . flowers very well, but my sister, who
_____   works in a flower shop, is an . . ? . . at it.

_____ 3–4. Rodney acts as though he isn't afraid of anything. But his closest
_____   friends know one of his most . . ? . . secrets. Rodney feels great . . ? . .
                                  when he sees a mouse.

_____ 5–6. Ved . . ? . . putting white carpet in his living room. Now the room
_____   looks so big that it seems almost . . ? . . .

_____ 7–8. Our teacher gave us very little homework this week, but I . . ? . . that
_____   in the weeks ahead, the class will not . . ? . . to be so easy.

Showing You Understand the Words

PART A

In the space at the left, write the letter of the choice that best completes the sentence or answers the question.

____ 1. If you have friends who are **experts** on cooking, you might
   a. decide it was dangerous to eat anything they make.
   b. get their help on a special meal you are planning.
   c. buy them a beginner's cookbook.

____ 2. You would probably feel **panic** if you woke up one morning and found that
   a. your pillow had fallen on the floor.
   b. light rain was falling outside.
   c. a big snake had wrapped itself around your feet.

____ 3. Which of the following do you think is a **personal** question?
   a. "How much money do you make?"
   b. "Where is the nearest gas station?"
   c. "Is there a bowling alley in town?"

____ 4. Which of the following might you do to show you **regret** that you had a fight with your friend?
   a. Say nothing until your friend says to you, "I'm sorry."
   b. Say to your friend, "You're really a fool."
   c. Call your friend and say, "I'm sorry."

PART B

In the space at the left, write the letter of the choice that best completes the sentence.

____ 5. If a husband and wife **arrange** the photos from their wedding, they will probably
   a. tear up the photos.
   b. throw the photos into a drawer.
   c. place the photos in an album.

____ 6. Someone who **continues** losing weight will probably
   a. buy larger-size clothing.
   b. keep wearing the same clothing he or she has always worn.
   c. buy smaller-size clothing.

____ 7. Something **hollow** that is often found on a breakfast table is
   a. a plate of bacon and eggs.
   b. a coffee cup.
   c. a newspaper.

____ 8. If an adult says to a child, "I **suppose** you are the one who broke the mirror," the adult
   a. has a feeling the child probably did it.
   b. is sure the child did it.
   c. is sure the child did not do it.

Adding Words to a Reading

A. Play Now, Pay Later

Read the following paragraph carefully. Then fill in each blank with a word from the box. Use each word once.

a. **arranged**	b. **continued**	c. **hollow**	d. **suppose**

Did you ever hear the story of the ants and the grasshopper? It goes like this. During the summer, the ants worked hard to prepare° for the winter. From sunup to sundown, they hid pieces of food in (1)_____ spaces off a main underground tunnel. For weeks, the ants (2)_____ to work hard. And what did the grasshopper do during this time? He played. He sang and danced and had a fine time. When the ants warned him that winter was coming, he just laughed and said, "I (3)_____ it will, but no one knows for sure. Anyway, there will always be plenty of food to eat. You'll see." But, of course, winter did come. The ants went into their tunnels and lived off the food that they had carefully (4)_____ there in neat piles. Soon the grasshopper knocked at their door. "I'm hungry!" he said. "Will you share your food with me?" The ants shook their heads. "Now maybe you are sorry about the way you spent the summer," they said. They shut the door on the grasshopper and left him alone and hungry in the snow.

B. A Man of Many Faces

Read the following paragraph carefully. Then fill in each blank with a word from the box. Use each word once.

a. **expert**	b. **panic**	c. **personal**	d. **regret**

If you ever have the chance, see the movie *The Great Imposter*. The movie tells the story of Ferdinand Demara, Jr., a very interesting man. Demara did not have much education. But he was very smart. When he wanted to learn about something, he read everything that he could find on the subject. In that way, he became an (5)_____ on many subjects. Many of the people who met Demara believed that he was a college teacher because he knew so much. In fact, Demara started acting as if he were a college professor and more. During his life, Demara held jobs as a doctor, prison warden, chef, priest, and lawyer. He was so good at all these jobs that nobody suspected° he was not the real thing. Sometimes someone would ask Demara a question like "How does it feel to be a doctor?" or "What made you become a prison warden?" Such (6)_____ questions made Demara feel nervous that someone might learn his secret. Many times, when he thought he might be caught, he felt so much fear and (7)_____ that he packed his belongings and moved somewhere else. Finally, he was caught and served time in jail. But even then, he did not (8)_____ that he had told all those lies in the past.

Using the Words When Writing and Talking

Now that you understand the meanings of the eight new words in the chapter, you are ready to use them on paper and in speaking. Complete each sentence below in a way that shows you really know what each **boldfaced** word means. Take a few minutes to think about your answer before writing it down and saying it out loud.

1. In my room, I like to neatly **arrange** _____

   _____

2. I hope that I will always **continue** to _____

   _____

3. Young children think their parents are **experts** in everything. But when kids get older, they ____

   _____

4. **Hollow** trees are important in a forest because _____

   _____

5. Everyone in the building felt **panic** when _____

   _____

6. If someone asks me a question that I think is too **personal**, I simply say, "_____

   _____."

7. I will always **regret** that _____

   _____

8. Since my friends didn't meet me when they said they would, I **supposed** _____

   _____

Scores	Adding One Word to an Item	_____%	Showing You Understand the Words	_____%
	Adding Two Words to an Item	_____%	Adding Words to a Reading	_____%

Number right: 8 = 100%, 7 = 88%, 6 = 75%, 5 = 63%, 4 = 50%, 3 = 38%, 2 = 25%, 1 = 13%
Enter your scores above and in the vocabulary performance chart on the inside back cover of the book.

admit	encourage
available	experiment
contribute	intimate
dull	portion

Learning Eight New Words

In the space at the left, write the letter of the meaning closest to that of each **boldfaced** word. Use the other words (the *context*) in each sentence to help you figure out the word's meaning.

1 admit
(ad-**mit**)
– verb

- People charged with a crime will sometimes **admit** their guilt. They hope that by saying, "Yes, I did it," they will receive a lighter sentence.
- When I found crumbs in her bedroom, my daughter **admitted** that she ate the last of the chocolate cake.

___*Admit* means   a. hide   b. enjoy   c. honestly tell

2 available
(uh-**vay**-luh-buhl)
– adjective

- At one time, jeans came only in blue and were called "blue jeans." Now they are **available** in dozens of colors.
- Asian foods are **available** at many stores in my neighborhood, but they are not sold in my sister's neighborhood.

___*Available* means   a. boring   b. easy to get   c. expensive

3 contribute
(kuhn-**trib**-yoot)
– verb

- Each winter, people are asked to **contribute** food and clothing to help the city's homeless.
- My history class is interesting because every student **contributes** his or her ideas.

___*Contribute* means   a. give   b. take away   c. find

4 dull
(**duhl**)
– adjective

- Darren says that his work is **dull** because he does the same simple things day after day.
- The movie was so **dull** that half the audience fell asleep and the rest went home early.

___*Dull* means   a. not interesting   b. fun   c. private

5 encourage
(en-**kur**-ij)
– verb

- To **encourage** a team to do better, a coach should not yell at the players all the time.
- My parents **encouraged** me to aim high and hope for the best.

___*Encourage* means   a. stop   b. shout at angrily   c. give hope to

6 experiment
(ek-**sper**-uh-ment)
– verb

- I like to **experiment** with new recipes, but sometimes I end up feeding the results to my dog.
- Last year, the teacher **experimented** with a completely different way to teach English to children from other countries.

___*Experiment* means   a. give   b. try something new   c. watch

7 intimate
(**in**-tuh-mit)
– adjective

- Most of us tell **intimate** things about ourselves only to those people we know well and trust completely.
- In a diary, people may write about thoughts they feel are too **intimate** to tell anyone.

___*Intimate* means   a. boring   b. private   .   c. false

8 portion
(**por**-shuhn)
– noun

- Every week, Lawrence puts a **portion** of his paycheck into the bank.
- Father was busy at the Thanksgiving table, cutting **portions** of the turkey for everyone.

___*Portion* means   a. all   b. nothing   c. part

Matching Words with Meanings

Here are the meanings, or *definitions*, of the eight new words. Write each word next to its meaning. The sentences above and on the facing page will help you decide on the meaning of each word.

1. _____   To tell the truth about something; to confess

2. _____   Boring

3. _____   To give something, such as money, help, or ideas

4. _____   A small part of something larger

5. _____   To make others feel they can do well; to help others get the courage to do something

6. _____   To try something new and different

7. _____   Easy to get, buy, or find; ready for use

8. _____   Having to do with inner feelings; private

BE CAREFUL: Don't go any further until you know the answers above are correct. Then you can use the meanings to help you in the following activities. After a while, you will know the words so well that you won't need to check the definitions at all.

Adding One Word to an Item

Complete each item below by writing one word from the box on the answer line at the left. Use each word once.

a. **admits**	c. **contributed**	e. **encouraged**	g. **intimate**
b. **available**	d. **dull**	f. **experimented**	h. **portions**

_____ 1. Everyone in our family . . ? . . something to the block fair. Dad baked pies, Mom brought tablecloths, and I played the guitar.

_____ 2. To lose weight, you don't have to give up all the foods you love. Just eat smaller . . ? . . of them.

_____ 3. I went to the video store to see if any good horror movies were . . ? . . .

_____ 4. I . . ? . . with driving a different route to work this morning to see if it would be faster.

_____ 5. Because of problems at home, Lorena planned to drop out of school. But her teachers . . ? . . her to keep going and not give up.

_____ 6. Jake likes to dance, but he . . ? . . that he is not very good at it.

_____ 7. Hakim thought the book would be . . ? . . . However, it was so exciting that he stayed up all night reading it.

_____ 8. Carlos is too shy to share his . . ? . . thoughts with anyone.

Adding Two Words to an Item

Complete each item below by writing **two** words from the box on the answer lines at the left. Use each word once.

a. **admit**	c. **contributed**	e. **encouraging**	g. **intimate**
b. **available**	d. **dull**	f. **experimenting**	h. **portions**

_____
_____ 1–2. Children from unhappy homes often keep . . ? . . secrets about family life to themselves. Caring adults can make the children feel better by . . ? . . them to talk about what is happening at home.

_____
_____ 3–4. If things get . . ? . . at a party, try . . ? . . with this idea for waking everyone up: Ask people to talk about their earliest memories.

_____
_____ 5–6. I don't like to . . ? . . it, but I have never . . ? . . anything to the toy drive that my neighborhood runs every year.

_____
_____ 7–8. Here's what to do when you have two hungry kids and only one candy bar . . ? . . . Have one child cut the candy bar into two . . ? . . and have the second child choose which piece he or she wants.

Showing You Understand the Words

PART A

In the space at the left, write the letter of the choice that best completes the sentence or answers the question.

____ 1. You would probably hate to **admit** that you
   a. care for your family.
   b. bought a new car.
   c. cheated on a test.

____ 2. Which of the following would you want to have **available** during the worst snowstorm of the year?
   a. An air conditioner
   b. Warm boots
   c. A bathing suit

____ 3. If you want to **experiment** with your hairstyle, you might
   a. get the same haircut you always get.
   b. wear a hat.
   c. get a different haircut.

____ 4. If you hear a friend's **intimate** life story, you probably will
   a. end up with a better understanding of the person.
   b. never know much about the person.
   c. wish your friend had told the truth.

PART B

In the space at the left, write the letter of the choice that best completes the sentence.

____ 5. If each member of the football team **contributed** to winning the game, it's likely that
   a. one star player did it all.
   b. everyone on the team deserves thanks.
   c. many players never showed up for practice.

____ 6. People trying to read a very **dull** book might
   a. fall asleep.
   b. laugh out loud.
   c. be kept awake by all the action.

____ 7. To **encourage** workers, a boss might say,
   a. "You are the best staff anyone could ask for."
   b. "You workers think the world owes you a living!"
   c. "I'm leaving work early. I'll see you sometime tomorrow."

____ 8. Someone who gave away a **portion** of his dinner did which of the following?
   a. Gave away all of his dinner
   b. Gave away most of his dinner
   c. Gave away some of his dinner

Adding Words to a Reading

A. Soaps Are for Me!

Read the following paragraph carefully. Then fill in each blank with a word from the box. Use each word once.

a. **admit**	b. **dull**	c. **encourage**	d. **intimate**

People often laugh at me for watching TV soap operas. Let them laugh. I like the "soaps" for three reasons. First, sometimes my own life seems (1)_____, with the same boring jobs to do every day at home and at work. But the soaps are always exciting. People hop from one romance to the next, get into all kinds of difficulty, and come down with strange illnesses. Second, the soaps let me be nosy without getting into trouble. I (2)_____ it. To be truthful, I like hearing about the private lives and inner thoughts of people on the soaps. But I would never want my own friends or family to tell me such (3)_____ things. How could I look them in the face again? The soaps are a safe way to get all the interesting "inside dirt" on people. Third, the soaps (4)_____ me to deal with my own problems. Compared with what goes on in a soap opera, my own troubles seem minor°. What if I did have a little fight with my husband? At least I don't have two lovers and their jealous wives to worry about, my brother hasn't been missing for ten years (he lives downstairs), and I haven't got some terrible disease.

B. Keeping the Customer Happy

Read the following paragraphs carefully. Then fill in each blank with a word from the box. Use each word once.

a. **available**	b. **contributed**	c. **experiment**	d. **portions**

I'm a waiter in a restaurant. It's not a fancy place, but it's nice. Every so often, we run out of desserts that are on the menu. A customer orders apple pie, and I have to say, "Sorry, we're out of it." The customers don't like that, and sometimes they even get mad at me. So I went to the boss and (5)_____ an idea. Here's what I said: "If we're out of a dessert, why not offer the customer something that is (6)_____—but serve it at half price?"

The boss started to laugh. "We would lose too much money!"

"No, we won't," I said. "Getting paid half for a few (7)_____ of apple pie or chocolate pudding a couple of times a week won't cost us much. And with each serving, we make a customer happy, and a happy customer is a loyal° customer who will come back over and over again."

"All right," my boss said. "Let's (8)_____. Let's try your idea for a month and see how it works."

So that's what we're doing. Now, instead of just saying, "Sorry, we're all out," I tell the customer, "We're all out of strawberry ice cream today, but we do have vanilla fudge. And to show you how sorry we are, we're serving that at half price."

Using the Words When Writing and Talking

Now that you understand the meanings of the eight new words in the chapter, you are ready to use them on paper and in speaking. Complete each sentence below in a way that shows you really know what each **boldfaced** word means. Take a few minutes to think about your answer before writing it down and saying it out loud.

1. Most people find it difficult to **admit** that _____

_____

2. The library book was not **available** because _____

_____

3. When I go to a party, I like to **contribute** something, such as _____

_____

4. The TV show was so **dull** that we _____

_____

5. To **encourage** children to believe in themselves, parents should _____

_____

6. If you eat dinner at the house of a friend who is **experimenting** with spicy food, you _____

_____

7. A young girl writing in her diary might write an **intimate** thought about _____

_____

8. I threw away a small **portion** of the pizza because _____

_____

Scores	Adding One Word to an Item	_____%	Showing You Understand the Words	_____%
	Adding Two Words to an Item	_____%	Adding Words to a Reading	_____%

Number right: 8 = 100%, 7 = 88%, 6 = 75%, 5 = 63%, 4 = 50%, 3 = 38%, 2 = 25%, 1 = 13%
Enter your scores above and in the vocabulary performance chart on the inside back cover of the book.

compete	envy
contain	gradual
depend	intense
effective	involve

Learning Eight New Words

In the space at the left, write the letter of the meaning closest to that of each **boldfaced** word. Use the other words (the *context*) in each sentence to help you figure out the word's meaning.

1 compete
(kuhm-**peet**)
– verb

• When Kathy and I **compete** at checkers, she always wins.
• The two brothers **compete** at everything, even to see who can finish his dinner first.

___*Compete* means
    a. try to win   b. give up   c. share

2 contain
(kuhn-**tayn**)
– verb

• These boxes **contain** colorful shells that I found at the seashore.
• The bowl in the back of my refrigerator **contains** vegetables that are several months old.

___*Contain* means
    a. dislike   b. make   c. have inside

3 depend
(di-**pend**)
– verb

• When life gets difficult, it helps if you can **depend** on friends to cheer you up.
• Leon **depends** on his neighbor to watch his sons while he is at work.

___*Depend on* means
    a. wait for   b. rely on   c. turn away from

4 effective
(uh-**fek**-tiv)
– adjective

• This medicine is so **effective** that I haven't coughed once since I took it.
• Exercise is an **effective** way to improve health and get more energy.

___*Effective* means
    a. late   b. slow   c. good

5 envy
(**en**-vee)
– verb

• Many people **envy** movie stars because they are so rich and famous, but famous people often lead sad lives.
• Children often **envy** grownups because adults can stay up as late as they like.

___*Envy* means
    a. look like   b. have more than   c. wish to have the same as

6 gradual
(**graj**-yoo-uhl)
– adjective

- Although we might not see it from one day to the next, there is a **gradual** change as spring turns into summer.
- Over the months, we enjoyed watching Tiger's **gradual** growth from tiny kitten to adult cat.

____ *Gradual* means
a. happening slowly   b. becoming smaller   c. happening quickly

7 intense
(in-**tens**)
– adjective

- The birth of a healthy baby boy brought Elise and Jorge **intense** happiness.
- Many people felt **intense** sadness when Princess Diana was killed.

____ *Intense* means
a. little   b. not important   c. deep

8 involve
(in-**volv**)
– verb

- The teachers work hard to **involve** every student in the school play, either as an actor or as a singer.
- I found it helpful to **involve** my parents when I was trying to decide which apartment to rent.

____ *Involve* means
a. keep out   b. bring in   c. make angry

Matching Words with Meanings

Here are the meanings, or *definitions*, of the eight new words. Write each word next to its meaning. The sentences above and on the facing page will help you decide on the meaning of each word.

1. _____ Happening little by little

2. _____ Going as planned or wished; working well

3. _____ To try hard to win over others; to try to outdo others

4. _____ Deeply felt

5. _____ To hold inside

6. _____ To wish to have what someone else has

7. _____ To make someone or something a part of

8. _____ To have faith in someone or something; to rely

BE CAREFUL: Don't go any further until you know the answers above are correct. Then you can use the meanings to help you in the following activities. After a while, you will know the words so well that you won't need to check the definitions at all.

Adding One Word to an Item

Complete each item below by writing one word from the box on the answer line at the left. Use each word once.

a. **competes**	c. **depend**	e. **envies**	g. **intense**
b. **contains**	d. **effective**	f. **gradual**	h. **involved**

_____ 1. The sun makes such a . . ? . . trip through the sky each day that we never really see it moving.

_____ 2. I feel sorry for whoever is playing tennis with Sarah. Whenever Sarah . . ? . ., she usually wins.

_____ 3. Because they wanted to find ways to end the fighting, the two warring countries . . ? . . many nations in the peace process.

_____ 4. I . . ? . . on my dog to wake me every morning in time for work.

_____ 5. Shopping for clothes in secondhand stores is an . . ? . . way to save money.

_____ 6. Because he works outside in the summer heat, Scott . . ? . . people who work in air-conditioned offices.

_____ 7. When the runner lost the race, her face showed . . ? . . disappointment.

_____ 8. My jewelry box . . ? . . paper clips, pencils, nail files, and chewing gum. Oh, yes, the box has some jewelry in it, too.

Adding Two Words to an Item

Complete each item below by writing **two** words from the box on the answer lines at the left. Use each word once.

a. **competed**	c. **depend**	e. **envy**	g. **intense**
b. **contained**	d. **effective**	f. **gradual**	h. **involve**

_____
_____ 1–2. When I was a kid, I used to . . ? . . my friend because his lunch box always . . ? . . a candy bar, while mine had only a piece of fruit.

_____
_____ 3–4. It turned out to be a good idea to . . ? . . my three-year-old daughter in feeding our cat. She gets . . ? . . joy from having such a grown-up job.

_____
_____ 5–6. Omar used to lose when he . . ? . . at chess, but then he found a more . . ? . . way to play. Now he wins almost every game.

_____
_____ 7–8. When children are very young, they . . ? . . on adults for everything, but as they grow, with the . . ? . . passing of time, kids slowly learn to do things for themselves.

Showing You Understand the Words

PART A

In the space at the left, write the letter of the choice that best completes the sentence or answers the question.

___ 1. If you **compete** in a pie-eating contest, which of these do you do?
   a. You make pies for the contest.
   b. You judge the contest.
   c. You try to win the contest.

___ 2. If you know what a box **contains**, you
   a. need to open it to see what's inside.
   b. don't need to open it to see what's inside.
   c. ask someone to tell you what's inside.

___ 3. You would be most likely to **envy** a person who had just
   a. lost a job.
   b. won a vacation to Hawaii.
   c. made a dentist appointment.

___ 4. To make a **gradual** change to a low-fat diet, you would
   a. start eating high-fat foods.
   b. add one or two low-fat foods to your diet each week or two.
   c. begin right away to eat only low-fat foods.

PART B

In the space at the left, write the letter of the choice that best completes the sentence.

___ 5. A person who **depends** on the bus to get to work
   a. hopes the bus will come on time.
   b. never takes the bus.
   c. drives in a car pool.

___ 6. A dishwashing liquid is **effective** if it
   a. does a poor job of cleaning the dishes.
   b. costs more than other brands.
   c. gets the dishes really clean.

___ 7. A husband and wife who feel **intense** sadness at the thought of moving probably have
   a. good friends in the neighborhood.
   b. neighbors they don't get along with.
   c. a new apartment they don't like much.

___ 8. When children in a family are **involved** in making an important decision, they
   a. are not asked what they think.
   b. are asked what they think.
   c. are told to leave the room.

Adding Words to a Reading

A. A Fake "Cure"

Read the following paragraphs carefully. Then fill in each blank with a word from the box. Use each word once.

a. **contained**	b. **depended**	c. **effective**	d. **involve**

Have you ever heard anybody say, "That's just snake oil"? The term "snake oil" means "fake medicine." People claim° that it can cure an illness, but it doesn't really do anything. The term comes from the 1800s, when "medicine shows" would travel from town to town, selling homemade "cures." People believed in the medicine because the seller would often (1)_____ several sick people in the show. They would be called out of the audience and "cured" after taking a big drink of the medicine. Of course, the "sick" people weren't really sick. They were in good health and worked for the medicine show.

These so-called medicines were said to be (2)_____ for everything from baldness to cancer. However, the "medicine" bottles really (3)_____ useless liquids, anything from cactus juice to vinegar to, yes, snake oil. Because most people lived too far from town to see a real doctor, they bought many bottles of this fake medicine. They (4)_____ on it to keep their families healthy. By the time they found out that the medicine didn't work, the people running the medicine show would be many miles away—cheating the next group of townspeople.

B. The Jobs Everyone Hates

Read the following paragraph carefully. Then fill in each blank with a word from the box. Use each word once.

a. **compete**	b. **envy**	c. **gradual**	d. **intense**

Most people don't like to do housework very much. They (5)_____ those who have the money to hire someone else to do the work. Which housework jobs do people hate most? Nearly 1,400 people were asked that question. Many said they did not like dusting or doing the laundry. But the largest number of people said their most (6)_____ dislike was for washing the dishes and cleaning the bathroom. These two kinds of housework easily won the "prizes" for the worst jobs. Nothing else could (7)_____ with them. Many people also said that they used to like to cook. But as the years went by, a (8) _____ change took place. People got more and more tired of preparing° meals. For them, the kitchen became a place to stay out of. Maybe that's the reason fast-food restaurants do such good business.

Using the Words When Writing and Talking

Now that you understand the meanings of the eight new words in the chapter, you are ready to use them on paper and in speaking. Complete each sentence below in a way that shows you really know what each **boldfaced** word means. Take a few minutes to think about your answer before writing it down and saying it out loud.

1. I knew everyone was ready to **compete** when _____

   _____

2. My pockets **contain** _____

   _____

3. For me, a good friend is one I can **depend** on to _____

   _____

4. An **effective** way to lose weight is to _____

   _____

5. Many people **envy** well-known athletes because _____

   _____

6. The growth of a tree is so **gradual** that _____

   _____

7. I felt **intense** happiness when _____

   _____

8. If you want to **involve** young children in helping around the house, you should _____

   _____

Scores	Adding One Word to an Item	_____%	Showing You Understand the Words	_____%
	Adding Two Words to an Item	_____%	Adding Words to a Reading	_____%

Number right: 8 = 100%, 7 = 88%, 6 = 75%, 5 = 63%, 4 = 50%, 3 = 38%, 2 = 25%, 1 = 13%
Enter your scores above and in the vocabulary performance chart on the inside back cover of the book.

UNIT

3

Review Activities

On the next ten pages are activities to help you review the words you learned in Unit Three. You may do these activities in any order.

• Completing a Crossword Puzzle #1

• Completing a Crossword Puzzle #2

• Choosing the Best Word to Complete an Item

• Adding a Word to an Item, Parts A and B

• Finding the Same or the Opposite Meaning

• Using the Words When Writing and Talking

Completing a Crossword Puzzle #1

The box at the right lists twenty-four words from Unit Three. Using the meanings at the bottom of the page, fill in these words to complete the puzzle that follows.

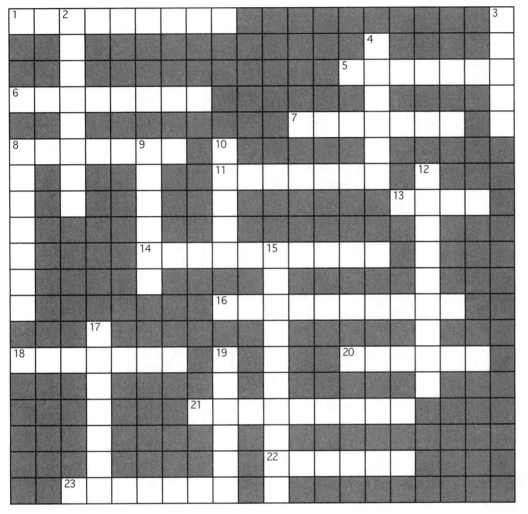

admit
advice
available
cautious
contribute
defeat
defect
disgust
dismiss
dull
experiment
guarantee
ideal
impossible
inspect
intimate
involve
locate
necessary
opinion
permit
prevent
provide
resolve

ACROSS

1. Very important to something else; needed
5. To make a strong decision to do something
6. Having to do with inner feelings; private
7. To let someone leave; to send away
8. To give something that people need
11. To cause someone to have a feeling of sickness or strong dislike
13. Boring
14. To give something, such as money, help, or ideas
16. To try something new and different
18. To look at something closely in order to find problems or errors
20. To gain a victory over someone or something
21. Easy to get, buy, or find; ready for use
22. To find something
23. To make someone or something a part of

DOWN

2. Not taking chances; careful
3. Perfect; meeting every need or wish
4. To let someone do something
8. To keep someone from doing something
9. A problem or mistake that keeps something from being perfect
10. To tell the truth about something; to confess
12. A promise (by a seller to a buyer) to fix or replace something that breaks
15. Not able to be done
17. What someone thinks or feels about something
19. A helpful idea about how to do something

Completing a Crossword Puzzle #2

The box at the right lists twenty-four words from Unit Three. Using the meanings at the bottom of the page, fill in these words to complete the puzzle that follows.

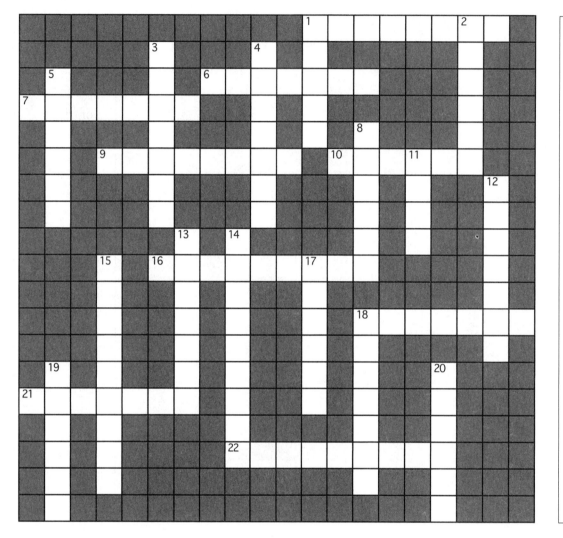

amazed
arrange
compete
confident
contain
continue
depend
donate
effective
effort
encourage
envy
expert
gradual
hollow
intense
panic
personal
portion
purpose
regret
sincere
suppose
uncertain

ACROSS

1. Having to do with a person's life and feelings; private
6. To put something in order
7. To try hard to win over others; to try to outdo others
9. To keep on doing something; to not stop
10. To have faith in someone or something; to rely
16. Sure of something; certain
18. To guess that something is true or will happen
21. To hold inside
22. To make others feel they can do well; to help others get the courage to do something

DOWN

1. A sudden feeling of great fear
2. Very surprised
3. Deeply felt
4. Happening little by little
5. Being empty inside
8. To be sorry; to feel bad about something that happened

11. To wish to have what someone else has
12. The reason for something; the goal
13. A small part of something larger
14. Going as planned or wished; working well
15. Not sure; in doubt
17. Hard work; trying hard
18. Honest; truthful
19. To give something in order to help others
20. Someone who knows a lot about a subject

Choosing the Best Word to Complete an Item

On the answer line at the left, write the word that best completes each item.

_____ 1. Carrie did not call a plumber when the pipes in her basement froze. She
was . . ? . . she could fix the problem herself.
   a. intense   b. confident   c. personal

_____ 2. Because she thinks it is . . ? . . to do the same kind of exercise every
day, Shannon sometimes runs, sometimes swims, and sometimes rides
her bike.
   a. amazed   b. gradual   c. dull

_____ 3. Although penguins are birds, it is . . ? . . for them to fly. Their bodies
are too large and their wings are too little.
   a. ideal   b. gradual   c. impossible

_____ 4. I always go to Marie's Hair Salon because Marie is an . . ? . . in cutting
curly hair like mine.
   a. expert   b. effort   c. advice

_____ 5. When the ice on the pond gets to be six inches deep, the owner . . ? . .
people to ice skate there.
   a. experiments   b. contains   c. permits

_____ 6. You can buy frozen strawberries anytime, but fresh ones are . . ? . . for
only a few months in the summer.
   a. available   b. hollow   c. necessary

_____ 7. Because John is my closest friend, I can talk to him about the . . ? . .
parts of my life.
   a. effective   b. ideal   c. intimate

_____ 8. Since the new baby down the street is all dressed in pink, I . . ? . . that
the baby is a girl.
   a. envy   b. suppose   c. dismiss

_____ 9. Peter ate so many . . ? . . of the cherry pie that there was little left for
the rest of the family.
   a. efforts   b. purposes   c. portions

_____ 10. The children put their money together to buy their mother a birthday
present. Even the four-year-old . . ? . . a nickel.
   a. continued   b. contributed   c. contained

_____ 11. Lori had to . . ? . . that she was the one who had broken the arm of her
grandfather's favorite chair.
   a. envy   b. admit   c. locate

_____ 12. The weather report says there will be a . . ? . . warming this week, with
the temperature slowly rising from the 40s into the 60s.
   a. sincere   b. intimate   c. gradual

(Continues on next page)

_____ 13. There used to be only one long-distance telephone company, but now companies like MCI, Sprint, and AT&T all . . ? . . to get people's business.

    a. disgust   b. contain   c. compete

_____ 14. Even though it will be hard, Karen has . . ? . . to put some money from each of her paychecks into a savings account.

    a. contained   b. involved   c. resolved

_____ 15. Because I have no car, I have to . . ? . . on a neighbor for a ride to work.

    a. prevent   b. inspect   c. depend

_____ 16. The teachers . . ? . . the classes at different times for lunch. The first-graders go out at 12 o'clock, the second-graders at 12:30, and so on.

    a. encourage   b. locate   c. dismiss

_____ 17. To make a toy drum, you can use anything . . ? . . that has a lid, such as an empty oatmeal box.

    a. hollow   b. intense   c. uncertain

_____ 18. Peeling apples, rolling out a crust, and cleaning up afterward is a lot of . . ? . . , but the taste of apple pie is worth all the work.

    a. effort   b. guarantee   c. advice

_____ 19. Hiram taped sheets of plastic over his windows to . . ? . . cold air from coming into the house.

    a. prevent   b. donate   c. disgust

_____ 20. When Mrs. Ricardo visited her grandson, she was . . ? . . to see that he had grown five inches in just six months.

    a. amazed   b. cautious   c. intimate

_____ 21. I . . ? . . my brother's singing voice. He sings like a bird, while I sound like a frog.

    a. resolve   b. suppose   c. envy

_____ 22. It is my . . ? . . that my husband makes the world's best chocolate cake.

    a. purpose   b. panic   c. opinion

_____ 23. The apartment we looked at today seems . . ? . . . It is just the right size, it is neat and clean, and the rent is not too high.

    a. cautious   b. ideal   c. personal

_____ 24. The lost man stared at the city map for a long time, trying to . . ? . . Park Avenue.

    a. locate   b. dismiss   c. involve

Score	Choosing the Best Word to Complete an Item	_____%

Adding a Word to an Item

PART A

Complete each item below by writing one word from the box on the answer line at the left. Use each word once.

a. **advice**	d. **defeated**	g. **encourages**	j. **necessary**
b. **contain**	e. **disgust**	h. **inspect**	k. **panic**
c. **continues**	f. **donate**	i. **intense**	l. **regret**

_____ 1. Instead of letting old clothes hang in the closet, . . ? . . them to a homeless shelter so they can be used by others.

_____ 2. If you . . ? . . buying that purple and gold dress, you should return it to the store.

_____ 3. Even if you are unhappy with your job, my . . ? . . is not to quit until you have another one.

_____ 4. We will go to the shore this weekend if the sunny weather . . ? . . that long.

_____ 5. Please don't . . ? . . under my bed. I don't want you to see the balls of dust there.

_____ 6. When the doctor told Mr. and Mrs. Rojas that their son was going to live, they smiled with . . ? . . happiness.

_____ 7. Balloons float upward because they . . ? . . a gas that is lighter than air.

_____ 8. Since I did not see the end of the movie, I do not know if the humans . . ? . . the aliens, or if the aliens took over the Earth.

_____ 9. Before you paint the living room, it will be . . ? . . to take the old wallpaper off the walls.

_____ 10. Mrs. Evans . . ? . . her students by telling them what they are good at, not by yelling at them for their mistakes.

_____ 11. Professional athletes . . ? . . many people by getting so much money and then complaining about their jobs.

_____ 12. As soon as an airplane leaves the ground, some people feel a great deal of . . ? . . and are not able to relax until the plane lands safely.

(Continues on next page)

PART B

Complete each item below by writing one word from the box on the answer line at the left. Use each word once.

a. **arranged**	d. **effective**	g. **involves**	j. **purpose**
b. **cautious**	e. **experiment**	h. **personal**	k. **sincere**
c. **defect**	f. **guarantee**	i. **provide**	l. **uncertain**

_____ 13. One . . ? . . of most tests is to help students see how much they know about a subject.

_____ 14. When you buy a CD from that store, you get a . . ? . . that the CD will be replaced if anything ever goes wrong with it.

_____ 15. There are lots of things I like about Rick, but he has one big . . ? . . . He believes he is right about everything.

_____ 16. Apple trees . . ? . . fruit to eat as well as much-needed shade on hot, sunny days.

_____ 17. The little girl . . ? . . her crayons in two piles—one with the colors she liked, the other with the colors she did not like.

_____ 18. I teach my children to be . . ? . . about petting strange dogs, even if the dogs seem friendly.

_____ 19. When Kareem makes soup, he likes to . . ? . . by adding different herbs and spices.

_____ 20. I like the people I work with, but I don't talk to them about . . ? . . things such as problems in my marriage.

_____ 21. Paula wants to surprise her father with a nice gift for his birthday, but she is . . ? . . about what he would like.

_____ 22. To prove that he is . . ? . . about quitting smoking, James promises to pay each of his children ten dollars if he ever has another cigarette.

_____ 23. The concert at school tonight . . ? . . students from the fourth and fifth grades, but not from the sixth and seventh.

_____ 24. Borrowing money from friends and not returning it is an . . ? . . way to lose their friendship.

Scores	Part A (Adding a Word) _____%	Part B (Adding a Word) _____%

Number right in each part: 12 = 100%, 11 = 92%, 10 = 83%, 9 = 75%, 8 = 67%; 7 = 58%, 6 = 50%, 5 = 42%; 4 = 33%, 3 = 25%. 2 = 17%, 1 = 8%
Enter your scores above and in the vocabulary performance chart on the inside back cover of the book.

Finding the Same or the Opposite Meaning

PART A

In the space at the left, write the letter of the choice that correctly completes each sentence. In most cases, the correct answer will have the **same** or **almost the same** meaning as the **boldfaced** word.

____ 1. If you are **amazed** at the low price of an apartment, you
    a. are surprised at how little it costs.   b. are worried about what it costs.
    c. are not sure what it costs.

____ 2. A **confident** person is often heard saying things like,
    a. "This is boring."   b. "I doubt that I can do this."
    c. "I am sure that I can do this."

____ 3. If the Eagles **defeat** the Cowboys in a football game, the Eagles
    a. beat the Cowboys.   b. never play the Cowboys.
    c. lose to the Cowboys.

____ 4. If a smell **disgusts** you, then it
    a. pleases you.   b. surprises you.
    c. makes you feel sick.

____ 5. A job that takes **effort** is one that
    a. pays well.   b. is hard to do.
    c. is very easy.

____ 6. If you talk about **intimate** matters with your coworkers, then you talk with them about
    a. your private life.   b. helpful ideas.
    c. things that are perfect.

____ 7. A **portion** of pie is
    a. no pie at all.   b. the whole pie.
    c. a piece of pie.

____ 8. If you **provide** friends with a place to sleep, you
    a. ask them for a place to sleep.   b. don't let them stay with you.
    c. give them a place to sleep.

____ 9. If you have a **purpose** for talking to your neighbors, you have
    a. no special reason for talking to them.   b. a clear reason for talking to them.
    c. a dislike for talking to them.

____10. If you did something that you now **regret**, you feel
    a. sorry about what happened.   b. bored with what happened.
    c. good about what happened.

____11. If you **resolve** to get more exercise, you
    a. do not need to get more exercise.   b. do not want to get more exercise.
    c. decide that you are really going to exercise more often.

(Continues on next page)

___12. If you **suppose** that a friend dyes her hair, it means that you
    a. wish that she wouldn't color it.   b. believe that she probably colors it.
    c. know for sure that she colors it.

PART B
In the space at the left, write the letter of the choice that is the **opposite** of the **boldfaced** word.

___13. The opposite of **cautious** is
    a. not easy   b. not cold   c. not careful

___14. The opposite of **continue** is
    a. stop   b. shout   c. push

___15. The opposite of **effective** is
    a. not working well   b. not looking   c. not hearing

___16. The opposite of **gradual** is
    a. very sad   b. very busy   c. all at once

___17. The opposite of **hollow** is
    a. not scary   b. not empty   c. not funny

___18. The opposite of **impossible** is
    a. able to repeat   b. able to see   c. able to happen

___19. The opposite of **locate** is
    a. not speak   b. not find   c. not wish

___20. The opposite of **necessary** is
    a. not needed   b. not honest   c. not strong

___21. The opposite of **panic** is
    a. calmness   b. doubt   c. hope

___22. The opposite of **permit** is
    a. not care   b. not let   c. not see

___23. The opposite of **sincere** is
    a. not weak   b. not strong   c. not truthful

___24. The opposite of **uncertain** is
    a. sure   b. straight   c. soft

Scores	Part A (Same Meanings) _____%	Part B (Opposite Meanings) _____%

Number right in each part: 12 = 100%, 11 = 92%, 10 = 83%, 9 = 75%, 8 = 67%; 7 = 58%, 6 = 50%, 5 = 42%; 4 = 33%, 3 = 25%. 2 = 17%, 1 = 8%
Enter your scores above and in the vocabulary performance chart on the inside back cover of the book.

Using the Words When Writing and Talking

The items below will help you use many of the words in this unit on paper and in conversation. Feel free to use **any tense of a boldfaced verb** and to make a **boldfaced noun plural**. (See pages 249–251 and 252.)

1. Using the word **admit**, write or talk about something that most people do not like to tell about themselves. For instance, you may feel that many people don't like to say that they eat too much, lose their temper easily, or have trouble saving money.

2. Using the word **advice**, write or talk about a time you gave someone an idea to help solve a problem. For example, you may have given a friend a way to work out a difficulty at home, on the job, or in a relationship.

3. Using the word **arrange**, write or talk about the order in which you have put (or plan to put) the furniture in one room where you live. You might describe how you have set up your bedroom or how you want your living room to look.

4. Using the word **available**, write or talk about some nonfood items that you can find easily in most large supermarkets—for example, soap, light bulbs, and movies to rent.

5. Using the word **compete**, write or talk about a time that you tried to beat someone at a game. Maybe you bowled with a family member, shot pool with a friend, or played cards with a roommate.

6. Using the word **contain**, write or talk about several items that are inside your refrigerator.

7. Using the word **contribute**, write or talk about someone who has given something that has made other people happier or better off. You might describe a famous person, like Martin Luther King, Jr., or someone you know firsthand—for example, a friend, neighbor, relative, or teacher.

8. Using the word **defect**, write or talk about a time when something was wrong with an item you bought. Maybe the zipper on a new jacket broke or the controls on your new air conditioner didn't work.

9. Using the word **depend**, tell about someone you can trust to be there for you. The person might baby-sit for your child, give you a ride to work, or listen to you when you need to talk.

10. Using the word **dismiss**, write or talk about a time when one person sent several other people away. Maybe a teacher let a class out early, a boss told employees they could leave work before the end of the day, or a doctor let a patient go home from the hospital.

11. Using the word **donate**, write or talk about a time that you gave something that helped another person. You might have given time, money, clothing, books, or a typewriter.

12. Using the word **dull**, write or talk about someone or something that you do not find at all interesting. It might be a book, a movie, a TV show, or your weekend plans.

13. Using the word **encourage**, write or talk about what parents and teachers can do to help kids feel they can do well in school. You might explain what you think adults can say or do to help kids try their best.

(Continues on next page)

14. Using the word **envy**, write or talk about a time you wanted something that someone else had. Perhaps you wanted a toy that belonged to another child or the happy family life enjoyed by a close friend.

15. Using the word **experiment**, write or talk about a time when you tried doing something you had never done before. Maybe you tried a new way of studying, exercising, dressing, or cooking a meal.

16. Using the word **expert**, write or talk about one subject that you know a good deal about. It could be a subject you studied in school, learned at work, or picked up as a hobby.

17. Using the word **guarantee**, write or talk about something that will be fixed or replaced for free if it ever breaks down. It might be a computer, car, radio, TV, or washing machine.

18. Using the word **ideal**, write or talk about something that seems perfect to you. It could be your favorite ice cream, a beautiful spot on a beach, or a perfect way to relax after a hard day.

19. Using the word **inspect**, write or talk about a time you looked closely at something. Maybe it was your car after it had been washed, some secondhand furniture you were thinking of buying, or your living room before guests arrived for a party.

20. Using the word **intense**, write or talk about a time when you had deep feelings. You might describe a time that was frightening, happy, sad, or thankful.

21. Using the word **involve**, write or talk about an activity that you were part of when it was being planned. Perhaps you helped plan a party, family vacation, or special meal.

22. Using the word **opinion**, write or talk about the way you feel about something. It could be your favorite (or least favorite) movie, TV show, or restaurant. Or you might tell what you think is the biggest problem these days with schools, parents, children, bosses, or companies.

23. Using the word **personal**, write or talk about what you do when you have a private problem you would like to solve. Maybe you talk to a close friend, speak to a relative, or write down your thoughts in a journal.

24. Using the word **prevent**, write or talk about something that you have tried to stop from happening. Maybe you tried to keep someone from getting hurt, from borrowing your clothes, or from finding out about a surprise you had planned.

Unit Four

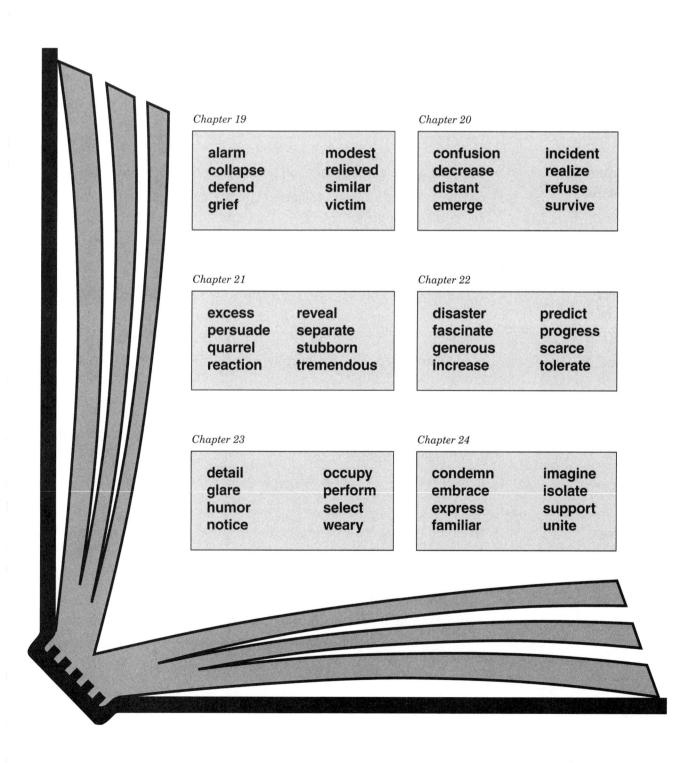

Chapter 19

alarm	modest
collapse	relieved
defend	similar
grief	victim

Chapter 20

confusion	incident
decrease	realize
distant	refuse
emerge	survive

Chapter 21

excess	reveal
persuade	separate
quarrel	stubborn
reaction	tremendous

Chapter 22

disaster	predict
fascinate	progress
generous	scarce
increase	tolerate

Chapter 23

detail	occupy
glare	perform
humor	select
notice	weary

Chapter 24

condemn	imagine
embrace	isolate
express	support
familiar	unite

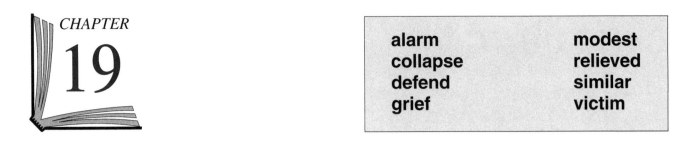

Learning Eight New Words

In the space at the left, write the letter of the meaning closest to that of each **boldfaced** word. Use the other words (the *context*) in each sentence to help you figure out the word's meaning.

1 alarm
(uh-**larm**)
– verb

____*Alarm* means

- Did it **alarm** you when our doorbell rang in the middle of the night?
- We were **alarmed** when we heard that a second-grader in our neighborhood was taken away by a stranger.

    a. scare   b. please   c. relax

2 collapse
(kuh-**laps**)
– verb

____*Collapse* means

- The earthquake caused many tall buildings in the city to **collapse**.
- On the first night of our camping trip, the tent **collapsed** on top of us and woke us all up.

    a. build   b. stay safe   c. fall down

3 defend
(di-**fend**)
– verb

____*Defend* means

- A mother bear is always ready to **defend** her cubs against danger.
- Nikki takes karate lessons so she can **defend** herself if anyone tries to hurt her.

    a. give up   b. keep safe   c. harm

4 grief
(**greef**)
– noun

____*Grief* means

- Rhetta felt a lot of **grief** when her grandmother died.
- With **grief** in his heart, David buried his dog Brownie, who had been his good friend for fifteen years.

    a. sadness   b. happiness   c. boredom

5 modest
(**mod**-ist)
– adjective

____*Modest* means

- Even though she has won prizes for her paintings, Cara is **modest** about being such a good artist.
- It must be hard for movie stars to stay **modest** when people are always telling them how wonderful they are.

    a. not working hard   b. not thinking too   c. thinking too
       at something   highly of oneself   highly of oneself

6 relieved
(ri-**leevd**)
– adjective

• We were **relieved** to learn that no one was hurt in the bus accident.

• Juan was **relieved** when the teacher called on someone else to answer the hard question.

___*Relieved* means   a. unhappy   b. not caring   c. made less worried

7 similar
(**sim**-uh-lur)
– adjective

• The guitar and banjo are **similar** in several ways. They both have long necks and strings that are played with the fingers.

• Joe and his dad sound so **similar** on the phone that I can't tell them apart.

___*Similar* means   a. not bragging   b. good-looking   c. alike

8 victim
(**vik**-tuhm)
– noun

• For a crime **victim**, going to court and seeing the person who hurt him or her can be as scary as the crime itself.

• The Red Cross helps the **victims** of floods, earthquakes, and fires.

___*Victim* means   a. person who   b. person who hurts   c. person who
                          is harmed   someone else   helps others

Matching Words with Meanings

Here are the meanings, or *definitions*, of the eight new words. Write each word next to its meaning. The sentences above and on the facing page will help you decide on the meaning of each word.

1. _____   Great sadness; sorrow

2. _____   Not thinking too highly of oneself; not proud; humble

3. _____   To keep safe from harm; to protect

4. _____   A person who is hurt or done wrong to

5. _____   Alike; like another in some ways

6. _____   To fall down or fall to pieces

7. _____   No longer worried

8. _____   To make afraid

BE CAREFUL: Don't go any further until you know the answers above are correct. Then you can use the meanings to help you in the following activities. After a while, you will know the words so well that you won't need to check the definitions at all.

Adding One Word to an Item

Complete each item below by writing one word from the box on the answer line at the left. Use each word once.

a. **alarmed**	c. **defend**	e. **modest**	g. **similar**
b. **collapsed**	d. **grief**	f. **relieved**	h. **victims**

_____ 1. The children used blocks to build a tower more than three feet high, but it . . ? . . before anyone saw it.

_____ 2. I bet your family is . . ? . . that you decided not to take the job which is several hundred miles away.

_____ 3. Hot peppers and sweet peppers look . . ? . . but taste very different.

_____ 4. The sight of a car rolling down the hill without a driver . . ? . . everyone.

_____ 5. When you go walking in the woods, wear long pants and long sleeves to . . ? . . yourself against poison ivy.

_____ 6. More than six million Jews were . . ? . . of the Nazis during World War II.

_____ 7. When Martin came into the room, we knew he had very bad news. His . . ? . . showed on his face.

_____ 8. Because my parents taught me to be . . ? . ., I never bragged about how well I did in school.

Adding Two Words to an Item

Complete each item below by writing **two** words from the box on the answer lines at the left. Use each word once.

a. **alarm**	c. **defend**	e. **modest**	g. **similar**
b. **collapsed**	d. **grief**	f. **relieved**	h. **victim**

_____
_____ 1–2. Mr. Turner was so . . ? . . that he was surprised when he won the best-teacher award. When he died a year later, his students felt real . . ? . . .

_____
_____ 3–4. I don't want to . . ? . . you, but if you carry your wallet in your back pocket, you may become a robbery . . ? . . .

_____
_____ 5–6. Many old towns in Europe had walls built around them to . . ? . . the people who lived there against enemies. Now, most of those walls are falling apart or have . . ? . . .

_____
_____ 7–8. I felt bad about breaking my grandmother's favorite plate, so I was . . ? . . when I saw a . . ? . . one I could buy and give her.

Showing You Understand the Words

PART A

In the space at the left, write the letter of the choice that best completes the sentence or answers the question.

____ 1. Which of these sights would **alarm** you?
   a. A visit from little children on Halloween
   b. A beautiful beach
   c. A stranger driving away in your car

____ 2. If you are feeling so sick that you think you might **collapse**, you would probably
   a. go to work.
   b. call a doctor.
   c. invite friends to dinner.

____ 3. If a teacher tells you that she likes a paper you have written, which of the following might you say if you are **modest**?
   a. "I knew you would like it."
   b. "Thanks. I wasn't sure how it turned out, but I'm glad you liked it."
   c. "I bet it was the best in the class."

____ 4. Your relatives from another state are driving to visit you. It's getting dark and they are two hours late. You feel **relieved** when they
   a. call and say, "We'll be there in ten minutes."
   b. call you from a hospital emergency room.
   c. never show up.

PART B

In the space at the left, write the letter of the choice that best answers the question.

____ 5. Which of the following would **defend** a country at war?
   a. Children
   b. Soldiers
   c. Senior citizens

____ 6. Which of these would bring **grief** to most people?
   a. A raise at work
   b. A visit from a loved relative
   c. The death of a close friend

____ 7. Which two words have a **similar** sound?
   a. ring / necklace
   b. better / butter
   c. north / west

____ 8. A man was arrested, put on trial, and jailed after robbing many homes. Who were his **victims**?
   a. The police who arrested him
   b. The people whose homes he robbed
   c. The judge who put him in jail

Adding Words to a Reading

A. A Young Librarian

Read the following paragraphs carefully. Then fill in each blank with a word from the box. Use each word once.

a. **collapse**	b. **grief**	c. **modest**	d. **similar**

Aja Henderson is a young girl who lives in Louisiana. Ever since Aja was little, she has loved to read. For her birthday and at holiday time, Aja always asked for books. And she always used any money she saved to buy more books. Because of all her books, Aja never felt alone. Her books kept her company. When she read a funny story, she laughed. When she read a really sad one, she felt (1)_____.

After collecting for a few years, Aja had so many books that her family teased her, saying that their house might (2)_____ from all the heavy books she owned. Then one day Aja found out something that bothered her. The other kids in her neighborhood could not enjoy books as much as she did. They did not read much, and there was no public° library nearby. So Aja came up with an idea. She would begin her own library! And that is exactly what Aja did.

At first, Aja was nervous that the neighborhood kids would not come to her library. But when several kids began stopping by her house to look through her books, she relaxed. After a while, all the neighborhood kids started to borrow books from her. In fact, today so many kids come to borrow her books that Aja gives the kids library cards (3)_____ to the ones that real libraries use. Aja even helps some of the children learn to read. Everyone thinks Aja's library is wonderful. But she is (4)_____ about what she has done. "Just seeing other kids learn to love reading is thanks enough for me," she says.

B. No More Harm

Read the following paragraph carefully. Then fill in each blank with a word from the box. Use each word once.

a. **alarmed**	b. **defend**	c. **relieved**	d. **victims**

Pam Lynchner is an example of someone who fought against something she thought was wrong. In 1990, Lynchner was hurt badly when a man mugged her. The man was caught. Because he had been arrested twice before for mugging, he was sentenced to twenty years in jail. Lynchner was (5)_____ to know that she was no longer in danger. But the feeling did not last. Just two years later she was (6)_____ by the news that the man who had mugged her had been set free. To make it even worse, the man tried to sue Lynchner. He said that being in jail had been difficult and painful for him. Lynchner was distressed° that the man was out of jail and making problems for her. She began to talk to other (7)_____ of crime. She heard many other stories about criminals who got out of jail early and kept bothering the people they had hurt. Lynchner wanted to do something about this, so she started a group to (8)_____ the rights of those who had been harmed. She called her group "Justice for All." The group works to keep criminals from getting out of jail early. "Justice for All" now has more than five thousand members.

Using the Words When Writing and Talking

Now that you understand the meanings of the eight new words in the chapter, you are ready to use them on paper and in speaking. Complete each sentence below in a way that shows you really know what each **boldfaced** word means. Take a few minutes to think about your answer before writing it down and saying it out loud.

1. Two things that **alarm** me are _____

    _____

2. The bridge **collapsed** when _____

    _____

3. People need to **defend** themselves against _____

    _____

4. The whole country felt **grief** when _____

    _____

5. If someone received the highest grade in the class and wanted to sound **modest**, he or she might say, " _____

    _____."

6. When I go to the dentist for a checkup, I am **relieved** when _____

    _____

7. One way in which school and work are **similar** is _____

    _____

8. In the news, I heard about a **victim** who _____

    _____

Scores	Adding One Word to an Item	_____%	Showing You Understand the Words	_____%
	Adding Two Words to an Item	_____%	Adding Words to a Reading	_____%

Number right: 8 = 100%, 7 = 88%, 6 = 75%, 5 = 63%, 4 = 50%, 3 = 38%, 2 = 25%, 1 = 13%
Enter your scores above and in the vocabulary performance chart on the inside back cover of the book.

confusion	incident
decrease	realize
distant	refuse
emerge	survive

Learning Eight New Words

In the space at the left, write the letter of the meaning closest to that of each **boldfaced** word. Use the other words (the *context*) in each sentence to help you figure out the word's meaning.

1 **confusion**
(kuhn-**fyoo**-shuhn)
– noun

- The poor directions caused so much **confusion** that everyone arrived late for the party.
- The instructions for putting the toy together were missing, so at first I felt great **confusion**.

___*Confusion* means

    a. feeling of danger   b. feeling of not knowing what to do   c. feeling of peace

2 **decrease**
(di-**kreess**)
– verb

- Putting ice on an injury helps **decrease** pain and swelling.
- To **decrease** your chances of getting sick, you should eat healthy foods and get plenty of exercise.

___*Decrease* means

    a. make less   b. make greater   c. keep the same

3 **distant**
(**diss**-tuhnt)
– adjective

- Some of the bright spots in the sky are **distant** planets that are millions of miles away.
- If we listened closely, we could hear the low rumble of a **distant** train moving toward us.

___*Distant* means

    a. nearby   b. not at all close   c. different

4 **emerge**
(i-**murj**)
– verb

- Today, I saw a tiny brown mouse **emerge** from a small hole in one of our kitchen cabinets. When it saw me, it ran back into the hole.
- The story was about a two-headed monster that **emerged** from the forest at midnight to scare the town's children.

___*Emerge* means

    a. stay still   b. get lost   c. come out

5 **incident**
(**in**-si-duhnt)
– noun

- To stop an **incident** from happening, the police told the angry men to calm down and go home.
- The last **incident** I had with my car was two months ago when the battery went dead.

___*Incident* means

    a. time of trouble   b. time of happiness   c. time of resting

6 **realize**
(**ree**-uh-liiz)
– verb

- My children's teachers **realize** that I can't attend after-school meetings.
- Mr. Ramirez groaned "Oh, no" when he **realized** he had locked his keys in his car.

___*Realize* means
    a. hope
    b. know
    c. write

7 **refuse**
(ri-**fyooz**)
– verb

- Despite all the warnings about high-fat foods, many people **refuse** to give up eating rich, heavy meals.
- My sister **refused** to stop eating her Halloween candy even though she felt sick from eating all the sugar.

___*Refuse to* means
    a. decide not to
    b. forget about
    c. want to

8 **survive**
(sur-**viiv**)
– verb

- Seat belts and air bags help people **survive** serious car crashes.
- In 1912, when the great ship *Titanic* sank, 1500 people died, but another 712 **survived** the accident.

___*Survive* means
    a. live through
    b. forget
    c. cause

Matching Words with Meanings

Here are the meanings, or *definitions*, of the eight new words. Write each word next to its meaning. The sentences above and on the facing page will help you decide on the meaning of each word.

1. _____ To come into view; to come out into the open

2. _____ Something bad or upsetting that happens; a disturbing event

3. _____ Far away

4. _____ A feeling that things are mixed up and not at all clear

5. _____ To make or become less

6. _____ To understand that something is true

7. _____ To make a strong decision not to do something

8. _____ To stay alive through a dangerous time

BE CAREFUL: Don't go any further until you know the answers above are correct. Then you can use the meanings to help you in the following activities. After a while, you will know the words so well that you won't need to check the definitions at all.

Adding One Word to an Item

Complete each item below by writing one word from the box on the answer line at the left. Use each word once.

a. **confusion**	c. **distant**	e. **incidents**	g. **refuses**
b. **decreases**	d. **emerged**	f. **realizes**	h. **survive**

_____ 1. No one knew what was going on at the new restaurant. Because of all the . . ? . . , three tables received the wrong orders, and our waiter forgot about us completely.

_____ 2. We are lucky to live at a time when there are telephones. They let us speak to friends and relatives living in even the most . . ? . . places.

_____ 3. The rain stopped, and the sun . . ? . . from behind a dark storm cloud.

_____ 4. Do you think Robert . . ? . . that his shirt and tie look terrible together?

_____ 5. No matter how many times we tell our puppy not to chew on our couch pillows, she still . . ? . . to stop.

_____ 6. Because my parents lived through a fire that killed others, they often ask themselves, "Why did we . . ? . . when others died?"

_____ 7. Putting more police on the streets . . ? . . crime.

_____ 8. Although the large crowd at the football game was noisy, no . . ? . . were reported between fans of the two teams.

Adding Two Words to an Item

Complete each item below by writing **two** words from the box on the answer lines at the left. Use each word once.

a. **confusion**	c. **distant**	e. **incidents**	g. **refused**
b. **decrease**	d. **emerged**	f. **realized**	h. **survived**

_____
_____ 1–2. The thick fog and heavy rain caused so much . . ? . . for drivers that Mary had to . . ? . . her driving speed to make sure she didn't pass her street.

_____
_____ 3–4. In the morning, when Stephen . . ? . . from his tent and saw half-eaten food all over, he . . ? . . that an animal had visited his campsite during the night.

_____
_____ 5–6. The plane crash was so . . ? . . from any town that it took hours before police began to look for anyone who might have . . ? . . .

_____
_____ 7–8. After two . . ? . . at the playground when fights broke out, many parents . . ? . . to let their kids go there anymore.

Showing You Understand the Words

PART A

In the space at the left, write the letter of the choice that best completes the sentence.

___ 1. At your job, you might want to **decrease** your
   a. vacation time.
   b. pay.
   c. long drive to work every day.

___ 2. If you take a trip to a **distant** lake, you will have
   a. a long drive to get there.
   b. a short drive to get there.
   c. a short walk to get there.

___ 3. You should **refuse** to pay a store bill if you
   a. lost your checkbook.
   b. bought everything listed on the bill.
   c. bought nothing listed on the bill.

___ 4. You probably would not **survive**
   a. playing with a puppy.
   b. a swim with a group of hungry sharks.
   c. a visit from your favorite relative.

PART B

In the space at the left, write the letter of the choice that best completes the sentence or answers the question.

___ 5. Drivers on a superhighway would feel **confusion** if
   a. they bought a cold drink at a rest stop.
   b. all the exit signs had been taken away.
   c. their cars were in perfect working order.

___ 6. When musicians **emerge** on stage, they
   a. hide under the stage.
   b. come out in front of the curtain.
   c. stay in a dressing room.

___ 7. Which of the following **incidents** would make most people stay away?
   a. A parade
   b. A circus
   c. A bank robbery

___ 8. Children will **realize** that candy is sweet when they
   a. see someone else eat it.
   b. taste it for themselves.
   c. leave it in their pockets.

Adding Words to a Reading

A. Is He Man or Machine?

Read the following paragraph carefully. Then fill in each blank with a word from the box. Use each word once.

a. **confusion**	b. **distant**	c. **emerges**	d. **refuses**

My friend Bob loves computers. His whole life centers around them. If Bob wants to buy something, he clicks a couple of keys and finds what he wants. When he wants to meet new people, he types messages to (1)_____ computer lovers, many of whom live hundreds, even thousands, of miles away. They "talk" for hours on the computer but never meet each other in person. Sitting at the computer, Bob hardly ever (2)_____ from his room to go outside. I'm nervous about what's happening to Bob. He feels cozy and relaxed with his computer but not around real people. I try to tell him that this isn't good. I tell him that spending so much time with his computer will prevent° him from having a full life. But he disagrees and (3)_____ to listen to what I am saying. One day, the electricity will go out or his computer will break down. Maybe at this point, when he feels great (4)_____, Bob will be forced to connect with human beings rather than with a machine.

B. Struck by Lightning

Read the following paragraph carefully. Then fill in each blank with a word from the box. Use each word once.

a. **decrease**	b. **incident**	c. **realized**	d. **survived**

Who said lightning does not strike the same place twice? Roy Sullivan knows that isn't true. Sullivan, a forest ranger in Virginia, has been a victim° of lightning seven times. Over the years, Sullivan's shoulder, stomach, eyebrows, and ankles were burned. Once he was hit while sitting in his truck. The bolt pushed him out the door and threw him to the ground. During another (5)_____, lightning struck his head, burned a hole in the hat he was wearing, set his hair on fire, moved down his body, and left through the toes of his boots. Somehow, Sullivan (6)_____ all these strikes. Once he (7)_____ that lightning had a way of finding him, Sullivan made a special plan to (8)_____ his family's chances of being struck. Whenever a storm came near, he would go—all alone—into the kitchen and would make his wife and kids go into the basement, far from him. Sullivan died in 1983 at the age of 71. His death had nothing to do with lightning.

Using the Words When Writing and Talking

Now that you understand the meanings of the eight new words in the chapter, you are ready to use them on paper and in speaking. Complete each sentence below in a way that shows you really know what each **boldfaced** word means. Take a few minutes to think about your answer before writing it down and saying it out loud.

1. I was left feeling great **confusion** when _____

   _____

2. One reason a company might **decrease** a person's salary is _____

   _____

3. Many people like to travel to **distant** lands because _____

   _____

4. This morning I saw a bee **emerge** from _____

   _____

5. The scariest **incident** that ever happened to me was when _____

   _____

6. People in an accident may not **realize** they are hurt until _____

   _____

7. Young people often **refuse** to listen to what their parents say because _____

   _____

8. The people in the town **survived** the flood because _____

   _____

Scores	Adding One Word to an Item	_____%	Showing You Understand the Words	_____%
	Adding Two Words to an Item	_____%	Adding Words to a Reading	_____%

Number right: 8 = 100%, 7 = 88%, 6 = 75%, 5 = 63%, 4 = 50%, 3 = 38%, 2 = 25%, 1 = 13%
Enter your scores above and in the vocabulary performance chart on the inside back cover of the book.

excess	reveal
persuade	separate
quarrel	stubborn
reaction	tremendous

Learning Eight New Words

In the space at the left, write the letter of the meaning closest to that of each **boldfaced** word. Use the other words (the *context*) in each sentence to help you figure out the word's meaning.

1 excess
(**ek**-sess)
– adjective

* Several restaurants in town give their **excess** food to groups that feed the poor.
* I will paint the living room first, and if there is any **excess** paint, I'll do the hallway.

___*Excess* means

 a. leftover   b. good   c. used

2 persuade
(pur-**swayd**)
– verb

* Nathan wants to drop out of school, but his parents are trying to **persuade** him to stay.
* Advertising often **persuades** people to buy many things they don't need.

___*Persuade* means

 a. get someone   b. stop   c. leave
  to do something

3 quarrel
(**kwar**-uhl)
– noun

* Jamal and Michael have not spoken to each other for five years, ever since they had a bad **quarrel** about money.
* The neighbors' **quarrel** was very loud. Their yelling and screaming made me think they might hurt each other, so I called the police.

___*Quarrel* means

 a. reason   b. fight   c. dream

4 reaction
(ree-**ak**-shuhn)
– noun

* Whenever our cat is petted, her **reaction** is to purr.
* If something comes flying toward your face, your **reaction** will be to pull back quickly.

___*Reaction* means

 a. something that happens   b. action that   c. more of something
  because of something else   is hard to do   than is needed

5 reveal
(ri-**veel**)
– verb

* If I promise to keep it a secret, will you **reveal** what you are getting Dora for her birthday?
* My grandma never **revealed** her age to us; she said only that she was "over forty."

___*Reveal* means

 a. hide   b. forget   c. tell

6 separate
(**sep**-uh-rayt)
– verb

• In cooking class, we learned how to **separate** eggs by cracking them and putting the yolks in one bowl and the whites in another.

• To get the noisy kids to be quiet, the teacher **separated** them so they were sitting far away from each other.

___*Separate* means

    a. bring together   b. make larger   c. put apart

7 stubborn
(**stuhb**-urn)
– adjective

• The **stubborn** boy would not go to bed, even though the baby sitter kept asking him to.

• It is hard to work with **stubborn** people. They are not willing to listen to others or look at different ways of doing things.

___*Stubborn* means

    a. easy to   b. not wanting to   c. quick to learn
      get along with   do something

8 tremendous
(tri-**men**-duhss)
– adjective

• The blue whale is a **tremendous** animal. Its tongue alone can weigh up to 8,900 pounds.

• Outer space is so **tremendous** that no one can really understand its size.

___*Tremendous* means

    a. friendly   b. ugly   c. big

Matching Words with Meanings

Here are the meanings, or *definitions*, of the eight new words. Write each word next to its meaning. The sentences above and on the facing page will help you decide on the meaning of each word.

1. _____   Very large

2. _____   Something that is done because something else is done first

3. _____   To use words to get someone to think or do something

4. _____   Not wanting to change or give in

5. _____   Extra; more than is needed

6. _____   To put or move two or more things apart; to put in different places

7. _____   A fight with words; an argument

8. _____   To make something known

BE CAREFUL: Don't go any further until you know the answers above are correct. Then you can use the meanings to help you in the following activities. After a while, you will know the words so well that you won't need to check the definitions at all.

Adding One Word to an Item

Complete each item below by writing one word from the box on the answer line at the left. Use each word once.

a. **excess**	c. **quarrels**	e. **revealed**	g. **stubborn**
b. **persuade**	d. **reaction**	f. **separates**	h. **tremendous**

_____ 1. The class cheered when the teacher . . ? . . that I had won the contest.

_____ 2. Although butterflies don't look strong, every year they fly the . . ? . . distance from Canada all the way down to Mexico.

_____ 3. When the boss yelled at Sara, her . . ? . . was to cry.

_____ 4. The donkey is a . . ? . . animal. If it doesn't want to move, it won't.

_____ 5. You cannot say anything that will . . ? . . me to go see that horror movie—I don't enjoy being afraid.

_____ 6. Children may argue a lot, but they soon forget their . . ? . . and play together happily.

_____ 7. Every morning at work, Rita . . ? . . the mail into three piles—one for the company president, one for the vice president, and one for the office manager.

_____ 8. My family grows fruit. We eat most of it and sell the . . ? . . fruit at a roadside stand.

Adding Two Words to an Item

Complete each item below by writing **two** words from the box on the answer lines at the left. Use each word once.

a. **excess**	c. **quarrel**	e. **revealed**	g. **stubborn**
b. **persuade**	d. **reaction**	f. **separate**	h. **tremendous**

_____ 1–2. My little sister eats only vanilla ice cream. I tried to . . ? . . her to taste
_____ other flavors, but she is so . . ? . . she won't take even a tiny bite.

_____ 3–4. When the . . ? . . burst of fireworks filled the sky, everyone's . . ? . .
_____ was to say, "Ooooohhhh!"

_____ 5–6. Every year, the library sells its . . ? . . books. Employees . . ? . . the
_____ books into two piles and sell hardcover books for a dollar and
paperback books for fifty cents.

_____ 7–8. When Irina learned that Glenn had . . ? . . her secret to his friend, they
_____ had a big . . ? . . .

Showing You Understand the Words

PART A

In the space at the left, write the letter of the choice that best completes the sentence.

___ 1. To **persuade** your friends to go to a movie, tell them
    a. the acting is really bad.
    b. the story is boring.
    c. you will pay for their tickets.

___ 2. You can tell that people are having a **quarrel** when you hear
    a. angry voices.
    b. laughter.
    c. the sounds of dancing.

___ 3. Your **reaction** to a good joke might be
    a. to leave the room.
    b. to smile or laugh.
    c. to say "I don't get it."

___ 4. Like most children, when you were young, you probably **revealed** your happiness by
    a. sitting very quietly.
    b. looking sad.
    c. jumping up and down.

PART B

In the space at the left, write the letter of the choice that best completes the sentence.

___ 5. If people have a party and end up with **excess** lemonade, they
    a. have to make some more.
    b. should add ice to make the lemonade cooler.
    c. may give some to their neighbors.

___ 6. Pets may need to be **separated** if
    a. they begin to fight whenever they are together.
    b. they sleep quietly when they are around each other.
    c. they do not look at each other.

___ 7. Yoko and Emi argued. Yoko said she wanted to be friends again. Emi was **stubborn** and said,
    a. "You'll always be my best friend."
    b. "I'm sorry. I was wrong."
    c. "I will never be your friend."

___ 8. If a teacher gives students a **tremendous** amount of homework, the students
    a. can finish in just a few minutes.
    b. will be doing homework for a long time.
    c. don't have any homework.

Adding Words to a Reading

A. Whose Fault Is It?

Read the following paragraph carefully. Then fill in each blank with a word from the box. Use each word once.

a. **persuade**	b. **quarrel**	c. **revealed**	d. **stubborn**

Mrs. Harris looked very upset. When I asked her what was wrong, she answered "Nothing." But soon she (1)_____ what was happening. "My daughters, Maya and Tracy, have had a big fight," she said. "The (2)_____ started over a skirt. Maya had a new skirt that Tracy wanted to wear on a date. Since Maya wasn't home, Tracy took the skirt without asking. When Maya discovered° what Tracy had done, she took Tracy's favorite sweater and wore it to school. There, by accident, some ketchup got spilled on the sweater. Now both girls are really angry at each other. Tracy is too (3)_____ to say she should not have taken the skirt without asking. But Maya is just as bad. She says it is Tracy's fault that the sweater got dirty. I'm trying to (4)_____ both girls to say they are sorry, but neither of them will. If they don't make up pretty soon, they're going to drive me crazy!"

B. Forests Full of Life

Read the following paragraph carefully. Then fill in each blank with a word from the box. Use each word once.

a. **excess**	b. **reaction**	c. **separated**	d. **tremendous**

Forests are beautiful. Trees stretch high in the air, making a leafy green roof. Below, small young trees dot the forest floor. One of the most interesting things about a forest is the way new trees get planted. Small animals, like squirrels and chipmunks, pick up seeds that have fallen from the trees to the ground. These animals gather more seeds than they can eat. They take the (5)_____ seeds and bury them to eat later. That is how seeds get (6)_____ from the trees they grew on, sometimes by hundreds of miles. Often the animals forget about the seeds they buried and never go back to eat them. As the months go by, the rain, sunlight, and rich soil act upon the seeds. The (7)_____ of the seeds is to grow upward until they emerge° above the ground. Over the years, some of the tiny plants grow into (8)_____

trees. Their branches of the big trees become home for the same kinds of animals that

planted them long ago.

Using the Words When Writing and Talking

Now that you understand the meanings of the eight new words in the chapter, you are ready to use them on paper and in speaking. Complete each sentence below in a way that shows you really know what each **boldfaced** word means. Take a few minutes to think about your answer before writing it down and saying it out loud.

1. Because we had **excess** food after the party, we _____

   _____

2. Most parents try to **persuade** their children to _____

   _____

3. The two neighbors got into a **quarrel** when _____

   _____

4. What is the **reaction** of most people to the birth of a baby? They _____

   _____

5. When the police questioned them, the couple **revealed** _____

   _____

6. Before putting clothes in a washer, you should **separate** _____

   _____

7. I get upset when people are so **stubborn** that they _____

   _____

8. The new mall is so **tremendous** that _____

   _____

Scores	Adding One Word to an Item _____%	Showing You Understand the Words _____%
	Adding Two Words to an Item _____%	Adding Words to a Reading _____%

Number right: 8 = 100%, 7 = 88%, 6 = 75%, 5 = 63%, 4 = 50%, 3 = 38%, 2 = 25%, 1 = 13%
Enter your scores above and in the vocabulary performance chart on the inside back cover of the book.

disaster	predict
fascinate	progress
generous	scarce
increase	tolerate

Learning Eight New Words

In the space at the left, write the letter of the meaning closest to that of each **boldfaced** word. Use the other words (the *context*) in each sentence to help you figure out the word's meaning.

1 disaster
(duh-**zass**-tur)
– noun

- The family party turned into a **disaster** when two cousins got into a bad fight and had to go to the hospital.
- Every year, hurricanes, floods, and other natural **disasters** cause thousands of people to lose their homes.

___*Disaster* means   a. something that causes harm   b. something interesting   c. something that turns out well

2 fascinate
(**fass**-uh-nayt)
– verb

- It's easy to see that cars **fascinate** Nelson. His room is filled with car magazines.
- The dog's wagging tail **fascinates** the baby. She keeps trying to grab it.

___*Fascinate* means   a. bore greatly   b. frighten   c. interest greatly

3 generous
(**jen**-ur-uhss)
– adjective

- Nick is very **generous** with his new car—he lets his friends drive it whenever they ask.
- The **generous** couple gave each of their nephews a hundred-dollar check at graduation.

___*Generous* means   a. willing to share   b. selfish   c. bad-tempered

4 increase
(in-**kreess**)
– verb

- If you smoke, you greatly **increase** your chances of getting heart disease.
- My little brother still does not understand that study **increases** one's chances for good grades.

___*Increase* means   a. make smaller   b. make greater   c. get rid of

5 predict
(pri-**dikt**)
– verb

- Many scientists **predict** that one day we will find life on Mars.
- Dora **predicted** that her baby would be a girl, but she was wrong.

___*Predict* means   a. lie   b. tell ahead of time   c. forget

6 progress
(**prog**-ress)
– noun

• I have made real **progress** with my driving lessons. Now I can park my car on the street without hitting the curb.

• Tia is making excellent **progress** in learning English.

____*Progress* means   a. mistakes   b. friends   c. movement
                                                                                         toward a goal

7 scarce
(**skairss**)
– adjective

• So many elephants have been killed for their ivory that the animals have become **scarce**.

• Peaches were **scarce** this year because bad weather destroyed most of the crop.

____*Scarce* means   a. easily found   b. famous   c. few in number

8 tolerate
(**tol**-uh-*rayt*)
– verb

• My mother does not **tolerate** TV watching at dinner time. She wants us to sit around the table and talk together.

• There is a no-smoking rule where I work. The only place where smoking is **tolerated** is the parking lot.

____*Tolerate* means   a. let happen   b. stop   c. hide

Matching Words with Meanings

Here are the meanings, or *definitions*, of the eight new words. Write each word next to its meaning. The sentences above and on the facing page will help you decide on the meaning of each word.

1. _____   To make greater or larger; to add to

2. _____   Movement toward a goal

3. _____   Few in number; hard to find; rare

4. _____   To say what one thinks will happen in the future

5. _____   A happening that causes loss and suffering

6. _____   To interest someone greatly; to hold someone's interest

7. _____   Happy to give or share; unselfish

8. _____   To let something go on without trying to stop it; to put up with

BE CAREFUL: Don't go any further until you know the answers above are correct. Then you can use the meanings to help you in the following activities. After a while, you will know the words so well that you won't need to check the definitions at all.

Adding One Word to an Item

Complete each item below by writing one word from the box on the answer line at the left. Use each word once.

a. **disaster**	c. **generous**	e. **predict**	g. **scarce**
b. **fascinates**	d. **increased**	f. **progress**	h. **tolerate**

_____ 1. The flu that hit the United States in 1918 was a . . ? . . that killed more than 500,000 Americans.

_____ 2. People who have . . ? . . hearts always find time to help others.

_____ 3. Lifting weights has greatly . . ? . . my strength.

_____ 4. Some parents do not . . ? . . their children's using swear words.

_____ 5. The builders are making good . . ? . . with my aunt's new home—the roof is on already.

_____ 6. People think that the stars can help them . . ? . . what is going to happen in their lives.

_____ 7. Mr. Beck is a hard teacher. A lot of students in his class receive C's. A's are really . . ? . . .

_____ 8. I laughed the other day when I heard someone say, "Work . . ? . . me. I can sit and look at it for hours."

Adding Two Words to an Item

Complete each item below by writing **two** words from the box on the answer lines at the left. Use each word once.

a. **disasters**	c. **generous**	e. **predict**	g. **scarce**
b. **fascinated**	d. **increase**	f. **progress**	h. **tolerates**

_____
_____ 1–2. Since no one can . . ? . . when an earthquake will happen, it is one of the most feared of all . . ? . . .

_____
_____ 3–4. Tonya is such a . . ? . . person that she . . ? . . her neighbor's coming over almost every day to borrow something.

_____
_____ 5–6. Nicki's boss cares about her education. He says he won't . . ? . . her hours at her job until she makes better . . ? . . at school.

_____
_____ 7–8. The movie *Gorillas in the Mist* is about a woman named Dian Fossey. Apes and gorillas . . ? . . Fossey, and she was angry that they were becoming . . ? . . because of illegal hunting.

Showing You Understand the Words

PART A

In the space at the left, write the letter of the choice that best completes the sentence or answers the question.

___ 1. Which of the following do you think is a **disaster**?
   a. A fire that killed several people
   b. A good meal
   c. A job opening that sounds perfect

___ 2. If a friend's story about a fight with a coworker **fascinates** you, you might say,
   a. "I don't think this is any of my business."
   b. "Really! What happened then?"
   c. "This is boring. Who cares?"

___ 3. Two friends ask you to lend them ten dollars each. Because you feel **generous**, you might say,
   a. "I don't have any extra money."
   b. "Why should I?"
   c. "I'll be glad to give you a loan."

___ 4. To **increase** your weight, you should
   a. step on a scale.
   b. stop eating dessert.
   c. eat more at each meal.

PART B

In the space at the left, write the letter of the choice that best completes the sentence or answers the question.

___ 5. People who say that they can **predict** the future mean that they
   a. can change the future.
   b. know what is going to happen in the future.
   c. never think about the future.

___ 6. If people make **progress** in their schoolwork, they probably
   a. study at home every day.
   b. never study at home.
   c. make believe they are studying at home.

___ 7. If jobs are **scarce** in one part of the country, they are
   a. easy to get.
   b. high-paying.
   c. hard to find.

___ 8. Which of the following will most teachers *not* **tolerate**?
   a. A lot of noise and running around
   b. A time when kids are quiet
   c. The rules of good grammar

Adding Words to a Reading

A. An Animal in Danger

Read the following paragraphs carefully. Then fill in each blank with a word from the box. Use each word once.

a. **disaster**	b. **fascinated**	c. **scarce**	d. **tolerate**

For thousands of years, tigers have (1)_____ human beings. Carvings made in Russia six thousand years ago show that people there thought of the tiger as a god. Children across the world have grown up hearing stories, songs, and poems about tigers. Such stories tell of the animal's strength, beauty, and danger. But today this beautiful cat faces a problem that is alarming° to scientists. The tiger is becoming (2)_____. It is dying out so fast that many scientists say there will soon be no tigers in the wild. The only ones left will be in zoos. This would be a real (3)_____ for animal lovers around the world.

Why are the tigers dying out? They are being killed for their skins, bones, and other body parts. People throughout the world believe that tiger parts make strong medicine. The whiskers, the eyes, the claws, and the bones are used to treat different sicknesses. A hundred years ago, there were about 150,000 tigers in the world. Today there may be as few as 5,000. Many countries no longer (4)_____ the killing of the tiger. But it may be too late to save this beautiful animal.

B. The Simple Life of the Amish

Read the following paragraphs carefully. Then fill in each blank with a word from the box. Use each word once.

a. **generous**	b. **increase**	c. **predict**	d. **progress**

The Amish are members of a church that was formed in the late 1600s. They live in Pennsylvania, Ohio, Indiana, and other states. Their traditions° have not changed much over the years. They believe that human beings should live simply. They dress the same way the Amish did three hundred years ago. Living mostly on farms, they use horses instead of tractors to do the work. They do not have electricity or drive cars.

The Amish want their children to go to school. They want to see them do well and make (5)_____ in reading, writing, and arithmetic. But they believe that higher education is not needed. So Amish children leave school after the eighth grade. Most Amish marry at a young age, live on farms, and have large families.

Many outsiders have trouble understanding how the Amish can live without cars, electricity, VCRs, and phones. Some people (6)_____ that in the future, the Amish will have trouble holding onto their young people. And it is true that some young people leave the Amish church, wanting to (7)_____ their freedom. But many Amish are very happy. They are (8)_____ people who share what they have with one another. To them, non-Amish people rush around too much and miss the simple joys of life.

Using the Words When Writing and Talking

Now that you understand the meanings of the eight new words in the chapter, you are ready to use them on paper and in speaking. Complete each sentence below in a way that shows you really know what each **boldfaced** word means. Take a few minutes to think about your answer before writing it down and saying it out loud.

1. One of the worst **disasters** I ever saw was _____

   _____

2. I have always been **fascinated** by _____

   _____

3. Some people are so **generous** that they _____

   _____

4. One way that people can **increase** their energy is _____

   _____

5. One of the things that I **predict** will happen in the next one hundred years is _____

   _____

6. To make **progress** studying vocabulary, it is a good idea to _____

   _____

7. Tickets to the rock concert were **scarce** because _____

   _____

8. In my home, one thing I will not **tolerate** is _____

   _____

Scores	Adding One Word to an Item	_____%	Showing You Understand the Words	_____%
	Adding Two Words to an Item	_____%	Adding Words to a Reading	_____%

Number right: 8 = 100%, 7 = 88%, 6 = 75%, 5 = 63%, 4 = 50%, 3 = 38%, 2 = 25%, 1 = 13%
Enter your scores above and in the vocabulary performance chart on the inside back cover of the book.

detail	occupy
glare	perform
humor	select
notice	weary

Learning Eight New Words

In the space at the left, write the letter of the meaning closest to that of each **boldfaced** word. Use the other words (the *context*) in each sentence to help you figure out the word's meaning.

1 detail
(**dee**-tayl)
– noun

___*Detail* means

• The student's report was very good except for one **detail**—the word *flower* was spelled wrong.

• Because the United States dollar bill has so many tiny **details**, it is hard to copy.

a. end   b. part   c. color

2 glare
(**glair**)
– verb

___*Glare* means

• My dog-hating neighbors **glare** at me whenever I take Lassie for a walk.

• Instead of yelling, my father silently **glared** at me when I came home two hours late.

a. choose   b. smile   c. give an angry look

3 humor
(**hyoo**-mur)
– noun

___*Humor* means

• The movie was supposed to be funny, but I could see no **humor** in it.

• Our English teacher likes to begin each class with **humor**, such as a joke or a funny story.

a. lesson   b. anger   c. something funny

4 notice
(**noh**-tiss)
– verb

___*Notice* means

• Did you **notice** how sad Emily seemed today?

• Sitting in the food court at the mall, I **noticed** a small child who looked lost.

a. see   b. forget   c. choose

5 occupy
(**ok**-yuh-pii)
– verb

___*Occupy* means

• Several silver and blue fish **occupy** a small glass bowl in the living room.

• Chen was upset to find roaches **occupying** every drawer in his new apartment.

a. break   b. clean   c. live in

6 perform
(pur-**form**)
– verb

- The children get their allowance only if they **perform** their jobs around the house.
- I hope that I **performed** well on yesterday's English test.

____*Perform* means   a. do   b. fail   c. leave

7 select
(si-**lekt**)
– verb

- A salesclerk helped me **select** a watch for my father's birthday.
- The child **selected** a blue crayon from the box and then drew a picture of his dog.

____*Select* means   a. break   b. lose   c. pick out

8 weary
(**wihr**-ee)
– adjective

- After her baby was born, Lucy was happy but **weary**.
- You must have been up too late last night. You look **weary**.

____*Weary* means   a. sad   b. wide awake   c. needing rest

Matching Words with Meanings

Here are the meanings, or *definitions*, of the eight new words. Write each word next to its meaning. The sentences above and on the facing page will help you decide on the meaning of each word.

1. _____   To look at in an angry way

2. _____   Something that makes people laugh

3. _____   To live in

4. _____   To see and understand something that is happening

5. _____   To choose

6. _____   Tired; worn out in body or mind

7. _____   To do something

8. _____   A small part; a single item

BE CAREFUL: Don't go any further until you know the answers above are correct. Then you can use the meanings to help you in the following activities. After a while, you will know the words so well that you won't need to check the definitions at all.

Adding One Word to an Item

Complete each item below by writing one word from the box on the answer line at the left. Use each word once.

a. **detail**	c. **humor**	e. **occupy**	g. **selected**
b. **glared**	d. **notice**	f. **performed**	h. **weary**

_____ 1. I don't know the people who . . ? . . the apartment across the hall.

_____ 2. Janet planned her party carefully, not forgetting a single . . ? . . .

_____ 3. The doctor who is taking out Tony's tonsils has . . ? . . the operation many times before.

_____ 4. When the cashier walked away to make a phone call, the people waiting in the check-out line . . ? . . at her.

_____ 5. After finishing the five-mile race, Gina fell on the grass, too . . ? . . to take another step.

_____ 6. When Phil got sticky gum all over the bottom of his expensive new shoes, he could have gotten angry. Instead he laughed at the . . ? . . of it all.

_____ 7. The movie director interviewed more than fifty actors before he . . ? . . one for the starring role.

_____ 8. We were so busy at work that we did not . . ? . . it had begun to snow.

Adding Two Words to an Item

Complete each item below by writing **two** words from the box on the answer lines at the left. Use each word once.

a. **details**	c. **humor**	e. **occupy**	g. **select**
b. **glared**	d. **noticed**	f. **perform**	h. **weary**

_____ 1–2. Tara . . ? . . at her unkind landlord when he told her that she could not
_____ . . ? . . her apartment anymore.

_____ 3–4. When I . . ? . . my neighbor's children laughing at my new haircut, I
_____ knew other people would also see the . . ? . . in how silly I looked.

_____ 5–6. The blues singer is . . ? . . from traveling almost every day of the year.
_____ But in order to make a living, she must . . ? . . her act night after night.

_____ 7–8. "When you . . ? . . a subject for your paper," said the teacher, "choose
_____ something you know a lot about. Then you can include many interesting . . ? . . in your paper."

Showing You Understand the Words

PART A

In the space at the left, write the letter of the choice that best completes the sentence or answers the question.

___ 1. Driving on your street, you are hit by another car. You would most likely **glare** at
   a. the person who drove the car that hit you.
   b. a police officer who came to help.
   c. a small child standing by the road.

___ 2. You are most likely to find **humor**
   a. at a circus.
   b. at a funeral.
   c. at the doctor's office.

___ 3. If you are wearing a good-looking new jacket, you probably want people to **notice**
   a. that you spilled some ketchup on the front.
   b. that it fits you perfectly.
   c. that you lost a button on the sleeve.

___ 4. Which of the following would you probably **select** to wear on a snowy day?
   a. A T-shirt
   b. A warm jacket
   c. A pair of sandals

PART B

In the space at the left, write the letter of the choice that best completes the sentence or answers the question.

___ 5. The **details** of a book's story are
   a. what happens in the story.
   b. the front and back covers of the book.
   c. the people who wrote the book.

___ 6. A group of cows would probably **occupy**
   a. a barn.
   b. a small house.
   c. a supermarket.

___ 7. Many dog owners get their pets to **perform**
   a. miracles.
   b. large jobs around the house.
   c. a small trick like "sit" or "stay."

___ 8. Which of these would help a **weary** person?
   a. Taking a long trip in a car
   b. Taking a nap
   c. Studying for a test

Adding Words to a Reading

A. Taking a Break with TV

Read the following paragraph carefully. Then fill in each blank with a word from the box. Use each word once.

a. **humor**	b. **noticed**	c. **select**	d. **weary**

Most men and women work hard—sometimes at jobs they don't like—to bring money home to their families. After a hard day on the job and a long ride home, these people feel (1)_____. So after dinner, when they finally have some leisure°, they like to use that time by relaxing in front of the TV. Have you ever (2)_____ the kind of TV show they like to watch? Often they (3)_____ lighthearted shows about families much like their own. For many people, these shows are fun to watch and bring much needed (4)_____ into their lives. By watching shows that make them laugh, people get a break from their everyday problems.

B. Working and Living Together

Read the following paragraph carefully. Then fill in each blank with a word from the box. Use each word once.

a. **details**	b. **glare**	c. **occupy**	d. **perform**

Taking care of a home is not easy. People who (5)_____ a house or apartment know that there are many jobs that must get done. To help out, every family needs to (6)_____ a number of jobs to keep the house in good order. Dishes need to be washed, repairs need to be made, laundry must be done, and trash must be thrown out. Sometimes small jobs like dusting or vacuuming go undone because they seem like unimportant (7)_____. From time to time, quarrels° may break out over who is to do what. For example, a brother and sister may (8)_____ at each other because each thinks it is the other's turn to clean the bathroom. Mother may yell at Father for throwing his dirty laundry on the floor. Father may get angry at Mother for leaving dirty dishes in the sink. Every home will have some problems. But members of the family must learn to work out their differences. As they do, the ties—and the love—between them will grow stronger and stronger.

Using the Words When Writing and Talking

Now that you understand the meanings of the eight new words in the chapter, you are ready to use them on paper and in speaking. Complete each sentence below in a way that shows you really know what each **boldfaced** word means. Take a few minutes to think about your answer before writing it down and saying it out loud.

1. The **details** I like most on that old house are _____

   _____

2. The instructor **glared** at me because _____

   _____

3. Some people have no sense of **humor**. When they hear a joke, they _____

   _____

4. One thing I usually **notice** about people is _____

   _____

5. A family of mice might **occupy** _____

   _____

6. A server in a restaurant **performs** many jobs, such as _____

   _____

7. The best gift I ever **selected** was _____

   _____

8. My mother looked **weary** when _____

   _____

Scores	Adding One Word to an Item	_____%	Showing You Understand the Words	_____%
	Adding Two Words to an Item	_____%	Adding Words to a Reading	_____%

Number right: 8 = 100%, 7 = 88%, 6 = 75%, 5 = 63%, 4 = 50%, 3 = 38%, 2 = 25%, 1 = 13%
Enter your scores above and in the vocabulary performance chart on the inside back cover of the book.

condemn	imagine
embrace	isolate
express	support
familiar	unite

Learning Eight New Words

In the space at the left, write the letter of the meaning closest to that of each **boldfaced** word. Use the other words (the *context*) in each sentence to help you figure out the word's meaning.

1 condemn
(kuhn-**dem**)
– verb

- Most doctors **condemn** smoking, especially around children.
- The preacher **condemned** television shows that are full of sex and violence.

___*Condemn* means   a. help   b. give thanks for   c. speak strongly against

2 embrace
(em-**brayss**)
– verb

- In Latin America, men often hug when they meet each other, but in the United States, most men do not **embrace** each other.
- At the airport, a man **embraced** a woman tightly before saying goodbye.

___*Embrace* means   a. speak in an angry way   b. push away   c. put one's arms around

3 express
(ek-**spress**)
– verb

- A friendly wave is one way to **express** that you are glad to see someone.
- Ann's cat **expressed** its dislike for me by hissing and showing its teeth.

___*Express* means   a. make feelings known   b. whisper   c. picture in one's mind

4 familiar
(fuh-**mil**-yur)
– adjective

- Because its restaurants are in many countries, McDonald's is **familiar** to people all over the world.
- I grew up in this small town, so just about every street here is **familiar** to me.

___*Familiar* means   a. far away   b. often seen or heard   c. sad

5 imagine
(i-**maj**-uhn)
– verb

- To warm myself when it is cold outside, I often **imagine** that I am sitting by a nice warm fire.
- Nervous about sleeping in a strange room, my little brother began to **imagine** that there was a tiger under the bed.

___*Imagine* means   a. picture in the mind   b. forget   c. remember

6 isolate
(**ii**-suh-*layt*)
– verb

- If I feel a need to be away from others, I **isolate** myself by going into my bedroom and locking the door.
- When Robbie got chicken pox, his parents **isolated** him in his room so their other kids would not get sick.

___*Isolate* means

    a. put into a group   b. teach   c. put by oneself
       with everyone else

7 support
(suh-**port**)
– verb

- When somebody dies, people often **support** the family by sending flowers.
- After Nita's twins were born, her friends **supported** her by bringing her meals and doing her housework.

___*Support* means

    a. show caring for   b. blame   c. meet

8 unite
(yoo-**niit**)
– verb

- Each year, my relatives from all over the country **unite** at my grandmother's house for a big family party.
- Many small streams **unite** to form the large river that flows by my house.

___*Unite* means

    a. join together   b. fight   c. keep alone

Matching Words with Meanings

Here are the meanings, or *definitions*, of the eight new words. Write each word next to its meaning. The sentences above and on the facing page will help you decide on the meaning of each word.

1. _____ To say strongly that something is wrong or bad

2. _____ To keep someone or something apart from others

3. _____ To hug someone

4. _____ To help someone by saying or doing nice, caring things

5. _____ To picture something in one's mind

6. _____ To come together

7. _____ Often seen or heard; well-known

8. _____ To show one's feelings through words or actions

BE CAREFUL: Don't go any further until you know the answers above are correct. Then you can use the meanings to help you in the following activities. After a while, you will know the words so well that you won't need to check the definitions at all.

Adding One Word to an Item

Complete each item below by writing one word from the box on the answer line at the left. Use each word once.

a. **condemn**	c. **expressed**	e. **imagine**	g. **support**
b. **embraced**	d. **familiar**	f. **isolates**	h. **united**

_____ 1. Because Jessie grew up in a big city, the sounds of heavy trucks, car horns, and police sirens are . . ? . . to her.

_____ 2. People in town . . ? . . the high school's basketball team by attending games and cheering loudly.

_____ 3. It is nice to . . ? . . a world without wars.

_____ 4. Many people on the block . . ? . . to form a Neighborhood Watch group.

_____ 5. Marsha . . ? . . her new doll as if it were a long-lost love.

_____ 6. The zookeeper . . ? . . new animals until he is sure they have no diseases.

_____ 7. When children behave badly, adults should . . ? . . what the children do, not the children themselves.

_____ 8. Because he was shy, George . . ? . . his love for Sarah by writing her a letter.

Adding Two Words to an Item

Complete each item below by writing **two** words from the box on the answer lines at the left. Use each word once.

a. **condemn**	c. **express**	e. **imagine**	g. **support**
b. **embraced**	d. **familiar**	f. **isolate**	h. **united**

_____
_____ 1–2. When I went to Jeff's funeral, I didn't know how to . . ? . . my feelings in words. So I just went to his parents and quietly . . ? . . them.

_____
_____ 3–4. Because I live in a city where I don't know anyone, I sometimes like to . . ? . . that I see friendly, . . ? . . faces from my childhood.

_____
_____ 5–6. People on our block . . ? . . drugs and have . . ? . . to force drug dealers to move out of the neighborhood.

_____
_____ 7–8. Because her illness is catching, Janine has to . . ? . . herself at home. But her friends . . ? . . her by calling often and sending cards and gifts.

Showing You Understand the Words

PART A

In the space at the left, write the letter of the choice that best completes the sentence.

____ 1. You would probably **condemn** someone for saying something
    a. nice about someone you like.
    b. you agreed with.
    c. bad or hurtful about someone you like.

____ 2. If someone's face is **familiar** to you, you
    a. never saw it before.
    b. don't like how it looks.
    c. feel you have seen it before.

____ 3. If you like to **isolate** yourself when you study, you might
    a. find a quiet spot in the library, away from everyone else.
    b. take your books so you can study on a crowded bus.
    c. invite friends to study with you.

____ 4. If friends are feeling unhappy, you might **support** them by
    a. telling them their troubles are their own fault.
    b. staying away from them.
    c. listening to them tell you what is bothering them.

PART B

In the space at the left, write the letter of the choice that best completes the sentence or answers the question.

____ 5. If two people **embrace** each other, they probably
    a. are angry at one another.
    b. like or love each other.
    c. fight all the time.

____ 6. Which of the following **expresses** surprise?
    a. "Please come in."
    b. "Wow! What a shock!"
    c. "Take a seat."

____ 7. Young children **imagine** scary monsters that grown-ups
    a. do not see.
    b. have no trouble seeing.
    c. believe are real.

____ 8. If neighbors **unite** to build a community playground, they
    a. can't decide whether a playground is needed.
    b. don't want a playground.
    c. work together to build the playground.

Adding Words to a Reading

A. The Horror of Hate

Read the following paragraph carefully. Then fill in each blank with a word from the box. Use each word once.

a. **condemn**	b. **imagined**	c. **isolated**	d. **united**

During World War II, Adolf Hitler, the leader of Germany, had a horrible idea. In his mind, he (1)_____ a world with a "perfect race." Who would be in this perfect race? People like the Germans—blond, blue-eyed people. Many Germans liked Hitler's ideas and (2)_____ with him in his Nazi party. The Nazis thought that most other people were not good enough to live. For example, they hated people who were Jewish, or physically ill, or retarded, or homosexuals. The Nazis took all these people from their homes. Many were killed right away. Others were (3)_____ in terrible prison camps. In the camps, many more were killed, and others were forced to work. Many of those workers did not survive.° By the end of the war, the Nazis had killed millions of people. It is scary to think that even today there are "hate groups" like the Nazis in countries around the world. It is up to people of all backgrounds and beliefs to (4)_____ the hateful thinking of such groups.

B. Taking Time for Thanks

Read the following paragraph carefully. Then fill in each blank with a word from the box. Use each word once.

a. **embraced**	b. **expressed**	c. **familiar**	d. **support**

Last week, I got a letter that had (5)_____ handwriting on it. Though I knew I had seen the writing before, I wasn't sure whose it was. When I opened the letter, I was surprised to see it was from a friend I had not heard from in a while. I was even more surprised to read what she wrote. In her letter, my friend (6)_____ her thanks for a small favor I did a year ago. At that time, she and her brothers and sisters flew into town to be with their dying mother. I had cooked them some meals and done some shopping to (7)_____ the family during that hard time. "I was so upset when Mother died that I don't know if I ever really thanked you," my friend wrote. "I want you to know how much your help meant to me at that time of grief°." Her letter made me feel great. It also made me think about all the people I am thankful for in my life. Do I take the time to let them know that I am grateful? I decided to start right at home. When my daughter came home from school that day, I (8)_____ her and said, "Thank you for being a wonderful kid."

I am going to try to remember to say "thank you" more often.

Using the Words When Writing and Talking

Now that you understand the meanings of the eight new words in the chapter, you are ready to use them on paper and in speaking. Complete each sentence below in a way that shows you really know what each **boldfaced** word means. Take a few minutes to think about your answer before writing it down and saying it out loud.

1. Two things that I **condemn** are _____

    _____

2. I would probably **embrace** someone who _____

    _____

3. Puppies **express** their happiness by _____

    _____

4. When someone moves to a new city, seeing a **familiar** face _____

    _____

5. To chase away a bad mood, I like to **imagine** myself _____

    _____

6. When a child fights in class, the teacher might **isolate** him or her by _____

    _____

7. If my neighbors were in the hospital after a car accident, I might **support** them by _____

    _____

8. The workers in a company sometimes **unite** to _____

    _____

Scores	Adding One Word to an Item	_____%	Showing You Understand the Words	_____%
	Adding Two Words to an Item	_____%	Adding Words to a Reading	_____%

Number right: 8 = 100%, 7 = 88%, 6 = 75%, 5 = 63%, 4 = 50%, 3 = 38%, 2 = 25%, 1 = 13%

Enter your scores above and in the vocabulary performance chart on the inside back cover of the book.

Review Activities

On the next ten pages are activities to help you review the words you learned in Unit Four. You may do these activities in any order.

• Completing a Crossword Puzzle #1

• Completing a Crossword Puzzle #2

• Choosing the Best Word to Complete an Item

• Adding a Word to an Item, Parts A and B

• Finding the Same or the Opposite Meaning

• Using the Words When Writing and Talking

Completing a Crossword Puzzle #1

The box at the right lists twenty-four words from Unit Four. Using the meanings at the bottom of the page, fill in these words to complete the puzzle that follows.

alarm
confusion
decrease
detail
distant
emerge
excess
glare
grief
humor
incident
notice
occupy
perform
quarrel
reaction
refuse
reveal
select
separate
support
survive
tremendous
weary

ACROSS

3. To live in
5. Something that is done because something else is done first
7. Tired; worn out in body or mind
8. Great sadness; sorrow
12. Very large
15. Something that makes people laugh
16. To make something known
17. To come into view; to come out into the open
19. To help someone by saying or doing nice, caring things
20. To stay alive through a dangerous time
21. To choose
22. Something bad or upsetting that happens
23. Far away

DOWN

1. To make afraid
2. To see and understand something that is happening
4. To do something
6. To make or become less
8. To look at in an angry way
9. To make a strong decision not to do something
10. To put or move two or more things apart; to put in different places
11. A fight with words; an argument
13. A small part; a single item
14. A feeling that things are mixed up and not at all clear
18. Extra; more than is needed

Completing a Crossword Puzzle #2

The box at the right lists twenty-four words from Unit Four. Using the meanings at the bottom of the page, fill in these words to complete the puzzle that follows.

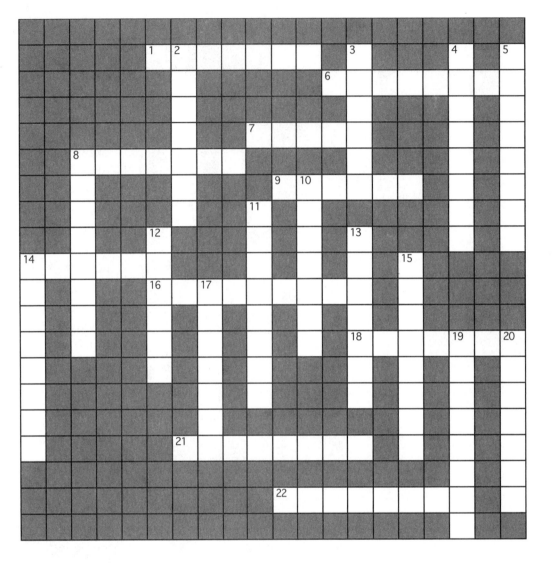

collapse
condemn
defend
disaster
embrace
express
familiar
fascinate
generous
imagine
increase
isolate
modest
persuade
predict
progress
realize
relieved
scarce
similar
stubborn
tolerate
unite
victim

ACROSS

1. To understand that something is true
6. To let something go on without trying to stop it
7. To come together
8. To say strongly that something is wrong or bad
9. A person who is hurt or done wrong to
14. Few in number; hard to find; rare
16. To interest someone greatly
18. To picture something in one's mind
21. Movement toward a goal
22. Happy to give or share; unselfish

DOWN

2. To show one's feelings through words or actions
3. Not thinking too highly of oneself; not proud; humble
4. Often seen or heard
5. To use words to get someone to think or do something
8. To fall down or fall to pieces

10. To keep someone or something apart from others
11. No longer worried
12. To keep safe from harm
13. To say what one thinks will happen in the future
14. Not wanting to change or give in
15. A happening that causes loss or suffering
17. Alike; like another in some ways
19. To make greater or larger; to add to
20. To hug someone

Choosing the Best Word to Complete an Item

On the answer line at the left, write the word that best completes each item.

_____ 1. When my spirits get low, I like to . . ? . . escaping to a warm, sunny island in the middle of the ocean.

    a. imagine   b. occupy   c. unite

_____ 2. I'm lucky. My family has always been there to . . ? . . me during the hard times.

    a. support   b. alarm   c. fascinate

_____ 3. When I am . . ? . . at the end of a long hot summer day, nothing makes me feel better than a frosty glass of iced tea.

    a. modest   b. weary   c. generous

_____ 4. Our company is making . . ? . . in hiring more women, but it still has a way to go.

    a. progress   b. details   c. confusion

_____ 5. Theo was afraid he had broken his ankle, so he was . . ? . . when the doctor told him it was just a sprain.

    a. stubborn   b. relieved   c. modest

_____ 6. Puppies and kittens . . ? . . young children. Kids seem to like anything that is smaller than they are.

    a. fascinate   b. separate   c. collapse

_____ 7. When Mrs. Diaz met her grandson for the first time, she rushed over and . . ? . . him tightly.

    a. embraced   b. defended   c. performed

_____ 8. The . . ? . . of the earthquake needed shelter, food, and medical care.

    a. quarrels   b. details   c. victims

_____ 9. The thick fog caused a . . ? . .—a fifteen-car accident on the bridge.

    a. disaster   b. detail   c. progress

_____ 10. I am trying to . . ? . . my teenage children to save some of the money they earn. So far, I have had no luck.

    a. predict   b. perform   c. persuade

_____ 11. Whenever I ask my wife to give up cigarettes, she . . ? . . at me in anger.

    a. emerges   b. glares   c. embraces

_____ 12. Although Tania is great in the kitchen, she is very . . ? . . about her cooking. She always says, "It wasn't hard to make. You could do it, too."

    a. familiar   b. scarce   c. modest

(Continues on next page)

_____ 13. Gina and Martin live on the first floor. Gina's parents . . ? . . the upstairs apartment.

    a. embrace   b. occupy   c. perform

_____ 14. Sirens screaming in the night always . . ? . . my children. They become so scared that I have to sit up with them until they fall back to sleep.

    a. select   b. notice   c. alarm

_____ 15. I have never understood why the roof of a river tunnel does not . . ? . . under the weight of all the water on top of it.

    a. reveal   b. collapse   c. survive

_____ 16. Did you ever . . ? . . how often the phone rings when you are taking a shower?

    a. notice   b. survive   c. reveal

_____ 17. To . . ? . . their homes from the forest fire, the owners sprayed their roofs with water.

    a. defend   b. perform   c. predict

_____ 18. Being able to laugh and see . . ? . . even at bad times can help you get through almost anything.

    a. humor   b. progress   c. grief

_____ 19. A good boss does not . . ? . . lateness or sloppy work.

    a. predict   b. isolate   c. tolerate

_____ 20. As we headed toward the parade, we could hear the . . ? . . sound of the band playing, even though we were almost half a mile away.

    a. stubborn   b. weary   c. distant

_____ 21. I could not decide which of three books to . . ? . ., so I bought all of them.

    a. emerge   b. select   c. separate

_____ 22. Everyone in our neighborhood . . ? . . the city's decision to close the police station on our street. We felt that the closing would put us in danger.

    a. revealed   b. condemned   c. survived

_____ 23. People who have bad heart problems are often . . ? . . in a special unit of a hospital. There they can receive the extra care they need.

    a. imagined   b. isolated   c. refused

_____ 24. Without your helpful map to guide us, we would have felt great . . ? . . trying to find our way to your new home.

    a. confusion   b. quarrel   c. victim

Score	Choosing the Best Word to Complete an Item	_____%

Number right: 24 = 100%, 23 = 96%, 22 = 92%, 21 = 88%, 20 = 83%; 19 = 79%, 18 = 75%, 17 = 71%; 16 = 67%, 15 = 63%. 14 = 58%, 13 = 54%, 12 = 50%, 11 = 46%, 10 = 42%, 9 - 38%, 8 = 33%, 7 = 29%, 6 = 25%, 5 - 21%, 4 = 17%, 3 = 13%, 2 = 8%, 1 = 4%
Enter your scores above and in the vocabulary performance chart on the inside back cover of the book.

Adding a Word to an Item

PART A

Complete each item below by writing one word from the box on the answer line at the left. Use each word once.

a. **details**	d. **express**	g. **predict**	j. **realize**
b. **emerged**	e. **incident**	h. **quarrel**	k. **stubborn**
c. **excess**	f. **perform**	i. **reaction**	l. **tremendous**

_____ 1. Sometimes my parents treat me like a child and do not seem to . . ? . . that I am a grownup.

_____ 2. An important study skill is being able to tell the difference between important main points and smaller, less important . . ? . . .

_____ 3. Kids often don't want to eat new foods and can be very . . ? . . about trying something even a little bit different.

_____ 4. I got a . . ? . . cut on my forehead when I banged into the windshield.

_____ 5. You cannot hope to . . ? . . well on a test if you had no sleep the night before.

_____ 6. After the thunderstorm, our dog . . ? . . from his hiding place under the bed.

_____ 7. There was so much . . ? . . food after the party that I did not have to cook for almost a week.

_____ 8. Marsha's knees help her . . ? . . the weather. When they hurt, she knows rainy weather is on the way.

_____ 9. When my sister told me she was getting a divorce, my first . . ? . . was to say that she was doing the wrong thing. But later I understood that she was doing what was best for her family.

_____ 10. There was a strange . . ? . . in our building yesterday. The glass in all the doors suddenly broke, even though nothing had hit them.

_____ 11. Melba and Joe had an argument on Saturday, but it was nothing serious—just a lovers' . . ? . . .

_____ 12. Because small children don't know how to . . ? . . anger in words, they sometimes show they are upset by hitting, kicking, and screaming.

(Continues on next page)

PART B

Complete each item below by writing one word from the box on the answer line at the left. Use each word once.

a. **decrease**	d. **grief**	g. **reveal**	j. **similar**
b. **familiar**	e. **increased**	h. **scarce**	k. **survive**
c. **generous**	f. **refused**	i. **separate**	l. **united**

_____ 13. Human beings can . . ? . . several weeks without food, but they can live only a few days without water.

_____ 14. When they do laundry, many people . . ? . . light- and dark-colored clothes. I just throw in everything all together.

_____ 15. My boss . . ? . . to give me a vacation because she needed extra help at the store.

_____ 16. Prices always seem to go up but never come down. It would be nice if they would . . ? . . every once in a while.

_____ 17. Most people feel deep . . ? . . when a pet dies.

_____ 18. When rain is . . ? . . during the growing season, farmers often lose their crops.

_____ 19. Crimes . . ? . . in our town last year. Police are trying to figure out why so many crimes took place these last twelve months.

_____ 20. The neighbors put aside their differences and . . ? . . to fight the plan to close a nearby park.

_____ 21. I don't mind coming home after being on vacation. It feels good to be back in my old . . ? . . routine.

_____ 22. If you say, "My good friend Jack would give me the shirt off his back," that is another way of saying he is very . . ? . . .

_____ 23. If you never drink Coke or Pepsi, you might think they taste . . ? . . . But those who drink a lot of soda say they don't taste a bit alike!

_____ 24. To protect the people whose homes had been robbed, the newspaper did not . . ? . . their names or addresses.

Scores	Part A (Adding a Word)	_____%	Part B (Adding a Word)	_____%

Number right in each part: 12 = 100%, 11 = 92%, 10 = 83%, 9 = 75%, 8 = 67%; 7 = 58%, 6 = 50%, 5 = 42%; 4 = 33%, 3 = 25%. 2 = 17%, 1 = 8%
Enter your scores above and in the vocabulary performance chart on the inside back cover of the book.

Finding the Same or the Opposite Meaning

PART A

In the space at the left, write the letter of the choice that has the **same** meaning as the **boldfaced** word.

_____ 1. The rising moon **emerged** from behind the trees. In other words, it
  a. stayed hidden.   b. was setting.
  c. came into view.

_____ 2. The fruit store has **excess** bananas. The store has
  a. too few bananas.   b. too many bananas.
  c. no bananas.

_____ 3. You write a note to someone saying, "I would like to **express** my thanks." That means you wish to
  a. put your thanks into words.   b. repeat your thanks.
  c. take back your thanks.

_____ 4. If friends tell you about an **incident** at a nearby school, they tell you about
  a. something bad that happened there.   b. the interesting courses there.
  c. the good teachers there.

_____ 5. If children **perform** their jobs around the house, they
  a. complain about doing the work.   b. do the work they should.
  c. don't do the work they should.

_____ 6. I **predicted** that both my roommates would move out by the end of the year. In other words, I said
  a. what I thought they would do in the future.   b. what I wished they would do.
  c. that I was angry about what they planned to do.

_____ 7. If two friends had a **quarrel** at a restaurant, they had
  a. no money to pay the check.   b. a good time there.
  c. an argument there.

_____ 8. My coworkers came up to me and asked, "What will your **reaction** be if the boss wants you to work the day shift from now on?" My coworkers wanted to know
  a. how I would answer the boss.   b. what my pay would be.
  c. what my work hours would be.

_____ 9. When we **realize** that the people we look up to are not perfect, we
  a. don't believe that they make mistakes.   b. understand that they make mistakes.
  c. have trouble believing that they make mistakes.

_____10. If friends tell you that you are **stubborn**, they mean that you
  a. are a good friend.   b. find it hard to change or give in.
  c. change your mind all the time.

(Continues on next page)

____11. If friends **support** you during a difficult time, they
    a. show their love and concern for you.   b. do nothing to help you.
    c. ask you if you can get along without their help.

____12. The new skyscraper downtown is a **tremendous** building. It's
    a. very large.   b. very new.
    c. smaller than anyone expected.

PART B

In the space at the left, write the letter of the choice that is the **opposite** of the **boldfaced** word.

____13. The opposite of **decrease** is
    a. smile   b. get larger   c. run fast

____14. The opposite of **distant** is
    a. neat   b. messy   c. close

____15. The opposite of **familiar** is
    a. strong   b. sharp   c. unknown

____16. The opposite of **grief** is
    a. joy   b. money   c. sadness

____17. The opposite of **increase** is
    a. get smaller   b. sit down   c. forget

____18. The opposite of **reveal** is
    a. hide   b. help   c. hurry

____19. The opposite of **scarce** is
    a. dry   b. wet   c. many

____20. The opposite of **separate** is
    a. dance   b. jump   c. join together

____21. The opposite of **similar** is
    a. smart   b. different   c. broken

____22. The opposite of **survive** is
    a. leave   b. repeat   c. die

____23. The opposite of **unite** is
    a. keep apart   b. watch   c. stay

____24. The opposite of **weary** is
    a. very small   b. full of energy   c. wanting to talk

Scores	Part A (Same Meanings) _____%	Part B (Opposite Meanings) _____%

Number right in each part: 12 = 100%, 11 = 92%, 10 = 83%, 9 = 75%, 8 = 67%; 7 = 58%, 6 = 50%, 5 = 42%; 4 = 33%, 3 = 25%. 2 = 17%, 1 = 8%
Enter your scores above and in the vocabulary performance chart on the inside back cover of the book.

Using the Words When Writing and Talking

The items below will help you use many of the words in this unit on paper and in conversation. Feel free to use **any tense of a boldfaced verb** and to make a **boldfaced noun plural**. (See pages 249–251 and 252.)

1. Using the word **alarm**, write or talk about a time that something scared you. Maybe you heard that a pill you take causes medical problems, or perhaps you saw a crowd get out of control at a rock concert.

2. Using the word **collapse**, write or talk about a time when you saw something fall apart. Perhaps a tent blew over, an old building came crashing down, or a pile of oranges in the supermarket tumbled to the floor.

3. Using the word **condemn**, write or talk about something that you feel very strongly is wrong and should be spoken out against. Maybe you think it is wrong that drunk driving isn't taken more seriously or that poor children go hungry.

4. Using the word **confusion**, write or talk about a time when things were unclear and mixed up. You might describe a busy store sale that had customers pushing each other to get the best items. Or you might describe how hard it was to get someone to fix a mistake in a bill that you had received.

5. Using the word **defend**, write or talk about a time that you (or someone else) protected a person or animal from harm. Maybe a friend came to your rescue when you were picked on as a child or you chased away children who were teasing a neighborhood dog.

6. Using the word **detail**, write or talk about a time that you paid careful attention to all the little things that need to be done when planning something important—for example, a wedding, a retirement party, or a special birthday.

7. Using the word **disaster**, write or talk about something that caused a lot of suffering. For example, you might describe a movie or a news story that showed a lot of people getting hurt, or you could tell what happened when a building near your home caught on fire.

8. Using the word **embrace**, write or talk about how friends or people in your family feel about hugging. Do some people always hug when they meet? Do others never hug?

9. Using the word **fascinate**, write or talk about something or someone that interests you and that you would like to know more about. It might be a subject in school, a place, or a person—for example, a teacher, movie or TV star, or world leader.

10. Using the word **generous**, write or talk about a person who has a big heart and always cares for and helps others.

11. Using the word **glare**, write or talk about a time when you looked at someone in an angry way. Perhaps the person didn't keep a secret or forgot to do something important.

12. Using the word **humor**, write or talk about something that makes you laugh, such as the silly things a friend does or the jokes that a family member tells.

13. Using the word **imagine**, write or talk about what you picture in your mind as the perfect vacation.

(Continues on next page)

14. Using the word **isolate**, write or talk about a time when a teacher, parent, or doctor might not let a child get together with other kids.

15. Using the word **modest**, write or talk about a time when you or another person did something well but did not brag about it. Maybe you got the highest grade on a test but did not tell anyone, or perhaps a friend won an award but let only a few people know.

16. Using the word **notice**, write or talk about a time when you saw something that no one else did. Maybe you saw someone stealing, or perhaps you found a mistake in something that everyone else thought was perfect.

17. Using the word **occupy**, write or talk about someone who lives in a house, apartment, or room near you.

18. Using the word **persuade**, write or talk about a time when you got a person to do what you wanted. Perhaps you got your parents to take you someplace special when you were a child, or maybe you got friends to try a restaurant you liked.

19. Using the word **progress**, write or talk about a goal that you are moving toward in your life. Your goal might be to become better at something, to learn to do something new, or to finish something you have begun.

20. Using the word **refuse**, write or talk about something you have decided you will never do. Perhaps you will not go on a roller coaster, eat a certain food, or see one kind of movie.

21. Using the word **relieved**, write or talk about a time that you were worried and then had that worry taken away. Perhaps you were afraid you were sick and then found out you were not. Or maybe you thought something was going to cost a lot of money and then learned it would not cost much at all.

22. Using the word **select**, write or talk about a time when you wanted many things but could not have everything you wanted. Maybe you were very hungry and wanted everything on a restaurant menu, or perhaps you liked every outfit you tried on in a store.

23. Using the word **tolerate**, write or talk about an action that you do not like and will not let happen. Maybe you don't let friends smoke in your house, copy your homework, or say mean things about other people.

24. Using the word **victim**, write or talk about a time that you (or someone else) was hurt by life or by another person. Perhaps relatives lost everything in a hurricane, your apartment was robbed, or a friend's car was stolen.

Unit Five

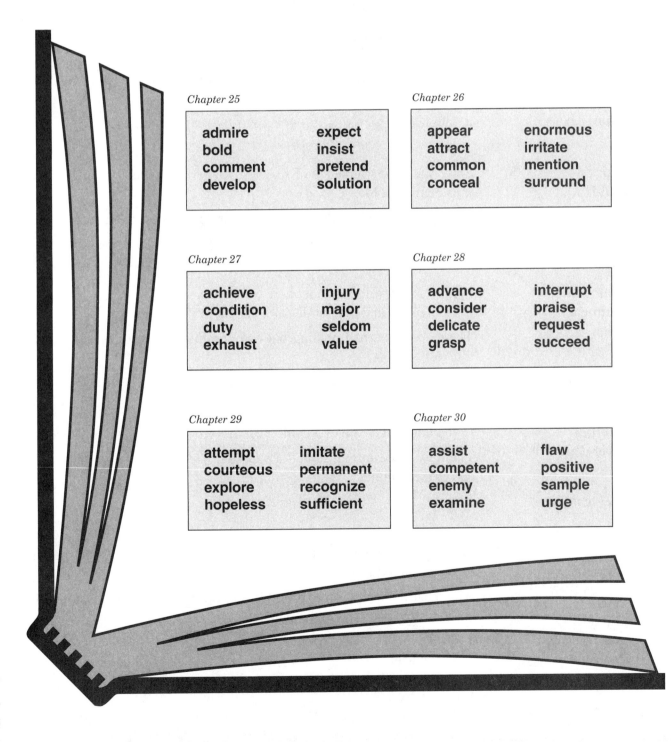

Chapter 25

admire	expect
bold	insist
comment	pretend
develop	solution

Chapter 26

appear	enormous
attract	irritate
common	mention
conceal	surround

Chapter 27

achieve	injury
condition	major
duty	seldom
exhaust	value

Chapter 28

advance	interrupt
consider	praise
delicate	request
grasp	succeed

Chapter 29

attempt	imitate
courteous	permanent
explore	recognize
hopeless	sufficient

Chapter 30

assist	flaw
competent	positive
enemy	sample
examine	urge

admire	expect
bold	insist
comment	pretend
develop	solution

Learning Eight New Words

In the space at the left, write the letter of the meaning closest to that of each **boldfaced** word. Use the other words (the *context*) in each sentence to help you figure out the word's meaning.

1 admire
(ad-**mii**-ur)
– verb

• Kids often think highly of athletes and musicians. It's too bad they don't **admire** their teachers as much.

• People **admired** the woman who went into the burning house to save a child.

___*Admire* means   a. laugh at   b. look up to   c. forget

2 bold
(**bohld**)
– adjective

• Since she is so frightened of roaches, Katherine thinks that anyone who kills them is **bold**.

• In the movie, the **bold** hero fights off purple monsters from outer space.

___*Bold* means   a. afraid   b. cruel   c. brave

3 comment
(**kohm**-ent)
– noun

• My coach's **comment** about how well I played in the soccer game made me feel proud and happy. He said, "Great job!"

• The newspapers had nothing but bad **comments** about the latest action movie.

___*Comment* means   a. something that is said   b. answer   c. spelling

4 develop
(di-**vel**-uhp)
– verb

• If you don't take care of a cold, it can **develop** into something worse.

• The ugly weed in our garden **developed** into a beautiful flower by the end of the summer.

___*Develop* means   a. grow   b. leave   c. dry

5 expect
(ek-**spekt**)
– verb

• Since my sister never remembers my birthday, I **expect** that she will forget it again this year.

• After hearing the weather report, we **expected** the storm to last all night, but it cleared up after fifteen minutes.

___*Expect* means   a. dislike very much   b. want   c. believe something will happen

6 insist
(in-**sist**)
– verb

___*Insist* means

- If friends are at my home around supper time, my mother will always **insist** they stay for dinner.
- Even though she looked sick, Renee **insisted** that she felt fine.

a. make believe   b. remind someone   c. say very strongly

7 pretend
(pri-**tend**)
– verb

___*Pretend* means

- Actors in a play **pretend** to be people they are not.
- I **pretended** to be pleased with the sweater that Uncle Fred gave me, but I really thought it was ugly.

a. make believe   b. grow   c. know

8 solution
(suh-**loo**-shuhn)
– noun

___*Solution* means

- Our problem is that we have twenty guests and only five chairs. The best **solution** is to have everyone sit on the floor.
- The **solution** to this week's crossword puzzle will be printed in next week's newspaper.

a. reason   b. question   c. answer

Matching Words with Meanings

Here are the meanings, or *definitions*, of the eight new words. Write each word next to its meaning. The sentences above and on the facing page will help you decide on the meaning of each word.

1. _____ To say something very strongly

2. _____ To think something will probably happen

3. _____ To act in a false way in order to fool someone; to make believe

4. _____ Not afraid

5. _____ An answer to a problem

6. _____ To grow little by little; to become

7. _____ To think highly of someone

8. _____ A statement that shows what a person thinks or feels

BE CAREFUL: Don't go any further until you know the answers above are correct. Then you can use the meanings to help you in the following activities. After a while, you will know the words so well that you won't need to check the definitions at all.

Adding One Word to an Item

Complete each item below by writing one word from the box on the answer line at the left. Use each word once.

a. **admire**	c. **comments**	e. **expected**	g. **pretended**
b. **bold**	d. **developed**	f. **insisted**	h. **solution**

_____ 1. When the police officer stopped me, I . . ? . . not to know I was going too fast.

_____ 2. I felt . . ? . . the day I told my boss I wanted a raise.

_____ 3. The math teacher asked, "Who can give me the . . ? . . to problem number four?"

_____ 4. I . . ? . . Gina for standing up to the bully who was teasing her.

_____ 5. After the superhighway was built nearby, the sleepy little town . . ? . . into a very busy city.

_____ 6. Darrell's girlfriend . . ? . . a bracelet for her birthday but got an engagement ring instead.

_____ 7. Part of the fun of watching sports on TV is listening to the announcer's . . ? . . .

_____ 8. The angry customer . . ? . . that she had been overcharged.

Adding Two Words to an Item

Complete each item below by writing **two** words from the box on the answer lines at the left. Use each word once.

a. **admire**	c. **comments**	e. **expect**	g. **pretends**
b. **bold**	d. **developed**	f. **insist**	h. **solutions**

_____
_____ 1–2. Marvin . . ? . . to like people but makes mean . . ? . . about them behind their backs.

_____
_____ 3–4. I . . ? . . the way that Joe and Lisa have worked to find . . ? . . to their marriage problems.

_____
_____ 5–6. Although Ralph was a shy, frightened child, he has . . ? . . into a . . ? . . adult who seems afraid of nothing.

_____
_____ 7–8. When I . . ? . . company to come, I . . ? . . that the children help me clean the apartment.

Showing You Understand the Words

PART A

In the space at the left, write the letter of the choice that best completes the sentence.

___ 1. Suppose you are at a party and see someone you would like to dance with. If you are **bold**, you might
    a. act as though you don't see the person.
    b. wait and hope the person will ask you to dance.
    c. say, "Hi! Would you like to dance?"

___ 2. If your friends make **comments** on your new hairstyle, you
    a. learn what they think of it.
    b. don't learn what they think of it.
    c. wish they would tell you what they think of it.

___ 3. If you **expect** rain, you probably will
    a. wash your car.
    b. plan a picnic.
    c. take an umbrella.

___ 4. If you had a headache, a **solution** to your problem might be
    a. loud noise.
    b. an aspirin.
    c. hard work.

PART B

In the space at the left, write the letter of the choice that best completes the sentence or answers the question.

___ 5. Which of the following might be said by a person who **admired** a movie?
    a. "I thought the movie would be better than it was."
    b. "I wish I had seen that movie."
    c. "What a great movie!"

___ 6. When a man's and a woman's feelings for each other **develop** into love, the two often decide to
    a. get married.
    b. stop speaking.
    c. stop dating.

___ 7. If someone **insists** that she knows the answer to a question, she
    a. is not sure of the answer.
    b. thinks that no one else knows the answer.
    c. feels strongly that she knows the answer.

___ 8. If someone **pretends** to be sick, he probably
    a. feels fine.
    b. is tall.
    c. needs to gain weight.

Adding Words to a Reading

A. A Surprising Change

Read the following paragraph carefully. Then fill in each blank with a word from the box. Use each word once.

a. **bold**	b. **developed**	c. **pretended**	d. **solution**

When I was a little girl, I had a neighbor named Nina, who was a very shy child. She used to hide behind her mother when she met someone new. In school, she never raised her hand to give answers. She would not even answer when the math teacher called on her for the (1)_____ to a problem. If Nina had to speak in front of the class, she (2)_____ to be sick and went to the nurse's office instead. When we were in fifth grade, Nina's family moved to another town. I didn't see her for many years. But when I met her again not long ago, I was surprised. Nina had (3)_____ from a shy little girl into a completely different adult. She has a good job selling beauty supplies to hair salons. She goes from salon to salon, showing shop owners the latest shampoos and hair colors. She is not a bit timid° anymore. Today, I would call Nina a (4)_____, outgoing woman. Isn't it surprising how much a person can change?

B. Just for Fun

Read the following paragraphs carefully. Then fill in each blank with a word from the box. Use each word once.

a. **admire**	b. **comment**	c. **expect**	d. **insisted**

Roberto and Maria went to look at new cars last Saturday. They asked their friend Anita to go along. "I didn't know you were getting a new car!" she said.

"We aren't," said Maria. "We don't (5)_____ to buy anything."

"Then why are you going?" Anita asked.

Roberto tried to explain. "It's fun to look at new cars, even when you can't buy one," he said. "We like to (6)_____ the new models and the new colors."

"Well, that sounds silly to me. It can't be any fun to look at things you can't buy," Anita said.

"Oh, but it is fun!" Maria (7)_____. "You should come with us and see."

But Maria could not persuade° Anita to go, so Maria and Roberto went alone. Later in the day, Roberto made a (8)_____ to Maria. He said, "I'm glad that you and I don't take life as seriously as Anita. Who cares if we can't buy a new car today? Spending the day together and daydreaming about the cars we would like to own is a great way to have fun."

Using the Words When Writing and Talking

Now that you understand the meanings of the eight new words in the chapter, you are ready to use them on paper and in speaking. Complete each sentence below in a way that shows you really know what each **boldfaced** word means. Take a few minutes to think about your answer before writing it down and saying it out loud.

1. I **admire** the way _____

    _____

2. A **bold** waiter or waitress might _____

    _____

3. If a friend makes a **comment** that hurts you, it's a good idea to _____

    _____

4. Over the past five years, the small shopping center has **developed** into _____

    _____

5. This week, I **expect** _____

    _____

6. If workers have a fever and a headache, their boss might **insist** _____

    _____

7. When I was little, I used to **pretend** that _____

    _____

8. A high-school principal may try to find a **solution** to _____

    _____

Scores	Adding One Word to an Item	_____%	Showing You Understand the Words	_____%
	Adding Two Words to an Item	_____%	Adding Words to a Reading	_____%

Number right: 8 = 100%, 7 = 88%, 6 = 75%, 5 = 63%, 4 = 50%, 3 = 38%, 2 = 25%, 1 = 13%
Enter your scores above and in the vocabulary performance chart on the inside back cover of the book.

appear	enormous
attract	irritate
common	mention
conceal	surround

Learning Eight New Words

In the space at the left, write the letter of the meaning closest to that of each **boldfaced** word. Use the other words (the *context*) in each sentence to help you figure out the word's meaning.

1 appear
(uh-**pihr**)
– verb

- My grandmother taught me not to judge people too quickly. Things are often not as they **appear**, she said.
- When John received the yellow tie with purple polka dots, he **appeared** happy, but I knew better.

___*Appear* means   a. look   b. think   c. dislike

2 attract
(uh-**trakt**)
– verb

- The sticky soda can on the floor started to **attract** ants.
- The music from the ice-cream truck **attracted** children from the whole neighborhood.

___*Attract* means   a. scare off   b. make angry   c. cause to come near

3 common
(**kom**-uhn)
– adjective

- The cold is so **common** that it makes millions of Americans miss work each year.
- Dogs used to be the country's most **common** pet, but today cats seem to be everyone's favorite.

___*Common* means   a. very large   b. strange   c. usual

4 conceal
(kuhn-**seel**)
– verb

- The thief wore a mask to **conceal** his face.
- I **concealed** my little brother's birthday present by burying it under a pile of clothes in his closet.

___*Conceal* means   a. bother   b. make sad   c. hide

5 enormous
(i-**nor**-muhss)
– adjective

- Joe's car is so **enormous** that he often has trouble finding a big enough parking space.
- Far bigger than elephants, the most **enormous** land animals ever to walk on Earth were dinosaurs.

___*Enormous* means   a. very small   b. very large   c. very good-looking

6 irritate
(**ihr**-uh-tayt)
– verb

- When James plays his new drums, the loud sounds he makes **irritate** the whole neighborhood.
- I **irritated** my boss when I didn't get to work on time and didn't call to say I would be late.

___*Irritate* means   a. help   b. calm down   c. bother

7 mention
(**men**-shuhn)
– verb

- I must not **mention** the surprise party to anyone at work. No one there can keep a secret.
- When Mrs. Ortiz talks to friends, she often **mentions** her brother, a well-known writer. She is very proud of him.

___*Mention* means   a. talk about   b. forget about   c. think about

8 surround
(suh-**round**)
– verb

- Piles of books and paper **surround** Eliza when she studies for exams.
- Like sharks, the TV reporters **surrounded** the couple so they could not move away and then asked them how they felt about the death of their children.

___*Surround* means   a. make happy   b. be all around   c. move away from

Matching Words with Meanings

Here are the meanings, or *definitions*, of the eight new words. Write each word next to its meaning. The sentences above and on the facing page will help you decide on the meaning of each word.

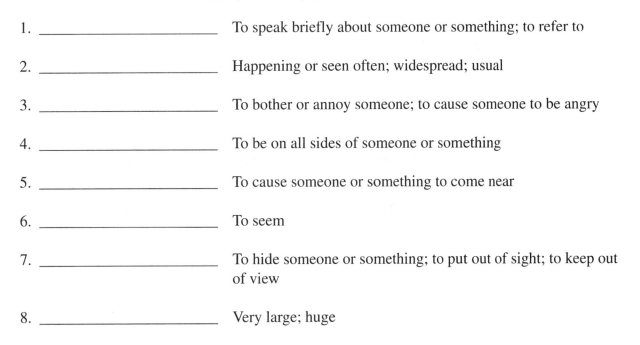

1. _____ To speak briefly about someone or something; to refer to

2. _____ Happening or seen often; widespread; usual

3. _____ To bother or annoy someone; to cause someone to be angry

4. _____ To be on all sides of someone or something

5. _____ To cause someone or something to come near

6. _____ To seem

7. _____ To hide someone or something; to put out of sight; to keep out of view

8. _____ Very large; huge

BE CAREFUL: Don't go any further until you know the answers above are correct. Then you can use the meanings to help you in the following activities. After a while, you will know the words so well that you won't need to check the definitions at all.

Adding One Word to an Item

Complete each item below by writing one word from the box on the answer line at the left. Use each word once.

| a. **appeared** | c. **common** | e. **enormous** | g. **mentioned** |
| b. **attract** | d. **conceal** | f. **irritate** | h. **surrounded** |

_____1. The hamburger was so . . ? . . that, served with cheese and bacon, it had more fat than one person should eat in a whole week.

_____2. The actors in the high-school play . . ? . . to be unsure about their lines.

_____3. Sally loves butterflies, so she plants flowers that . . ? . . them.

_____4. When I . . ? . . my wish to get a puppy, my landlord shook his head and said he did not want dogs in the building.

_____5. Carlos wore a hat to . . ? . . his new haircut from the rest of the world.

_____6. The best-liked and most . . ? . . flavors of ice cream are vanilla and chocolate.

_____7. My roommates . . ? . . me when they leave dirty dishes and half-eaten food on the kitchen table.

_____8. Three dogs . . ? . . the tree, barking at the cat sitting on a high branch overhead.

Adding Two Words to an Item

Complete each item below by writing **two** words from the box on the answer lines at the left. Use each word once.

| a. **appeared** | c. **common** | e. **enormous** | g. **mentioned** |
| b. **attracted** | d. **concealed** | f. **irritates** | h. **surrounded** |

_____ 1–2. When the burglars saw that they were . . ? . . by police, they dropped the jewelry they had . . ? . . in their clothing.

_____ 3–4. A . . ? . ., everyday problem that really . . ? . . me is drivers' keeping their radios on so loud that my house shakes as they pass by.

_____ 5–6. The . . ? . . sign on the side of the road . . ? . . many people to the opening of the new mall.

_____ 7–8. When I . . ? . . a new job opening at the place where I work, Pilar . . ? . . to be very interested.

Showing You Understand the Words

PART A

In the space at the left, write the letter of the choice that best completes the sentence or answers the question.

____ 1. After working in the hot sun all day, you would probably **appear**
   a. relaxed.
   b. happy.
   c. tired.

____ 2. You might **attract** a rabbit
   a. in a report on pets.
   b. with a carrot.
   c. by putting it in a box in the basement.

____ 3. If you are planning a surprise birthday party, you would **conceal** your plans from
   a. the person who is having a birthday.
   b. the guests who are coming.
   c. the person who is bringing the cake.

____ 4. Which of the following might **irritate** you if you are trying to relax?
   a. Cats meowing outside your window
   b. A soft blanket
   c. Quiet, sweet music

PART B

In the space at the left, write the letter of the choice that best completes the sentence or answers the question.

____ 5. Which of the following is a **common** happening on the weekend?
   a. Going to the movies
   b. Getting a divorce
   c. Saving a drowning person

____ 6. An **enormous** amount of water can be found in
   a. a cup.
   b. a puddle.
   c. an ocean.

____ 7. If a friend **mentions** George, that means he or she is
   a. hiding George.
   b. talking about George.
   c. doing something that bothers George.

____ 8. To **surround** a back yard with bushes, a person would need to plant bushes
   a. on all sides of the yard.
   b. along one side of the yard.
   c. at the back edge of the yard.

Adding Words to a Reading

A. Little Lies

Read the following paragraph carefully. Then fill in each blank with a word from the box. Use each word once.

a. **appear**	b. **common**	c. **conceal**	d. **mention**

If telling lies is wrong, why is it so (1)_____? One reason is that lying just a little bit makes it easier for people to talk to each other. When people meet for the first time, they often ask, "How are you?" even if they don't care. Such a question makes them (2)_____ interested and friendly. And no matter how angry or sad we feel, most of us answer, "I'm fine, thanks." Such social lies (3)_____ things we would rather not talk about and help keep conversations moving along. Another reason people lie is to be kind to others. Let's say someone you know gets a new haircut that you think looks terrible. You might act as though you did not see the haircut and not (4)_____ it at all. Or just to be nice, you might make a comment° such as, "I like your new haircut." In other words, even though we are taught as children that lying is wrong, sometimes it can be easier—and kinder—not to tell the whole truth.

B. Rudeness at the Movies

Read the following paragraph carefully. Then fill in each blank with a word from the box. Use each word once.

a. **attract**	b. **enormous**	c. **irritate**	d. **surround**

Most people like being scared, at least a little. After all, that is why movies with monsters or creepy ghosts (5)_____ millions of people into theaters each year. But sometimes the strangest things in the theater are not on screen. Instead, they are the people sitting next to you or behind you. For example, whenever I see a movie, there are always several rude people nearby who (6)_____ me by talking throughout the entire film. And do they speak about the movie? Never. They talk about an argument they had with a friend, a great party they went to, or their plans for later, when the movie is over. And if that isn't bad enough, the tallest person in the theater always chooses to sit right in front of me, blocking my view. I move this way and that, trying to see around the (7)_____ person in front of me. Then the people behind me get mad, start kicking the back of my seat, and yell at me to stop moving around so much. At this point, I begin to think that the reason these people come to the movies is not to see the movies. No, their real purpose° is to bother me. So when I go to a scary movie, I become afraid—not of monsters or of ghosts—but of the strange human beings that (8)_____ me in the theater.

Using the Words When Writing and Talking

Now that you understand the meanings of the eight new words in the chapter, you are ready to use them on paper and in speaking. Complete each sentence below in a way that shows you really know what each **boldfaced** word means. Take a few minutes to think about your answer before writing it down and saying it out loud.

1. A person would **appear** angry if _____

_____

2. The smell of freshly baked cookies **attracts** _____

_____

3. One **common** problem people have at work is _____

_____

4. A good way to **conceal** that you dislike someone is to _____

_____

5. We could tell that our guests had an **enormous** hunger because they _____

_____

6. At home, it **irritates** me when _____

_____

7. When I spoke to a friend this week, I **mentioned** _____

_____

8. Powerful people often **surround** themselves with _____

_____

Scores	Adding One Word to an Item	_____%	Showing You Understand the Words	_____%
	Adding Two Words to an Item	_____%	Adding Words to a Reading	_____%

Number right: 8 = 100%, 7 = 88%, 6 = 75%, 5 = 63%, 4 = 50%, 3 = 38%, 2 = 25%, 1 = 13%
Enter your scores above and in the vocabulary performance chart on the inside back cover of the book.

achieve	injury
condition	major
duty	seldom
exhaust	value

Learning Eight New Words

In the space at the left, write the letter of the meaning closest to that of each **boldfaced** word. Use the other words (the *context*) in each sentence to help you figure out the word's meaning.

1 achieve
(uh-**cheev**)
– verb

• In order to **achieve** their dreams of doing well in school, students must work hard and study every day.

• Sandra is a hard worker—I know that she will **achieve** great success in whatever she decides to do.

___*Achieve* means   a. lose   b. have trouble with   c. reach

2 condition
(kuhn-**dish**-uhn)
– noun

• After we fixed the broken steps and painted the shutters, the outside of the house was in good **condition**.

• With its flat tire and missing seat, the bike was in poor **condition**.

___*Condition* means   a. shape something is in   b. neighborhood   c. news

3 duty
(**doo**-tee)
– noun

• My dog thinks it is his **duty** to guard the house from any living thing— including me!

• When I was in grade school, my teacher gave me the **duty** of cleaning the chalkboard every day.

___*Duty* means   a. job   b. hobby   c. problem

4 exhaust
(eg-**zawst**)
– verb

• People who don't get enough sleep can **exhaust** themselves so much that they get sick.

• Jody works so hard that just watching her **exhausts** me.

___*Exhaust* means   a. make happy   b. make strong   c. make tired

5 injury
(**in**-juh-ree)
– noun

• The doctors used an x-ray machine to get a better look at Anne's ankle **injury**.

• Thanks to seat belts and air bags, people may have bad car accidents and still walk away without serious **injury**.

___*Injury* means   a. movement   b. harm   c. good health

6 major
(**may**-jur)
– adjective

- TV programs are sometimes stopped so that a **major** news story can be reported.
- The Lees are planning **major** repairs on their house, including putting on a new roof.

___*Major* means   a. small   b. not expensive   c. big

7 seldom
(**sel**-duhm)
– adverb

- Because foxes hunt at night, people **seldom** see these beautiful animals.
- An excellent employee is **seldom** late for work.

___*Seldom* means   a. every day   b. not often   c. on purpose

8 value
(**val**-yoo)
– noun

- This ring was not expensive, but it has a lot of **value** to me because it was a gift from my great-grandmother.
- The thieves stole the painting from the museum because the painting had great **value**.

___*Value* means   a. reason   b. color   c. worth

Matching Words with Meanings

Here are the meanings, or *definitions*, of the eight new words. Write each word next to its meaning. The sentences above and on the facing page will help you decide on the meaning of each word.

1. _____   The state or shape that something or someone is in

2. _____   Harm, often to the body

3. _____   Not often

4. _____   Something that someone has to do

5. _____   The worth of something—in money or in importance

6. _____   Important; large

7. _____   To reach a goal, often after hard work or difficulty

8. _____   To cause someone to become very tired

BE CAREFUL: Don't go any further until you know the answers above are correct. Then you can use the meanings to help you in the following activities. After a while, you will know the words so well that you won't need to check the definitions at all.

Adding One Word to an Item

Complete each item below by writing one word from the box on the answer line at the left. Use each word once.

a. **achieved**	c. **duty**	e. **injury**	g. **seldom**
b. **condition**	d. **exhausted**	f. **major**	h. **value**

_____ 1. Covered with broken bottles and other trash, the park was in bad . . ? . . .

_____ 2. Believe it or not, but a strong sneeze can cause . . ? . . to the back and neck.

_____ 3. My parents raised me to feel it is my . . ? . . to help those in need.

_____ 4. Angie needs a lot of sleep, so she . . ? . . stays up past 10 p.m.

_____ 5. Our school swimming team . . ? . . first place in the statewide contest.

_____ 6. Their house cost fifteen thousand dollars in 1975, but its . . ? . . has gone up greatly since then.

_____ 7. School was called off because of a . . ? . . snowstorm.

_____ 8. Lifting heavy loads all day in the hot sun . . ? . . Warren, who was not used to such hard work.

Adding Two Words to an Item

Complete each item below by writing **two** words from the box on the answer lines at the left. Use each word once.

a. **achieved**	c. **duty**	e. **injury**	g. **seldom**
b. **condition**	d. **exhaust**	f. **major**	h. **value**

_____
_____ 1–2. Because Juanita is careful to warm up before she runs, she . . ? . . gets a painful . . ? . . like a pulled muscle.

_____
_____ 3–4. Before a party, my neighbors . . ? . . themselves trying to make their home look perfect. That is silly. Their good health has more . . ? . . than a neat home.

_____
_____ 5–6. It is a pet owner's . . ? . . to make sure pets get the shots they need to protect them against . . ? . . illnesses.

_____
_____ 7–8. Malik and Thea bought an old, rundown house. Two years later, they had . . ? . . their goal of fixing all the problems so that the house was in good . . ? . . .

Showing You Understand the Words

PART A

In the space at the left, write the letter of the choice that best completes the sentence or answers the question.

____ 1. Which of the following is a **duty** that many people have?
    a. Watching TV
    b. Going to baseball games
    c. Doing the laundry

____ 2. Which of the following would be likely to **exhaust** you?
    a. Watching a movie
    b. Working for sixteen hours in a row
    c. Driving to the neighborhood dry cleaner

____ 3. If you **seldom** see your two closest friends, you probably
    a. live far away from them.
    b. live close to them.
    c. see them every day.

____ 4. How would you find out the **value** of a bracelet?
    a. Wash it in the sink
    b. Drop it to see if it breaks
    c. Ask a jeweler how much it is worth

PART B

In the space at the left, write the letter of the choice that best completes the sentence or answers the question.

____ 5. A person who **achieves** success as an athlete probably
    a. does not like sports.
    b. is skilled and hard-working.
    c. has not done well but keeps trying.

____ 6. Which of the following describes the **condition** of a car that is for sale?
    a. It needs new brakes and some body work.
    b. It once belonged to a man in California.
    c. It will be used to take people to the airport.

____ 7. Which of these is an **injury** that would make it hard for a person to play soccer?
    a. The person's soccer ball is missing.
    b. The person has no one to play with.
    c. The person has a broken leg.

____ 8. Which of these would be described as a **major** accident?
    a. One car lightly bumps into another.
    b. A train full of passengers falls into the river.
    c. A bus knocks over a garbage can.

Adding Words to a Reading

A. The Truth About Drinking

Read the following paragraph carefully. Then fill in each blank with a word from the box. Use each word once.

a. **achieve**	b. **conditions**	c. **injury**	d. **major**

"This one's for you!" "I love you, man." "It's a light beer for a heavy world." These are some of the lines used in beer ads on TV. Ads like these make drinking seem fun and good. They make young people begin to think that drinking is a way for them to (1)_____ happiness and success. These ads are not honest about the problems that drinking can cause. They never show the sickness, sadness, and loss of a job that are the real (2)_____ of many people who drink heavily. The ads never show someone dealing with a serious (3)_____ caused by a drunk driver. The ads never mention° the families broken up because of the violence of a person who drinks too much alcohol. In short, these flashy ads do not tell the truth about the (4)_____ difficulties that alcohol causes for people all over the world.

B. A Life Out of Balance

Read the following paragraph carefully. Then fill in each blank with a word from the box. Use each word once.

a. **duty**	b. **exhausts**	c. **seldom**	d. **value**

Being lazy is not a good thing. However, constant° work is not good either. Jerome is an example of someone who never stops working. He works so hard at his job that he (5)_____ himself. When he is at home, he is always fixing something in the house or working in the yard. Jerome loves his wife and children. He takes his (6)_____ to be a good husband and father very seriously. The problem is that Jerome (7)_____ spends any time with his family. He is always too busy working. Jerome knows the (8)_____ of hard work. Sadly, he does not understand that spending time with his family is worth a lot, too.

Using the Words When Writing and Talking

Now that you understand the meanings of the eight new words in the chapter, you are ready to use them on paper and in speaking. Complete each sentence below in a way that shows you really know what each **boldfaced** word means. Take a few minutes to think about your answer before writing it down and saying it out loud.

1. Parents should teach children that they can **achieve** their dreams if _____

    _____

2. The beach was in bad **condition**. It _____

    _____

3. The **duty** at home that I like the least is _____

    _____

4. Work that often **exhausts** me is _____

    _____

5. I would know an **injury** is bad if _____

    _____

6. A **major** problem in this country is _____

    _____

7. In the spring and summer, the leaves on a tree **seldom** drop off unless _____

    _____

8. Something I have that has great **value** to me is _____

    _____

Scores	Adding One Word to an Item	_____%	Showing You Understand the Words	_____%
	Adding Two Words to an Item	_____%	Adding Words to a Reading	_____%

Number right: 8 = 100%, 7 = 88%, 6 = 75%, 5 = 63%, 4 = 50%, 3 = 38%, 2 = 25%, 1 = 13%
Enter your scores above and in the vocabulary performance chart on the inside back cover of the book.

advance	interrupt
consider	praise
delicate	request
grasp	succeed

Learning Eight New Words

In the space at the left, write the letter of the meaning closest to that of each **boldfaced** word. Use the other words (the *context*) in each sentence to help you figure out the word's meaning.

1 advance
(ad-**vanss**)
– verb

- If our baseball team wins tonight, we will **advance** to first place.
- We watched as the dark clouds **advanced** toward us.

___*Advance* means   a. stop moving   b. move forward   c. move away

2 consider
(kuhn-**sid**-ur)
– verb

- If you **consider** the problem much longer, you will not have time to do anything about it.
- When he goes to a restaurant, Jeffrey carefully **considers** everything on the menu before ordering.

___*Consider* means   a. cover up   b. think about   c. want

3 delicate
(**del**-i-kit)
– adjective

- Mom's crystal plates are so **delicate** that we use them only for very special family dinners.
- Because infants' bones are **delicate**, babies should be handled gently.

___*Delicate* means   a. light in color   b. strong   c. hurt easily

4 grasp
(**grasp**)
– verb

- When people are learning to drive, they often **grasp** the steering wheel tightly.
- With large smiles on their faces, the children **grasped** the ice-cream cones and started eating right away.

___*Grasp* means   a. grab   b. slap   c. drop

5 interrupt
(*in*-tuh-**ruhpt**)
– verb

- Dad gets angry when phone calls **interrupt** our dinner.
- Fran often **interrupts** the teacher with silly questions.

___*Interrupt* means   a. calm   b. help   c. stop for a short time

6 praise
(prayz)
– verb

- Most people in town **praise** our hard-working new mayor.
- My sister **praises** the new science-fiction series on TV, but I don't like it at all.

___*Praise* means

a. leave alone   b. dislike   c. say good things about

7 request
(ri-**kwest**)
– noun

- You may borrow my car, but I have one **request**: Please fill the gas tank before you return the car to me.
- The singer took **requests** from people wanting to hear their favorite songs.

___*Request* means

a. problem   b. answer   c. something that is asked for

8 succeed
(suhk-**seed**)
– verb

- It takes both hard work and luck to **succeed** in show business.
- On his third try, Jason **succeeded** in passing his driver's test.

___*Succeed* means

a. do badly   b. do well   c. pay too much

Matching Words with Meanings

Here are the meanings, or *definitions*, of the eight new words. Write each word next to its meaning. The sentences above and on the facing page will help you decide on the meaning of each word.

1. _____ To grab something and hold it tightly

2. _____ To do well at something

3. _____ To move forward or ahead

4. _____ To say good things about someone or something

5. _____ Easily broken

6. _____ To stop something for a time

7. _____ Something that someone is asked to do

8. _____ To think carefully about something

BE CAREFUL: Don't go any further until you know the answers above are correct. Then you can use the meanings to help you in the following activities. After a while, you will know the words so well that you won't need to check the definitions at all.

Adding One Word to an Item

Complete each item below by writing one word from the box on the answer line at the left. Use each word once.

| a. **advanced** | c. **delicate** | e. **interrupted** | g. **request** |
| b. **considered** | d. **grasped** | f. **praised** | h. **succeeding** |

_____ 1. The movers packed the . . ? . . crystal glasses inside soft tissue paper to keep them from breaking.

_____ 2. Kim . . ? . . the job offer for a few days before deciding to accept it.

_____ 3. The librarian made a strange . . ? . . . He asked the students to make as much noise as possible.

_____ 4. With one hand, the hero . . ? . . the young boy and pulled him away from the giant shark.

_____ 5. A rainstorm . . ? . . the ball game for fifteen minutes.

_____ 6. The art teacher . . ? . . Ethan's beautiful drawing.

_____ 7. Each day, the soldiers packed up their supplies and . . ? . . further into the northern countries.

_____ 8. Joan must be . . ? . . at her new job. She has already gotten a big raise.

Adding Two Words to an Item

Complete each item below by writing **two** words from the box on the answer lines at the left. Use each word once.

| a. **advanced** | c. **delicate** | e. **interrupted** | g. **request** |
| b. **considered** | d. **grasp** | f. **praised** | h. **succeeded** |

_____ 1–2. I reminded my children that they shouldn't . . ? . . the kitten as if it
_____ were a toy. Its bones are . . ? . . and could break.

_____ 3–4. Before speaking to the group, I carefully . . ? . . what I wanted to say
_____ and then . . ? . . to the front of the room.

_____ 5–6. When the little girl finally . . ? . . in tying her shoelaces, her parents
_____ . . ? . . her warmly.

_____ 7–8. The teacher . . ? . . my report with the . . ? . . that I speak more loudly.
_____

Showing You Understand the Words

PART A

In the space at the left, write the letter of the choice that best completes the sentence or answers the question.

____ 1. If you **considered** quitting your job, you probably
    a. like your job a lot.
    b. don't like your job.
    c. have already left your job.

____ 2. Which of the following would you think of as **delicate**?
    a. A brick
    b. A city
    c. A flower stem

____ 3. If you want to **praise** a friend's cooking, which of these might you say?
    a. "This tastes burned."
    b. "What do you call this strange-looking dish?"
    c. "This is delicious."

____ 4. Which of these is a **request** that you might make to a waiter in a coffee shop?
    a. "This is a nice restaurant."
    b. "I like your shirt."
    c. "Please bring me a slice of apple pie and a cup of coffee."

PART B

In the space at the left, write the letter of the choice that best completes the sentence or answers the question.

____ 5. A child who finishes second grade **advances** into
    a. first grade.
    b. second grade.
    c. third grade.

____ 6. Which of these would most people want to **grasp**?
    a. A small tree covered with thorns
    b. A hundred-dollar bill
    c. A piece of moldy bread

____ 7. Which of these would **interrupt** a picnic?
    a. A rain shower
    b. A beautiful day
    c. Hot dogs and hamburgers

____ 8. Most people who **succeed** in school
    a. study hard at home.
    b. never study at home.
    c. forget to do their homework.

Adding Words to a Reading

A. Animals Were First

Read the following paragraph carefully. Then fill in each blank with a word from the box. Use each word once.

a. **advance**	b. **delicate**	c. **grasp**	d. **succeeded**

Many animals walked the Earth long before humans. The best-known of these animals were the dinosaurs. Some dinosaurs were enormous° and scary. When these big animals hunted, they would (1)_____ slowly, (2)_____ the hunted animal in their sharp claws, and tear it to pieces. But not all dinosaurs were this big. Some were the size of today's chickens. These small animals hunted for the eggs of other dinosaurs. With their pointy teeth, they would crack the (3)_____ shells they found and eat the tasty juices inside them. And their size made it easy for them to run away quickly from larger animals. Dinosaurs of all sizes died out millions of years ago. Scientists have come up with different reasons why dinosaurs stopped walking the Earth. But no one knows for sure what happened. However, some animals from several million years ago (4)_____ in living from those times until now. For example, the snakes, turtles, and crocodiles of today are almost exactly like the ones that lived in the time of the dinosaurs.

B. Call Waiting—Oh, No!

Read the following paragraph carefully. Then fill in each blank with a word from the box. Use each word once.

a. **considered**	b. **interrupt**	c. **praise**	d. **request**

Have you ever (5)_____ buying an answering machine or getting "call waiting"? Let me tell you what I think about these inventions. I used to hate telephone answering machines. I felt nervous talking to a machine. When I heard the (6)_____ "Please start talking after you hear the beep," I forgot what I wanted to say. But I have gotten over my fears and do not hate answering machines anymore. I can even (7)_____ them as being useful. After all, they do permit° people to pass along information even when nobody is able to answer the phone. However, I will never stop hating call waiting. Talking to people who have call waiting drives me crazy. When they hear the little beep that tells them someone else is calling, they (8)_____ our conversation and say, "Just a minute, please. I'll see who's calling and come right back." I am left holding onto the phone, thinking, "Why is the other person who called more important than I am?" To me, "call waiting" really means "I am *left* waiting."

Using the Words When Writing and Talking

Now that you understand the meanings of the eight new words in the chapter, you are ready to use them on paper and in speaking. Complete each sentence below in a way that shows you really know what each **boldfaced** word means. Take a few minutes to think about your answer before writing it down and saying it out loud.

1. If a river floods, the water might **advance** to _____

    _____

2. For a long time, I **considered** _____

    _____

3. One of the most **delicate** things I own is _____

    _____

4. People who get nervous on rides at amusement parks often **grasp** _____

    _____

5. One night my sleep was **interrupted** by _____

    _____

6. Parents should **praise** their kids when _____

    _____

7. A **request** that is often heard in my house is, " _____

    _____?"

8. I know I will **succeed** in _____

    _____

Scores	Adding One Word to an Item	_____%	Showing You Understand the Words	_____%
	Adding Two Words to an Item	_____%	Adding Words to a Reading	_____%

Number right: 8 = 100%, 7 = 88%, 6 = 75%, 5 = 63%, 4 = 50%, 3 = 38%, 2 = 25%, 1 = 13%
Enter your scores above and in the vocabulary performance chart on the inside back cover of the book.

attempt	imitate
courteous	permanent
explore	recognize
hopeless	sufficient

Learning Eight New Words

In the space at the left, write the letter of the meaning closest to that of each **boldfaced** word. Use the other words (the *context*) in each sentence to help you figure out the word's meaning.

1 attempt
(uh-**tempt**)
– verb

___*Attempt* means

- Don't **attempt** to ski without first taking lessons.
- Many climbers have **attempted** to reach the top of Mount Everest, but few have made it.

    a. repeat   b. try   c. remember

2 courteous
(**kur**-tee-uhss)
– adjective

___*Courteous* means

- It was **courteous** of you to give your seat to the old gentleman.
- When the spinach was passed, the **courteous** little girl said "No, thank you," but her rude brother said "Yuck!"

    a. silly   b. frightened   c. thoughtful

3 explore
(ek-**splor**)
– verb

___*Explore* means

- In the years ahead, humans will **explore** the planet Mars and possibly even live there.
- Our new kitten **explored** every inch of the apartment before deciding where to sleep.

    a. search   b. lose   c. fear

4 hopeless
(**hohp**-liss)
– adjective

___*Hopeless* means

- When the flood washed away their homes and everything they owned, the people in town felt **hopeless**.
- When my neighbor lost his job and wasn't able to pay his bills, he began to feel **hopeless**.

    a. happy   b. without hope   c. tired

5 imitate
(**im**-uh-tayt)
– verb

___*Imitate* means

- Because Rosa looks up to her big brother so much, she tries to **imitate** the way he walks and talks.
- It's best just to be yourself and not try to **imitate** anyone else.

    a. see   b. hide   c. copy

6 permanent
(**pur**-muh-nuhnt)
– adjective

• Kate did not want a **permanent** job; she wanted one that lasted only for the summer.

• When Bruce colored his hair green for Halloween, he didn't know the color was **permanent**. He thought it would wash out.

___*Permanent* means   a. good   b. new   c. long-lasting

7 recognize
(**rek**-uhg-*nize*)
– verb

• After not seeing your cousin for two years, do you think you will **recognize** her? Or have you forgotten how she looks?

• Jake **recognized** his neighbor immediately, even though she had lost a lot of weight.

___*Recognize* means   a. know from before   b. not like   c. lose

8 sufficient
(suh-**fish**-uhnt)
– adjective

• Do you have **sufficient** gas in the tank to drive home, or should we stop at the gas station?

• There is **sufficient** chicken for dinner tonight and for leftovers tomorrow night.

___*Sufficient* means   a. expensive   b. too much   c. enough

Matching Words with Meanings

Here are the meanings, or *definitions*, of the eight new words. Write each word next to its meaning. The sentences above and on the facing page will help you decide on the meaning of each word.

1. _____   To try hard to do something; to make an effort

2. _____   Lasting a long time

3. _____   Believing that things will turn out badly; having no hope

4. _____   To copy how someone else behaves; to act like someone else

5. _____   Enough; as much as is needed

6. _____   To travel around a new, unknown place to see what it is like

7. _____   To know someone or something from an earlier time

8. _____   Polite; having good manners

BE CAREFUL: Don't go any further until you know the answers above are correct. Then you can use the meanings to help you in the following activities. After a while, you will know the words so well that you won't need to check the definitions at all.

Adding One Word to an Item

Complete each item below by writing one word from the box on the answer line at the left. Use each word once.

| a. **attempts** | c. **explored** | e. **imitate** | g. **recognizes** |
| b. **courteous** | d. **hopeless** | f. **permanent** | h. **sufficient** |

_____ 1. My dog doesn't bark when I drive into the garage because she . . ? . . the sound of my car.

_____ 2. I get upset when I see my children . . ? . . the violence they see in movies.

_____ 3. Seeing all the difficulty I was having with my packages, the . . ? . . clerk offered to help me carry them.

_____ 4. Before they chose a place to camp, the hikers . . ? . . the woods to find the best spot.

_____ 5. Jeffrey and Linda bought a house together, so I guess they think their relationship will be . . ? . . .

_____ 6. I have . . ? . . cash to pay for my movie ticket and yours, too.

_____ 7. Even though the class is hard for her, Luisa . . ? . . to do her best.

_____ 8. The lost hikers felt . . ? . . when they couldn't find their way back to camp.

Adding Two Words to an Item

Complete each item below by writing **two** words from the box on the answer lines at the left. Use each word once.

| a. **attempted** | c. **explore** | e. **imitating** | g. **recognize** |
| b. **courteous** | d. **hopeless** | f. **permanent** | h. **sufficient** |

_____
_____ 1–2. You may feel very sad and even . . ? . . if you think that your problems are . . ? . . and will never change.

_____
_____ 3–4. I was pleased when my bossy little boy began . . ? . . the kind and . . ? . . ways of his uncle.

_____
_____ 5–6. Several hours is not . . ? . . time to . . ? . . a large city like Chicago; you need to spend at least two full days.

_____
_____ 7–8. Everyone at the Halloween party wore a costume, so it was hard to see who was who. We . . ? . . to . . ? . . our friends by their height and voices.

Showing You Understand the Words

PART A

In the space at the left, write the letter of the choice that best completes the sentence or answers the question.

____ 1. Which might you say if you **attempted** to end a phone call?
   a. "Let me tell you what happened to me today."
   b. "Fill me in on all that's going on in your life."
   c. "Thanks for calling. I'll let you go now."

____ 2. If you want to **explore** Walt Disney World, you need
   a. to know Mickey Mouse's life story.
   b. strong legs and lots of money.
   c. several tired children who hate long lines.

____ 3. Before you **imitate** your newly married cousins at a family party, it's best to make sure they
   a. are quiet and shy.
   b. are in a bad mood.
   c. have a sense of humor.

____ 4. Which is most likely to be a **permanent** part of your life?
   a. The house you buy
   b. A movie you rent
   c. Your underwear

PART B

In the space at the left, write the letter of the choice that best completes the sentence or answers the question.

____ 5. A **courteous** person who receives a terrible birthday present might say,
   a. "This is the worst present anyone ever gave me."
   b. "Is this a joke?"
   c. "How kind of you to think of me on my birthday."

____ 6. Which of these might make a person feel **hopeless**?
   a. Winning the lottery
   b. Getting a very serious illness
   c. Seeing a funny movie

____ 7. A grade school teacher who **recognizes** a student from long ago might say,
   a. "Sorry, but I don't remember you."
   b. "It's good to see you again."
   c. "What grade school did you go to?"

____ 8. If people have **sufficient** time to relax on the weekend, they usually return to work feeling
   a. rested.
   b. tired.
   c. angry at their coworkers.

Adding Words to a Reading

A. A Cab Driver for Now

Read the following paragraph carefully. Then fill in each blank with a word from the box. Use each word once.

a. **attempted**	b. **courteous**	c. **permanent**	d. **recognized**

   As soon as James drove his taxi up to the curb, he (1)_____ the man in the expensive suit. It was the guy who never gave him a good tip. Even so, James was (2)_____—he asked, "May I take your bags?" and opened the cab door for the man. During the ride, James (3)_____ to have a friendly talk, but the man said nothing in return. "Oh well," James said to himself. "That's OK." In his heart, James knew that driving a cab was not going to be (4)_____. From the time he was little, James had loved getting up in front of people. He had starred in every play his schools had put on—from grade school through high school. Being the center of attention made him happy. Deep down, James felt that he had the talent° needed to become a movie and TV star. And when he became rich and famous, James promised himself, he would always be friendly to cab drivers— and leave them a big tip!

B. Thoughts at the Mall

Read the following paragraph carefully. Then fill in each blank with a word from the box. Use each word once.

a. **explore**	b. **hopeless**	c. **imitate**	d. **sufficient**

   On Sunday afternoons, I often (5)_____ one of the nearby shopping malls. I enjoy eating in the food court and looking at all the people. It always makes me laugh to see the middle-school kids pretending° they are all grown-up. They dress the same as older kids and even (6)_____ the ways that high school kids talk. Most of all, though, when I am at the mall, I love to shop. But no matter how much money I bring, it is never (7)_____ for all the things I'd like to buy. In fact, I know that I will *never* have enough money to own everything I would like. That could make me feel sad, even (8)_____. But I don't let it. I know that no amount of money will buy what is really important: family and friends, health, and happiness. So I buy only those things I really need and forget the rest. Life is too short to worry about what you don't have.

Using the Words When Writing and Talking

Now that you understand the meanings of the eight new words in the chapter, you are ready to use them on paper and in speaking. Complete each sentence below in a way that shows you really know what each **boldfaced** word means. Take a few minutes to think about your answer before writing it down and saying it out loud.

1. The first time I **attempted** to speak in front of a large group, I _____

_____

2. Many people are not **courteous** drivers. When they drive, they _____

_____

3. We **explored** the attic because _____

_____

4. Fans would feel **hopeless** about their team if _____

_____

5. Sometimes I try to **imitate** the way _____

_____

6. I made a **permanent** change in my life when I _____

_____

7. We had trouble **recognizing** our old neighborhood because _____

_____

8. I saved for several months so I would have **sufficient** money to _____

_____

Scores	Adding One Word to an Item	_____%	Showing You Understand the Words	_____%
	Adding Two Words to an Item	_____%	Adding Words to a Reading	_____%

Number right: 8 = 100%, 7 = 88%, 6 = 75%, 5 = 63%, 4 = 50%, 3 = 38%, 2 = 25%, 1 = 13%
Enter your scores above and in the vocabulary performance chart on the inside back cover of the book.

assist	flaw
competent	positive
enemy	sample
examine	urge

Learning Eight New Words

In the space at the left, write the letter of the meaning closest to that of each **boldfaced** word. Use the other words (the *context*) in each sentence to help you figure out the word's meaning.

1 **assist**
(uh-**sisst**)
– verb

- Seeing-eye dogs are trained to **assist** people who have problems with sight.
- Neighbors and friends **assisted** the family whose house had burned down by giving them food, clothes, and money.

___*Assist* means   a. find   b. look at carefully   c. help

2 **competent**
(**kom**-pi-tuhnt)
– adjective

- After seeing him burn several pieces of toast, I knew that Aya was far from being a **competent** cook.
- Sandra is not good at tennis, but she is a **competent** skater.

___*Competent* means   a. dangerous   b. skillful   c. boring

3 **enemy**
(**en**-uh-mee)
– noun

- Even though Bob and I are friends, his dog growls at me as though I am an **enemy**.
- In the science-fiction movie I saw last night, the **enemy** of the human race is a large, purple monster that eats people.

___*Enemy* means   a. someone who   b. someone who   c. someone who
                     is perfect   is liked   is hated

4 **examine**
(eg-**zam**-uhn)
– verb

- In the supermarket, shoppers **examine** the fruit and vegetables to make sure they are fresh.
- The airline **examined** the airplane that crashed to find out what had caused the accident.

___*Examine* means   a. leave   b. use   c. look at carefully

5 **flaw**
(**flaw**)
– noun

- Because the sweater has a **flaw**, I was able to buy it at a really good price.
- No one is perfect. Everyone has **flaws**.

___*Flaw* means   a. something wrong   b. good part   c. good looks

6 positive
(**poz**-uh-tiv)
– adjective

• Part of a coach's job is to keep members of the team feeling **positive**, even when they are not winning.

• Myra is a **positive** person who always look on the bright side.

___*Positive* means   a. sad   b. healthy   c. hopeful

7 sample
(**sam**-puhl)
– noun

• The doctor took a **sample** of Jen's blood for testing.

• Before we painted the living room, we brought home **samples** of three different colors.

___*Sample* means   a. picture   b. little bit   c. large amount

8 urge
(**urj**)
– noun

• As she walked past a beauty salon, Lola felt a sudden **urge** to color her hair bright red.

• After lying around all day, I got the **urge** to go out running.

___*Urge* means   a. dislike   b. fear   c. strong wish

Matching Words with Meanings

Here are the meanings, or *definitions*, of the eight new words. Write each word next to its meaning. The sentences above and on the facing page will help you decide on the meaning of each word.

1. _____   To look at carefully

2. _____   Cheerful; upbeat; sure of oneself

3. _____   A sudden desire to do something

4. _____   Being good at something; able to do something well; skilled

5. _____   A problem or fault that keeps something from being perfect

6. _____   To help

7. _____   Someone whom one hates and wishes to harm

8. _____   A small part of something that shows what the whole is like

BE CAREFUL: Don't go any further until you know the answers above are correct. Then you can use the meanings to help you in the following activities. After a while, you will know the words so well that you won't need to check the definitions at all.

Adding One Word to an Item

Complete each item below by writing one word from the box on the answer line at the left. Use each word once.

a. **assisted**	c. **enemies**	e. **flaws**	g. **samples**
b. **competent**	d. **examined**	f. **positive**	h. **urge**

_____ 1. Max felt an . . ? . . to surprise his boyhood friend, whom he hadn't seen in years, with a phone call.

_____ 2. Guards at the department store worked with the police and . . ? . . them in the search for the shoplifter.

_____ 3. We returned two dishes to the store because several of them had small . . ? . . we had not seen when we bought them.

_____ 4. When someone is killed, the police always ask friends and family if the murdered person had any . . ? . . .

_____ 5. Studies show that people with a . . ? . . view of life are healthier than people who always look on the bad side.

_____ 6. Lonnie . . ? . . the wrapped gift closely, trying to guess what was inside.

_____ 7. Some ice-cream stores give customers . . ? . . of their flavors to taste.

_____ 8. After drinking alcohol, even a . . ? . . driver is unsafe behind the wheel.

Adding Two Words to an Item

Complete each item below by writing **two** words from the box on the answer lines at the left. Use each word once.

a. **assist**	c. **enemy**	e. **flaws**	g. **sample**
b. **competent**	d. **examined**	f. **positive**	h. **urge**

_____
_____ 1–2. Because the word "used" was stamped on the cover of the book, I . . ? . . its pages closely. Since I found no . . ? . . , I went ahead and bought the book.

_____
_____ 3–4. During wartime, people can be arrested if they . . ? . . someone who is believed to be the . . ? . . .

_____
_____ 5–6. When Brenda and Trisha ran for club president, I found it hard to decide who should get my vote. Both are hard-working and . . ? . . . I finally chose Brenda because she has such a . . ? . . , upbeat way about her.

_____
_____ 7–8. Watching her father eat a hot-fudge sundae, Anita felt a strong . . ? . . to eat ice cream and asked her father for a . . ? . . of his.

Showing You Understand the Words

PART A

In the space at the left, write the letter of the choice that best completes the sentence or answers the question.

____ 1. If your car broke down on the highway and people in another car **assisted** you, they probably
   a. yelled rudely at you.
   b. stopped and asked you how they could help.
   c. bumped into you.

____ 2. Your **enemy** is probably someone you
   a. like as a friend.
   b. like to visit.
   c. dislike very much.

____ 3. Which of these would you do if you **examined** a photograph?
   a. Hide it in a drawer
   b. Tear it up and throw it away
   c. Spend a long time looking at it

____ 4. If you have an **urge** to see some relatives who live far away, you probably
   a. don't like them.
   b. like them and miss them.
   c. are happy they don't live nearby.

PART B

In the space at the left, write the letter of the choice that best completes the sentence or answers the question.

____ 5. A very **competent** doctor is one
   a. who forgets what's wrong with the patient.
   b. who gives out the wrong medicine.
   c. who can be trusted to do a good job.

____ 6. Stores often sell clothes with **flaws**
   a. at a very high price.
   b. at low prices.
   c. only in the wintertime.

____ 7. It's a gray, rainy morning. Which of these might a person say if he or she has a **positive** way of looking at life?
   a. "Great! If it rains now, it will be beautiful later today."
   b. "It's going to rain all day and spoil my plans."
   c. "A day like this makes me want to crawl back to bed and pull the covers over my head."

____ 8. If someone wanted a **sample** of three desserts being served at a party, he or she would
   a. ask for a small slice of each.
   b. eat a large piece of just one dessert.
   c. eat three whole desserts.

Adding Words to a Reading

A. The Birth of the American Red Cross

Read the following paragraph carefully. Then fill in each blank with a word from the box. Use each word once.

a. **assist**	b. **enemy**	c. **examined**	d. **positive**

Clara Barton was a nurse who lived during the American Civil War (1861–1865). She knew what happened to soldiers during war. When they received an injury° from a bullet or knife, they had to lie on the battlefield until the battle was over. By then, many of them had bled to death. Because Clara wanted to (1)_____ the soldiers, she asked to go to the battlefield while the fighting was still going on. The officer in charge said no. But Clara did not take "no" for an answer. Instead of thinking nothing could be done for the soldiers, Clara was (2)_____. She said that many of them could be saved if she could just get to them. After listening to her, the officer decided to let her go. She and her nurses then worked day and night to help the hurt soldiers. They (3)_____ their wounds, gave them medicine, and used a cart pulled by horses to take them to a hospital. The nurses did not care which side the men fought for. To them, no man was an (4)_____. They were all just human beings who needed help. After the war was over, Clara started the American Red Cross. The Red Cross helps people during wartime. But it does much more. When there is an earthquake, a flood, or a fire, the Red Cross is there to help. And it is all because of Clara Barton.

B. To Spank or Not to Spank?

Read the following paragraphs carefully. Then fill in each blank with a word from the box. Use each word once.

a. **competent**	b. **flaw**	c. **sample**	d. **urge**

Do you think children should be spanked? Whenever a (5)_____ of adults is asked that question, there are many different answers. Some people say that children need to be spanked in order to learn to be good. Others say there is a (6)_____ in that idea. They say that all spanking does is teach kids to hit those who are smaller and weaker. They also say that spanked children don't really learn to be good—they simply learn to be afraid of spanking.

People who believe in spanking say that children who are not spanked always expect° to get what they want. Others say that (7)_____ parents find better ways to teach kids how to behave. For example, when such parents feel the

(8)_____ to spank a child who is behaving badly, they take a few minutes to cool down. Then they do one or more of the following: talk to the child about why the behavior was wrong, take away the child's favorite toy, keep the child from watching TV, or make the child take "time out" in his or her room. What do you think? Do you think these ideas work as well as spanking?

Using the Words When Writing and Talking

Now that you understand the meanings of the eight new words in the chapter, you are ready to use them on paper and in speaking. Complete each sentence below in a way that shows you really know what each **boldfaced** word means. Take a few minutes to think about your answer before writing it down and saying it out loud.

1. When people feel sad or depressed, friends can **assist** them by _____

    _____

2. When a waiter or waitress is **competent**, I _____

    _____

3. One way to make **enemies** is to _____

    _____

4. To see if my home needs cleaning, I **examine** _____

    _____

5. One **flaw** about myself that I would like to change is _____

    _____

6. A **positive** person is one who _____

    _____

7. Grocery stores often give shoppers **samples** of _____

    _____

8. On a recent weekend, I had a strong **urge** to _____

    _____

Scores	Adding One Word to an Item	_____%	Showing You Understand the Words	_____%
	Adding Two Words to an Item	_____%	Adding Words to a Reading	_____%

Number right: 8 = 100%, 7 = 88%, 6 = 75%, 5 = 63%, 4 = 50%, 3 = 38%, 2 = 25%, 1 = 13%
Enter your scores above and in the vocabulary performance chart on the inside back cover of the book.

Review Activities

On the next ten pages are activities to help you review the words you learned in Unit Five. You may do these activities in any order.

- Completing a Crossword Puzzle #1

- Completing a Crossword Puzzle #2

- Choosing the Best Word to Complete an Item

- Adding a Word to an Item, Parts A and B

- Finding the Same or the Opposite Meaning

- Using the Words When Writing and Talking

Completing a Crossword Puzzle #1

The box at the right lists twenty-four words from Unit Five. Using the meanings at the bottom of the page, fill in these words to complete the puzzle that follows.

admire
attempt
bold
comment
condition
courteous
develop
duty
examine
exhaust
expect
explore
hopeless
injury
major
permanent
pretend
recognize
seldom
solution
succeed
sufficient
urge
value

ACROSS

3. The worth of something—in money or importance
5. Not often
6. To look at carefully
8. To act in a false way in order to fool someone; to make believe
10. Important; large
12. Enough; as much as is needed
16. To know someone or something from an earlier time
19. Believing that things will turn out badly
21. To think something will probably happen
22. Polite; having good manners
23. Something that someone has to do
24. The state or shape that something or someone is in

DOWN

1. To do well at something
2. To travel around a new, unknown place to see what it is like
4. To think highly of someone
7. To try hard to do something; to make an effort
9. Not afraid
11. To grow little by little; to become
13. A sudden desire to do something
14. Lasting a long time
15. A statement that shows what a person thinks or feels
17. Harm, often to the body
18. An answer to a problem
20. To cause someone to become very tired

Completing a Crossword Puzzle #2

The box at the right lists twenty-four words from Unit Five. Using the meanings at the bottom of the page, fill in these words to complete the puzzle that follows.

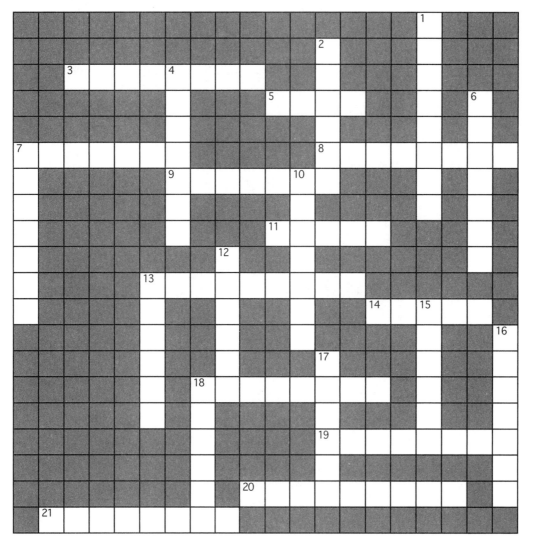

achieve
advance
appear
assist
attract
common
competent
conceal
consider
delicate
enemy
enormous
flaw
grasp
imitate
insist
interrupt
irritate
mention
positive
praise
request
sample
surround

ACROSS

3. To think carefully about something
5. A problem or fault that keeps something from being perfect
7. To cause something or someone to come near
8. To be on all sides of someone or something
9. To move forward or ahead
11. Someone whom one hates and wishes to harm
13. Being good at something
14. To grab something and hold it tightly
18. To bother or annoy someone
19. Cheerful; sure of oneself
20. To stop something for a time
21. Easily broken

DOWN

1. Very large; huge
2. To say good words about someone or something
4. To copy how someone else behaves
6. To speak briefly about someone or something
7. To reach a goal, often after hard work or difficulty
10. To hide someone or something; to keep out of view
12. To seem
13. Happening or seen often; widespread; usual
15. To help
16. Something that someone is asked to do
17. A small part of something that shows what the whole is like
18. To say something very strongly

Choosing the Best Word to Complete an Item

On the answer line at the left, write the word that best completes each item.

_____ 1. I went to the jewelry store in the mall to see if the ring I found on the street had any . . ? . . .

  a. duty   b. value   c. comment

_____ 2. The first time Wanda . . ? . . to ice skate, she fell down and broke her wrist.

  a. mentioned   b. attempted   c. requested

_____ 3. What started as a small argument between two people . . ? . . into a large fight with dozens of people getting hurt.

  a. developed   b. explored   c. pretended

_____ 4. All of us . . ? . . Gina because she does so well in school.

  a. admire   b. interrupt   c. conceal

_____ 5. My long hours at work . . ? . . me so much that all I want to do on the weekend is sleep.

  a. appear   b. exhaust   c. achieve

_____ 6. Tanya's little sister . . ? . . the new book tightly with both hands and said, "I love stories."

  a. insisted   b. grasped   c. achieved

_____ 7. Ben did not ask for help, but when we saw how much work he had to do, we chose to . . ? . . him.

  a. examine   b. imitate   c. assist

_____ 8. Although the old house needed a fresh coat of paint, overall it was in pretty good . . ? . . .

  a. condition   b. solution   c. flaw

_____ 9. When the rain turned to ice, there were several . . ? . . accidents on the turnpike.

  a. positive   b. major   c. courteous

_____ 10. Though twenty years had passed since the two old friends had been together, they . . ? . . each other right away at the grocery store.

  a. recognized   b. imitated   c. exhausted

_____ 11. The rock group . . ? . . so many people that the streets near the concert hall were filled with cars.

  a. attracted   b. considered   c. examined

_____ 12. I looked for a job for weeks but had no luck. In the beginning, I felt . . ? . ., but then then my mood improved.

  a. hopeless   b. bold   c. enormous

(Continues on next page)

_____ 13. Joseph . . ? . . several neighborhoods before deciding where he wanted to live.

      a. developed   b. achieved   c. explored

_____ 14. At first, I didn't have the . . ? . . to eat anything. But then I smelled the chocolate chip cookies baking in the oven, and I wanted to eat every single one of them.

      a. urge   b. solution   c. duty

_____ 15. You need to . . ? . . other people's feelings or you may say something that hurts someone badly.

      a. interrupt   b. attempt   c. consider

_____ 16. My grandparents have never needed or asked for help. But they did make one . . ? . . the other day. They asked if I could help them clean their basement.

      a. flaw   b. injury   c. request

_____ 17. Last winter, the flu was so . . ? . . that several schools and businesses closed their doors because so many people were sick.

      a. seldom   b. common   c. delicate

_____ 18. Even a tiny . . ? . . in the wing of an airplane can cause the plane to crash.

      a. flaw   b. sample   c. comment

_____ 19. After listening to Sheila's . . ? . . about how bad the new movie was, I changed my mind and decided to see something else.

      a. solution   b. condition   c. comment

_____ 20. Greg . . ? . . Janetta to say "no" when he asked her out on a date. He was happily surprised when she said "yes."

      a. expected   b. imitated   c. recognized

_____ 21. We were planning a surprise birthday party for Troy on Saturday night. All that day, we . ? . . that we did not know it was his birthday.

      a. requested   b. achieved   c. pretended

_____ 22. Malik's sleep was . . ? . . by the loud sound of hail smashing against his bedroom window.

      a. interrupted   b. concealed   c. assisted

_____ 23. In just a few hours, the . . ? . . blizzard brought more than two feet of snow to the city.

      a. permanent   b. delicate   c. enormous

_____ 24. It wasn't until the party was almost over that Carlos . . ? . . that he was moving to another state.

      a. attempted   b. mentioned   c. examined

Score	Choosing the Best Word to Complete an Item	_____%

Number right: 24 = 100%, 23 = 96%, 22 = 92%, 21 = 88%, 20 = 83%; 19 = 79%, 18 = 75%, 17 = 71%; 16 = 67%, 15 = 63%. 14 = 58%, 13 = 54%, 12 = 50%, 11 = 46%, 10 = 42%, 9 - 38%, 8 = 33%, 7 = 29%, 6 = 25%, 5 - 21%, 4 = 17%, 3 = 13%, 2 = 8%, 1 = 4%
Enter your scores above and in the vocabulary performance chart on the inside back cover of the book.

Adding a Word to an Item

PART A

Complete each item below by writing one word from the box on the answer line at the left. Use each word once.

a. **achieved**	d. **competent**	g. **enemies**	j. **permanent**
b. **advancing**	e. **courteous**	h. **injury**	k. **praised**
c. **appears**	f. **duties**	i. **irritated**	l. **sufficient**

_____ 1. The slow service and poor food . . ? . . Mr. and Mrs. Shahad so much that they complained to the restaurant manager.

_____ 2. Because Lonnie is such a . . ? . . student, his teacher asked him if he would like to tutor several younger children.

_____ 3. It took a lot of practice, but Andrea finally . . ? . . her goal. She beat her older brother at a game of basketball.

_____ 4. By saving her money for several months, Julia had . . ? . . cash to buy the leather jacket she wanted.

_____ 5. Although Rodney and Samuel were . . ? . . in grade school, they are best friends today.

_____ 6. In this light, my new jacket . . ? . . to be gray, but it is really blue.

_____ 7. The police were surprised that the Sung family walked away without a single . . ? . . from the three-car accident.

_____ 8. At a picnic, you have to eat quickly if you want to beat the army of ants that is . . ? . . toward your food.

_____ 9. Children behave better when they are . . ? . . and not yelled at and scolded all the time.

_____ 10. Even when customers are rude, Keisha tries hard to be . . ? . . and friendly.

_____ 11. Sara and Peter know their relationship is . . ? . . and will last forever.

_____ 12. Phil likes working at the movie theater, but he strongly dislikes one of his . . ? . .—picking up the trash that others leave behind.

(Continues on next page)

PART B

Complete each item below by writing one word from the box on the answer line at the left. Use each word once.

a. **bold**	d. **examined**	g. **positive**	j. **solution**
b. **concealed**	e. **imitates**	h. **sample**	k. **succeeded**
c. **delicate**	f. **insisted**	i. **seldom**	l. **surround**

_____ 13. Jim gets such a nice, . . ? . . feeling from cooking for others that he has decided to work several hours a week in a soup kitchen for the homeless.

_____ 14. We didn't plan to eat dinner at my grandparents' house, but my grandmother . . ? . . that we stay.

_____ 15. With two jobs and two night classes, Chen . . ? . . has time to relax.

_____ 16. Tamika was the only one in class who found the . . ? . . to the math problem.

_____ 17. After they . . ? . . the scene of the crime, the police were able to figure out how many people had robbed our apartment.

_____ 18. My sister . . ? . . the mess in her room by hiding it under her bed.

_____ 19. Although he was nervous about passing the test, Harry . . ? . . in getting his driver's license on the first try.

_____ 20. Brightly colored flowers and a pretty white fence . . ? . . the home of my dreams.

_____ 21. John tried a . . ? . . of Sandra's peanut butter pound cake. He liked it so much that he ate two big slices and took another slice home to enjoy later.

_____ 22. A butterfly's wings are so . . ? . . that they tear very easily.

_____ 23. My little sister often teases me when I am angry. She repeats every word I say and . . ? . . the way I act.

_____ 24. Some people thought Mario's plan to chase the bear away from the tent was brave and . . ? . ., but I thought it was stupid.

Scores Part A (Adding a Word) _____%	Part B (Adding a Word) _____%

Finding the Same or the Opposite Meaning

PART A
In the space at the left, write the letter of the choice that has the **same** meaning as the **boldfaced** word.

___ 1. If storm clouds are **advancing**, they are
   a. moving forward.   b. breaking up.
   c. moving away.

___ 2. Your coworkers **appear** to be happy when they learn you got a raise. They
   a. are very unhappy with the news.   b. seem pleased with the news.
   c. do not believe the news.

___ 3. If the smell of your dinner **attracts** your cats, the smell
   a. makes them come near you.   b. makes them run away from you.
   c. makes them sleepy.

___ 4. If you **conceal** a secret from your friends, you
   a. tell them the secret.   b. keep the secret hidden and don't tell it.
   c. hear them tell you the secret.

___ 5. When you **examine** a menu in a restaurant, you
   a. wave it in the air, as if to get rid of a fly.   b. pay no attention to it.
   c. look at it carefully to see what you want to order.

___ 6. If a day at work **exhausts** you, it
   a. makes you feel very tired.   b. gives you energy.
   c. disappoints you.

___ 7. If you get an **injury** while you are on vacation, you have gotten
   a. a present for someone.   b. a lot of rest.
   c. some sort of harm to the body.

___ 8. If the phone **interrupts** you while you are studying, it
   a. rings once and then is quiet.   b. is quiet and lets you work.
   c. stops you from doing your work for a while.

___ 9. If you get a **permanent** stain on your shirt, the stain will
   a. wash away easily.   b. stay there forever.
   c. wash away over a period of time.

___ 10. If you **recognize** several classmates from fifth grade, that means that you
   a. like them.   b. remember them from your school days.
   c. forget who they are.

___ 11. Someone who has a **sample** of a new kind of ice cream
   a. has a taste of the ice cream.   b. dislikes the ice cream.
   c. has a big box of the ice cream.

(Continues on next page)

___12. A person who **seldom** makes a mistake
    a. makes mistakes all the time.   b. hardly ever makes a mistake.
    c. never makes a mistake.

PART B

In the space at the left, write the letter of the choice that is the **opposite** of the **boldfaced** word.

___13. The opposite of **admire** is
    a. be sure of   b. talk about   c. think badly of

___14. The opposite of **bold** is
    a. angry   b. silly   c. scared

___15. The opposite of **delicate** is
    a. old   b. new   c. strong

___16. The opposite of **enemy** is
    a. student   b. friend   c. stranger

___17. The opposite of **enormous** is
    a. pretty   b. warm   c. small

___18. The opposite of **grasp** is
    a. let go   b. smile   c. shake

___19. The opposite of **hopeless** is
    a. feeling sad   b. looking forward to something   c. wanting to be honest

___20. The opposite of **irritate** is
    a. make happy   b. forget   c. ask

___21. The opposite of **positive** is
    a. excited   b. sad   c. straight

___22. The opposite of **succeed** is
    a. fail   b. act   c. win

___23. The opposite of **sufficient** is
    a. not enough   b. not boring   c. not expensive

___24. The opposite of **solution** is
    a. thought   b. problem   c. warning

Scores	Part A (Same Meanings) _____%	Part B (Opposite Meanings) _____%

Number right in each part: 12 = 100%, 11 = 92%, 10 = 83%, 9 = 75%, 8 = 67%; 7 = 58%, 6 = 50%, 5 = 42%; 4 = 33%, 3 = 25%. 2 = 17%, 1 = 8%
Enter your scores above and in the vocabulary performance chart on the inside back cover of the book.

Using the Words When Writing and Talking

The items below will help you use many of the words in this unit on paper and in conversation. Feel free to use **any tense of a boldfaced verb** and to make a **boldfaced noun plural**. (See pages 249–251 and 252.)

1. Using the word **achieve**, write or talk about a goal that you hope to reach some day. You might want to get a better job, learn a new language, or have a nicer apartment.

2. Using the word **assist**, write or talk about a time that you helped someone. Perhaps you baby-sat for neighbors so they could go job hunting, shoveled the snow on an elderly neighbor's sidewalk, or listened to a friend who needed to talk.

3. Using the word **attempt**, write or talk about the first time you tried to do something you knew would be difficult. Maybe you tried to ski, fix a broken bicycle, or speak in front of a large group.

4. Using the word **comment**, write or talk about a time when you said something that showed how you felt about someone or something. You may have said something like "You are so friendly. It's not surprising everyone likes you" or "I dislike the new restaurant in my neighborhood."

5. Using the word **common**, write or talk about something that young people often do nowadays. It might be going to the mall, listening to loud music, or saving money to buy good-looking clothes.

6. Using the word **competent**, write or talk about something that you do well. Maybe you are good at playing cards, cooking quick but good meals, or doing household repairs.

7. Using the word **condition**, write or talk about an elderly person that you know, and describe the shape the person is in. Is the person strong and active or fairly weak? Does he or she hear and see well or have difficulty hearing and seeing?

8. Using the word **consider**, write or talk about a decision you made after a lot of careful thought. It might have been a decision to leave a job, move to another town, or buy a new car.

9. Using the word **courteous**, write or talk about a time you were surprised by someone's good manners. Maybe a store clerk was helpful when you returned a shirt that had faded in the wash, or perhaps a driver slowed down so you could get onto a busy highway.

10. Using the word **develop**, write or talk about something that has grown and changed over the years. It could be a street, city, or school. It could even be a person.

11. Using the word **duty**, write or talk about something that everyone knows is your job at work or at home. Perhaps it is your job to do laundry at home or to repair machines at work.

12. Using the word **expect**, write or talk about a time when you thought something would happen a certain way, but it turned out very differently. You might describe a date you went on, a meeting you attended, or a movie you watched.

13. Using the word **explore**, write or talk about visiting someplace new. You might describe a vacation you took, a new neighborhood that you walked around in, or a shopping mall you visited.

14. Using the word **flaw**, write or talk about someone you like, even though there is something about the person you *don't* like. Perhaps the person has a bad temper, is always late, or spends money wildly.

(Continues on next page)

15. Using the word **imitate**, write or talk about the time that you saw children trying to act older than they really were. Maybe the children copied their parents or an older brother or sister.

16. Using the word **insist**, write or talk about a time you said something in a strong, firm way. Maybe you told your boss you *had* to have a raise, or perhaps you told your children they *had* to clean their rooms.

17. Using the word **major**, write or talk about a big change in your life. You might describe getting married, losing someone close to you, or returning to school.

18. Using the word **mention**, write or talk about a time a person told you something you didn't know. You might have learned that a neighbor was moving, a relative was getting divorced, or a friend was taking a new job.

19. Using the word **praise**, write or talk about how you felt when someone said nice things to you about the way you did something. Perhaps a teacher liked a paper you wrote, a boss said you had done a difficult job well, or friends told you how much they enjoyed your home-cooked meal.

20. Using the word **pretend**, write or talk about a time when you acted one way but really felt another way. Maybe you acted as though you liked an ugly present that someone gave you. Or perhaps you acted as though you were not upset when you really were.

21. Using the word **request**, write or talk about something that you plan to ask someone to do for you. You might want to ask a friend to baby-sit, ask a teacher for help with a problem, or ask neighbors to keep their cat out of your yard.

22. Using the word **surround**, write or talk about a place that has a fence around it. You might describe a back yard, a playing field, or a city park.

23. Using the word **urge**, write or talk about a time that you had a sudden wish to do something. Maybe it was something small (like eating a candy bar) or something big (like moving across the country).

24. Using the word **value**, write or talk about something of yours that means a lot to you, even though it is not worth a lot of money. It might be a photograph, a home-made birthday card from someone special, or a toy from your childhood.

For Extra Help

Forming Verb Tenses

This chart offers guidelines only for the verbs in this book. Check with your teacher for help forming the tenses of irregular verbs (for example, verbs like *go* or *see*).

Verbs Ending with a Consonant

Present Tense

I
You
We } *ask*
They

He, she, it   *asks*

Past Tenses: Add *-ed*

I
You
He, she, it   *asked*
We
They

I
You
We } **have** *asked*
They

He, she, it   **has** *asked*

I
You
He, she, it   **had** *asked*
We
They

Progressive Tenses: Add *-ing*

I   **am** *asking*

He, she, it   **is** *asking*

You
We } **are** *asking*
They

I
He, she, it   **was** *asking*

You
We } **were** *asking*
They

I
You
He, she, it   **will be** *asking*
We
They

I
You
We } **have been** *asking*
They

He, she, it   **has been** *asking*

I
You
He, she, it   **had been** *asking*
We
They

Verbs Having -*e* at the End

Present Tense

I
You
We   *decide*
They

He, she, it   *decides*

Past Tenses: Add -*d*

I
You
He, she, it   *decided*
We
They

I
You
We   **have *decided***
They

He, she, it   **has *decided***

I
You
He, she, it   **had *decided***
We
They

**Progressive Tenses:
Drop final *e* and add -*ing***

I   **am *deciding***

He, she, it   **is *deciding***

You
We   **are *deciding***
They

I
He, she, it   **was *deciding***

You
We   **were *deciding***
They

I
You
He, she, it   **will be *deciding***
We
They

I
You
We   **have been *deciding***
They

He, she, it   **has been *deciding***

I
You
He, she, it   **had been *deciding***
We
They

Verbs Having -*y* at the End

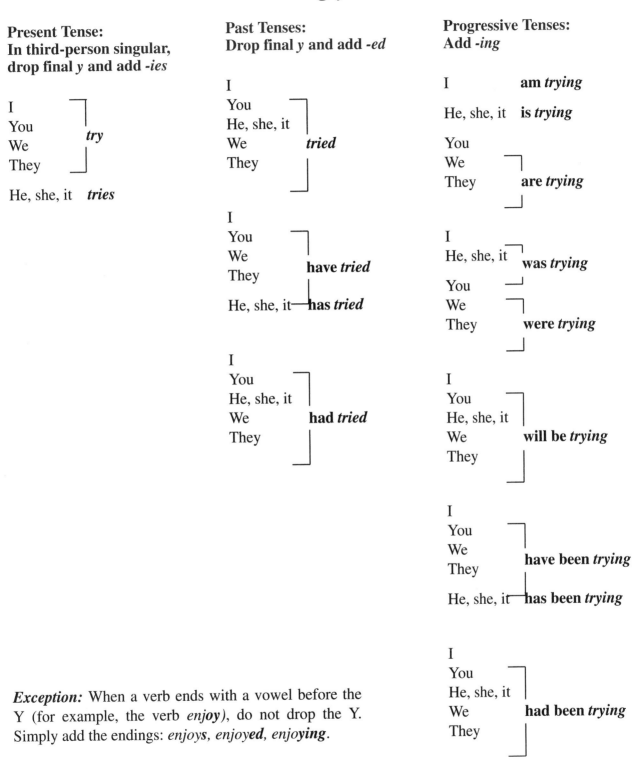

Present Tense:
In third-person singular,
drop final *y* and add -*ies*

I
You
We   *try*
They

He, she, it   *tries*

Past Tenses:
Drop final *y* and add -*ed*

I
You
He, she, it
We   *tried*
They

I
You
We
They   **have *tried***

He, she, it ⎯ **has *tried***

I
You
He, she, it
We   **had *tried***
They

Progressive Tenses:
Add -*ing*

I   **am *trying***

He, she, it   **is *trying***

You
We
They   **are *trying***

I
He, she, it **was *trying***
You
We
They   **were *trying***

I
You
He, she, it
We   **will be *trying***
They

I
You
We
They   **have been *trying***

He, she, it ⎯ **has been *trying***

I
You
He, she, it
We   **had been *trying***
They

Exception: When a verb ends with a vowel before the Y (for example, the verb *enjoy*), do not drop the Y. Simply add the endings: *enjoys, enjoyed, enjoying*.

Note: When a verb ends with a consonant (for example, the verb *plan*), you often double the final consonant when forming the past *(planned)* and progressive *(planning)* tenses. In both cases, the final *n* has been doubled before adding the tense ending. But this rule doesn't hold true for all verbs ending with a consonant. If you are not sure when to double the final consonant, check with your teacher or a dictionary.

Making Nouns Plural

Singular (**sing**-gyuh-lur) nouns name *one* person, place, or thing. **Plural** (**ploor**-uhl) nouns name *two or more* persons, places, or things. Most nouns can be made plural by adding *-s*.

Most Plurals: Add *-s*

Singular	Plural	Singular	Plural
hat	hats	student	students
teacher	teachers	cheese	cheeses

Some nouns form their plurals in other ways. A few of these are shown below. If you are not sure how to make a certain noun plural, check in a dictionary or ask your teacher.

Other Plurals

Nouns Ending in Consonant and *-y:*
Change *y* to *i* and add *-es*

Singular	Plural
cry	cries
party	parties
sky	skies
story	stories

Nouns Ending in *-ch, -sh, -ss,* or *-x:*
Add *-es*

Singular	Plural
church	churches
dish	dishes
class	classes
box	boxes

Some Nouns Ending in *-f* or *-fe:*
Change *f* or *fe* to *v* and add *-es*

Singular	Plural
leaf	leaves
knife	knives
life	lives
wife	wives

Some Nouns That Change Their Spelling

Singular	Plural
man	men
woman	women
child	children
mouse	mice

Limited Answer Key

Important Note: This answer key has the answers for the "Adding One Word to an Item" activity that is in each chapter. You should not look at these answers until you have tried your best to pick the word that should go in each sentence of this activity.

    If you use the answer key correctly, it will help you learn and remember the words in the chapter. It will also help you get ready for the other activities and tests, for which the answers are not given. To make this key easier to use, the titles of each chapter's readings are written after the chapter number.

Chapter 1 (The Nose Knows; Barbie: A Bad Example?)

Adding One Word to an Item

1. agreement
2. cancel
3. curious
4. prepare
5. flexible
6. odor
7. fact
8. suggests

Chapter 2 (Feeling Blue; A Late Love Letter)

Adding One Word to an Item

1. tension
2. produced
3. daily
4. experience
5. original
6. identify
7. negative
8. entertained

Chapter 3 (Ads That Lie; Horrible Hiccups!)

Adding One Word to an Item

1. minor
2. event
3. conclusion
4. attack
5. talent
6. volunteers
7. humble
8. protects

Chapter 4 (An Upsetting Dream; A King's Mistake)

Adding One Word to an Item

1. accused
2. precious
3. embarrassed
4. pleasant
5. inspires
6. public
7. unusual
8. claims

Chapter 5 (Be Proud of Your Age!; Making Anger Work for You)

Adding One Word to an Item

1. logical
2. benefited
3. rivals
4. delayed
5. emphasize
6. vacant
7. tempted
8. satisfy

Chapter 6 (How Not to Treat Customers; Stuck in the Middle)

Adding One Word to an Item

1. fortunate
2. motivated
3. suspect
4. leisure
5. opposes
6. definite
7. refers
8. specific

Chapter 7 (The Joy of Ice Cream; A Noisy Apartment)

Adding One Word to an Item

1. devour
2. distressed
3. modern
4. occasion
5. discovered
6. aware
7. constant
8. popular

Chapter 8 (Nuts in the Senate; Calling Dr. Leech)

Adding One Word to an Item

1. gratitude
2. ability
3. glanced
4. damage
5. failure
6. introduce
7. labor
8. create

Chapter 9 (TV and Violence; Are You Ready for a Pet?)

Adding One Word to an Item

1. intended
2. helpless
3. avoided
4. sociable
5. excuse
6. normal
7. includes
8. struggle

Chapter 10 (Help for Shy People; Not a Laughing Matter)

Adding One Word to an Item

1. previous
2. damp
3. loyal
4. approached
5. numerous
6. ignored
7. require
8. timid

Chapter 11 (Taking Risks; Bad Manners Hurt Everyone)

Adding One Word to an Item

1. furious
2. reversed
3. careless
4. capable
5. tradition
6. observes
7. resist
8. opportunity

Chapter 12 (Two Different Sisters; How "Honest Abe" Earned His Name)

Adding One Word to an Item

1. comfortable
2. persists
3. allow
4. distracted
5. respect
6. insulting
7. sensitive
8. wondered

Chapter 13 (Ready to Do Well; Advertising for a Date)

Adding One Word to an Item

1. confident
2. locate
3. purpose
4. uncertain
5. effort
6. donate
7. amazed
8. sincere

Chapter 14 (The Good and Bad Sides of Malls; As Good As It Looks?)

Adding One Word to an Item

1. guarantee
2. opinion
3. disgusts
4. inspected
5. resolves
6. dismissed
7. ideal
8. prevent

Chapter 15 (A Belief in Flying; She Tries Before She Buys)

Adding One Word to an Item

1. defects
2. cautious
3. advice
4. necessary
5. provide
6. impossible
7. defeated
8. permits

Chapter 16 (Play Now, Pay Later; A Man of Many Faces)

Adding One Word to an Item

1. regretted
2. personal
3. hollow
4. panic
5. expert
6. arranged
7. continue
8. supposed

Chapter 17 (Soaps Are for Me!; Keeping the Customer Happy)

Adding One Word to an Item

1. contributed
2. portions
3. available
4. experimented
5. encouraged
6. admits
7. dull
8. intimate

Chapter 18 (A Fake "Cure"; The Jobs Everyone Hates)

Adding One Word to an Item

1. gradual
2. competes
3. involved
4. depend
5. effective
6. envies
7. intense
8. contains

Chapter 19 (A Young Librarian; No More Harm)

Adding One Word to an Item

1. collapsed
2. relieved
3. similar
4. alarmed
5. defend
6. victims
7. grief
8. modest

Chapter 20 (Is He Man or Machine?; Struck by Lightning)

Adding One Word to an Item

1. confusion
2. distant
3. emerged
4. realizes
5. refuses
6. survive
7. decreases
8. incidents

Chapter 21 (Whose Fault Is It?; Forests Full of Life)

Adding One Word to an Item

1. revealed
2. tremendous
3. reaction
4. stubborn
5. persuade
6. quarrels
7. separates
8. excess

Chapter 22 (An Animal in Danger; The Simple Life of the Amish)

Adding One Word to an Item

1. disaster
2. generous
3. increased
4. tolerate
5. progress
6. predict
7. scarce
8. fascinates

Chapter 23 (Taking a Break with TV; Working and Living Together)

Adding One Word to an Item
1. occupy
2. detail
3. performed
4. glared
5. weary
6. humor
7. selected
8. notice

Chapter 24 (The Horror of Hate; Taking Time for Thanks)

Adding One Word to an Item
1. familiar
2. support
3. imagine
4. united
5. embraced
6. isolates
7. condemn
8. expressed

Chapter 25 (A Surprising Change; Just for Fun)

Adding One Word to an Item
1. pretended
2. bold
3. solution
4. admire
5. developed
6. expected
7. comments
8. insisted

Chapter 26 (Little Lies; Rudeness at the Movies)

Adding One Word to an Item
1. enormous
2. appeared
3. attract
4. mentioned
5. conceal
6. common
7. irritate
8. surrounded

Chapter 27 (The Truth About Drinking; A Life Out of Balance)

Adding One Word to an Item
1. condition
2. injury
3. duty
4. seldom
5. achieved
6. value
7. major
8. exhausted

Chapter 28 (Animals Were First; Call Waiting—Oh, No!)

Adding One Word to an Item
1. delicate
2. considered
3. request
4. grasped
5. interrupted
6. praised
7. advanced
8. succeeding

Chapter 29 (A Cab Driver for Now; Thoughts at the Mall)

Adding One Word to an Item
1. recognizes
2. imitate
3. courteous
4. explored
5. permanent
6. sufficient
7. attempts
8. hopeless

Chapter 30 (The Birth of the American Red Cross; To Spank or Not to Spank?)

Adding One Word to an Item
1. urge
2. assisted
3. flaws
4. enemies
5. positive
6. examined
7. samples
8. competent

Word List

ability, 62
accuse, 26
achieve, 212
admire, 200
admit, 128
advance, 218
advice, 116
agreement, 8
alarm, 152
allow, 86
amazed, 104
appear, 206
approach, 74
arrange, 122
assist, 230
attack, 20
attempt, 224
attract, 206
available, 128
avoid, 68
aware, 56
benefit, 32
bold, 200
cancel, 8
capable, 80
careless, 80
cautious, 116
claim, 26
collapse, 152
comfortable, 86
comment, 200
common, 206
compete, 134
competent, 230
conceal, 206
conclusion, 20

condemn, 182
condition, 212
confident, 104
confusion, 158
consider, 218
constant, 56
contain, 134
continue, 122
contribute, 128
courteous, 224
create, 62
curious, 8
daily, 14
damage, 62
damp, 74
decrease, 158
defeat, 116
defect, 116
defend, 152
definite, 38
delay, 32
delicate, 218
depend, 134
detail, 176
develop, 200
devour, 56
disaster, 170
discover, 56
disgust, 110
dismiss, 110
distant, 158
distract, 86
distressed, 56
donate, 104
dull, 128
duty, 212

effective, 134
effort, 104
embarrassed, 26
embrace, 182
emerge, 158
emphasize, 32
encourage, 128
enemy, 230
enormous, 206
entertain, 14
envy, 134
event, 20
examine, 230
excess, 164
excuse, 68
exhaust, 212
expect, 200
experience, 14
experiment, 129
expert, 122
explore, 224
express, 182
fact, 8
failure, 62
familiar, 182
fascinate, 170
flaw, 230
flexible, 8
fortunate, 38
furious, 80
generous, 170
glance, 62
glare, 176
gradual, 135
grasp, 218
gratitude, 63